Hockey Confidential

Hockey Confidential

INSIDE STORIES FROM PEOPLE
INSIDE THE GAME

BOB McKENZIE

Collins

Published by Collins, an imprint of HarperCollins Publishers Ltd

First edition

HarperCollins books may be purchased for educational, business,
or sales promotional use through our Special Markets Department.

HarperCollins Publishers Ltd
2 Bloor Street East, 20th Floor
Toronto, Ontario, Canada
M4W 1A8

www.harpercollins.ca

Library and Archives Canada Cataloguing in Publication
information is available upon request

ISBN 978-1-44341-832-4

Printed and bound in the United States of America
RRD 9 8 7 6 5 4 3 2 1

To Cindy, Mike and Shawn.
As Pops used to say, "Life is for the living."
Be mindful of the moments.

Contents

Preface

————

I cannot tell a lie. When the publisher of the book you hold in your hands first suggested to me the title, *Hockey Confidential,* I was a little uncomfortable with what I thought might be the connotation. What if someone thinks it's a tell-all book—the latter-day hockey equivalent of Jim Bouton's *Ball Four*? Or maybe even a personal career retrospective, spanning my more than 35 years covering and reporting on all things hockey? Because it's neither, and I wouldn't want anyone to be misled.

Of course, anyone who has followed my career path—from covering junior hockey for the Sault Ste. Marie (Ontario) *Star* to editor-in-chief of *The Hockey News* to *Toronto Star* hockey columnist to becoming the original Hockey Insider on The Sports Network (TSN) to @TSNBobMcKenzie having more than 750,000 followers on Twitter—would know my body of work tends to run towards the more conventional or conservative side of the spectrum. Tell-all? I don't think so. And while there may come a day when I'll recount what will end up being more than four decades' worth of personal and professional behind-the-scenes recollections in a book, this isn't it.

The truth, though, is I didn't have a better suggestion than *Hockey*

Confidential. And if I did, I'm not sure you would have bought *A Bunch of Stories Bob Would Like to Tell.* Not too catchy, now, is it? But if we're being honest here, that's essentially what *Hockey Confidential* is: a collection of hockey stories I find compelling, stories I would like to share.

If you read my first book, *Hockey Dad: True Confessions of a (Crazy?) Hockey Parent,* you'll see very quickly that this one is much different. *Hockey Dad* was an intensely personal first-person story about the good, the bad and the ugly of shepherding my two sons through the Canadian minor hockey system and beyond. For those who found *Hockey Dad* perhaps too narrow in its scope—that is, not dealing with stories from the NHL involving professional players and/or famous people—you'll be heartened to know *Hockey Confidential* should have broader appeal. Some of the names in the stories I tell on these pages will be instantly recognizable as amongst the biggest in the game, including Don Cherry, John Tavares, P.K. Subban, Steven Stamkos, Connor McDavid, Mark Lindsay and Jari Byrski.

Mark Lindsay and Jari Byrski? Come again?

Well, that's one of a number of reasons why the full title of the book—*Hockey Confidential: Inside Stories from People Inside the Game*—is actually an apt description. Mark Lindsay and Jari Byrski may not be household hockey names, but the fact that both work with and are well known to so many of the biggest stars and best players in the NHL means you should know them—and their stories—too.

I'd like to think there's more to this book than just hockey, that it has a greater meaning or application beyond the obvious hockey angles. It certainly does for me. For a guy whose life more or less revolves around all things puck, and mine does, I have no doubt there's plenty here for the hardcore hockey fan: John Tavares talking about the essence of scoring goals; Brandon Prust making sense of what it's really like to give or take punches in a hockey fight; and the colliding worlds of old and new in the growing debate on the place of advanced statistics—or #fancystats, as many have taken to calling them. But the longer I've been in this business, the older (and wiser, I'd like to think) I get, the more I think I've learned. Perhaps the closer I get to realizing my own mortality, the more I've come to appreciate and try to understand some grander or more universal themes of life and death and the meaning or purpose of our respective journeys.

To that end, the first chapter of this book is about hockey only to the extent that the subject is a well-known, dyed-in-the-wool hockey man who had a harrowing near-death experience and not only lived to talk about it publicly for the first time, but also offered a deeply personal perspective on how it impacted him and his view on the meaning of life.

Hockey Confidential, indeed.

You'll notice some other themes running through the book as well.

If life, and being around hockey, has taught me anything, it's not what you take or get as much as what you leave or give. So whether it's Mark Lindsay's ability to heal with his hands, Karl Subban's passion for aiding those less fortunate than his famous sons or Byrski's dedication to giving kids the confidence he so dearly lacked in his own childhood in Poland, these are stories I wanted to share with you. Trite as it may sound, if I'm going to go to the trouble of writing a book, I want it be a lasting legacy for my kids, who can pick it up long after I'm gone and know what it was I believed in, what my core values were and what mattered to me.

That's another common thread you'll find running throughout this project: the value of family within a hockey context—an 80-year-old Don Cherry sharing precious moments with his son, Tim, at the rink; rock star Gord Downie of the Tragically Hip communing with his brothers in a lifelong love affair with the Boston Bruins; the patriarchs of the Subban and Tavares families emigrating from Jamaica and Portugal, respectively, to become household hockey names and raise great Canadian superstars; to say nothing of a teenaged Connor McDavid leaning on his family and support system, including the incomparable Bobby Orr, to help cope with the pressures of being tabbed as the Next Big Thing in hockey; as well as Sheldon Keefe's dramatic personal struggle to leave behind a dark and troubled past to become a better man, son, brother, husband, father and hockey coach.

My original vision for this book was for it to be 25 to 40 chapters, 2,000 to 3,000 words each; but as I started telling some of the stories, they morphed into something entirely different—11 chapters in total, ranging anywhere from 3,000 to 15,000 words apiece. I started thinking of each chapter as its own mini-book, an opportunity to do something that is totally foreign to what my job has become—and, really, something that flies totally in the face of where media has gone.

Whether I'm appearing on television (where a 40-second comment is now deemed to be a major oration) or I'm on Twitter (tapping it out 140 characters at a time), it's become an attention-deficit disorder world. Don't get me wrong; that's not necessarily a criticism as much as it might be a lament. Hey, I'm as guilty as anyone of propagating the quick-hit, all-the-news-fit-to-print, so-long-as-it's-in-140-or-fewer-characters news feed. One of the reasons I got into journalism in the first place was because I wanted to be a storyteller, and I fear I've strayed from that, at least as the basis for what my job has become. My primary focus is to share news and information, and hopefully some perspective and insight along the way. The nature of the beast is that more output is better than less, but short is better than long, and really short is best of all. That isn't to say there aren't good long-form storytellers in our business, because there are, but I've either not had the opportunity to be one of them or wilfully neglected to do so. Until now, anyway.

I'm far from a wordsmith when it comes to writing—more of a

grinder than a natural talent. I have always envied those who seem to write so effortlessly. I've always been awestruck whenever I've read anything written by Michael Farber, whether it was back in his days as a columnist for the Montreal *Gazette* or later as a feature writer for *Sports Illustrated*. And I don't think I've ever read an NHL game story that could rival what Red Fisher did in his heyday covering the Canadiens for the *Gazette*. It was like poetry. I fully confess to having writer envy.

So *Hockey Confidential* is an indulgence for me. Maybe a bit of a risk, too, in that conventional media wisdom is that no one has time anymore to read long-form stories. I certainly hope that's not the case, and I'll just have to trust my instincts that it's not.

There are so many people I must thank, starting with Brad Wilson and the publishing team at HarperCollins. They've only ever shared my vision for *Hockey Confidential*, even when it started to take on a slightly different shape. An author couldn't have a more supportive, encouraging publisher, and for that, I thank them.

Nothing I do in any aspect of my life means anything without my family—my wife, Cindy, and my sons, Mike and Shawn. I started the *Hockey Confidential* process in August 2013 and didn't put it to bed until April 2014. It seemed like, with apologies to Cindy and all mothers out there, nine months of really hard labour. Squeezing it in to an all-too-busy "normal" work schedule at TSN meant I wasn't much of a husband or father for many of those months. There was even a time, in November 2013, on the night I had to go to the hospital emergency room with what was apparently a one-off case of atrial fibrillation (arrhythmia), when I wondered if this book, and the stress it was causing, might literally—and I do mean *literally*—kill me. Cindy, Mike and Shawn didn't just support me while I worked on it, they were my in-house focus group. No one in the McKenzie household—certainly not me—gets a free pass. I knew if my wife, a casual hockey fan at best, and my 28- and 25-year-old Xbox-generation sons found these stories interesting and not too long or plodding, *Hockey Confidential* was going to be just fine.

My book agent, Brian Wood, was also an invaluable editorial sounding board, but it's his expertise and counsel in a field I know nothing about—book publishing—that allowed me to concentrate solely on the task at hand. It never hurts to have an honest and trustworthy ally looking out for your best interests.

There were countless others, far too many to mention by name, who were instrumental in providing constructive criticism and helping to shape the final product you see before you. Also, to my bosses and colleagues at TSN, thank you for tolerating and accepting a sometimes distracted, fatigued or cranky Hockey Insider who maybe bit off more than he could chew during a tumultuous 2013–14 season that saw the hockey broadcasting business in Canada turned on its ear. TSN is, in a word, awesome. No better place in the world to hang your hat.

The greatest thanks, though, are owed to the people whose stories are told in these pages. These aren't my stories; they are their stories. I was merely fortunate enough to be able to tell them, but none of it would be possible without their trust, cooperation and incredible forthrightness to share that which, in many cases, they'd never shared before. Which works well for a book called *Hockey Confidential*.

I can't tell you how much I appreciated the hockey executive, who had a near-death experience, trusting me to tell his story publicly for the first time, as well as taking the time to relive in extreme detail such a traumatic event in his life. The same goes for Sheldon Keefe, who put up with numerous weather-related cancellations in the Ontario winter from hell, before finally doing an interview in London, Ontario, that was as candid as any in the book.

Don and Tim Cherry welcomed me as their guest to do something, strangely enough, no one had ever done before: stand alongside them while they watched a minor midget hockey game.

I emailed New York Islander superstar John Tavares hoping to get him and his uncle of the same name, a Canadian lacrosse legend, together for an interview before Hockey John went to training camp. One week later, we were all sitting in a Starbucks in Mississauga, Ontario, for a two-hour interview, which only underscores how incredibly giving and cooperative NHL superstars can be. Ditto for Montreal Canadien Brandon Prust, who worked around his injury rehabs and a busy schedule in 2013–14 to make time for me in Montreal on the eve of the playoffs to talk about his unlikely pro career as well as about fighting in hockey.

Karl Subban poured out his heart and soul to me in a long, all-encompassing interview at a Tim Hortons in Rexdale, Ontario; Mark Lindsay took time out from dissecting human cadavers to violate his own personal code of "staying hidden" to do an interview over dinner in Kingston, Ontario; Connor McDavid and his parents, Brian and Kelly, welcomed me to Erie, Pennsylvania, at a time when they were actually cancelling interviews and reducing Connor's media exposure; Gord Downie, front man for the Tragically Hip, did something he almost never does, talking in detail about his personal life and family members, over lunch on Danforth Avenue in Toronto; Tyler Dellow and myriad other advanced statistics gurus, including the legendary—and some would say mythical—Vic Ferrari, made themselves available on numerous occasions to repeatedly explain their craft to a guy who barely escaped Grade 12 math; and Jari Byrski welcomed me into his home, where his beloved wife died and where he thought seriously about taking his own life—and might have, if not for hearing my voice on television talking about a Steven Stamkos goal.

To all of them, and anyone else I interviewed as part of their stories, thank you so much. To all of you who have taken time and effort or spent your hard-earned money to read my work, you have my gratitude as well as a piece of my heart and soul, because that's what you'll find on each and every page.

I can only hope I did the stories justice, that you enjoy reading (what I now believe is the aptly named) *Hockey Confidential* as much as I enjoyed researching and writing it. As always, if there are any errors on these pages, either factual or by omission, just know there's only one guy to blame.

I'll see if I can find him.

CHAPTER 1

Not His Day to Die

*A Grizzled Hockey Guy Ponders the Meaning of Life,
and Death, After a Chilling Experience*

————

The man was drowning.

He was trapped.

His desperate attempts to escape—the punches, the kicks—had all failed.

The ice-cold water had filled the cab of the submerged tractor.

There was no air left to breathe.

His lungs were filling up with water.

He knew his life was down to its final seconds.

"I'm going to die in here," he thought. "I'm done. Is this how it ends?"

It was at that moment, panic-stricken in his mind, now floating on his side, encased in a watery tomb of glass and steel, that his entire life didn't so much flash before his eyes as his impending death did.

With no sense of time at all—it might have been just a fraction of a second, it might have been more than that, he just doesn't know—two visions came to the drowning man, stunning in their clarity and detail.

In the first, he could see his wife standing at the water's edge as the tractor and his lifeless body were pulled from the pond.

1

The second was his own funeral procession—the hearse, limousines and cars driving slowly past his family farmhouse on the road just across the open field from the pond in which he was now trapped and dying.

"I saw no flash of white light like they talk about," the man said. "I couldn't tell you how long I'd been in the water. Was it 45 seconds? A minute? Two? I don't know, but those visions, they seemed so real . . . I knew this was it, I was done if I didn't do something. If I didn't get out then, the visions would be real."

The drowning man gave one last desperate kick, using both his boots, to the side window panel of the tractor. Maybe it was fate—just not his day to die?—or perhaps it was simply that the water pressure on the glass had finally equalized from outside and inside the cab, but whatever it was, the large glass window popped free from its rubber moulding, offering escape.

The man frantically exited the cab, rose straight to the surface, crashed his head against shards of ice, coughed dirty pond water out of his lungs and gasped for air. Bleeding from his head, he crawled over the tractor's partially submerged arm and bucket, navigated his way to the snowy, reedy embankment and climbed up to solid ground.

The only vision he saw now was a most welcome one, and it was real: the bright noon-hour sun and cold, clear sky of a below-freezing winter's day in southwestern Ontario.

As he set out on the 500-metre trek to his farmhouse—wearing only a soaked T-shirt, sweat pants and boots—he traversed the snow-covered field to cross the road on which he had envisioned his own funeral procession. As he arrived at his house, he didn't feel the cold—didn't have any feelings, really, with the exception of one.

He was alive.

If Colin (Colie) Campbell had died on that sunny, clear and cold Friday January 8, 2010, on his farm near Tillsonburg, Ontario, he would have been eulogized for a life well lived, for an accomplished career in hockey as a player, coach and executive as well as that of an earnest and good family man—a husband, a father and a grandfather.

There would have been no shortage of friends or family or hockey people to pay tribute to a man who didn't quite make it to his 57th birthday but had lived a full and rich life nonetheless.

They would have talked of the 17-year-old boy who left Tillsonburg in 1970 to join Roger Neilson's Peterborough Petes, how the stocky five-foot-nine, 192-pound defenceman scrapped and battled his way to beat the odds to have a 12-year pro career that was based more on try than talent—but don't kid yourself, you didn't make the NHL in the 1970s without plenty of both.

They'd have told stories of his exploits as a Pete, winning the OHA championship in 1972, losing to the Cornwall Royals in the Memorial Cup final that year, playing alongside names such as Craig Ramsay, Stan Jonathan, Doug Jarvis and Bob Gainey in his three years with Neilson's Petes; going to the Vancouver Blazers of the fledging World Hockey Association for his first year of professional hockey and—accumulating triple-digit penalty minutes and zealously defending the front of his net against all foes in his trademark big-bucket helmet—doing what he would do for the Pittsburgh Penguins, Colorado Rockies, Edmonton Oilers, Vancouver Canucks and Detroit Red Wings over 11 well-travelled NHL seasons and 636 regular-season NHL games (25 goals, 128 points and 1,292 penalty minutes) in what was arguably the toughest, most menacing and intimidating and dangerous era of professional hockey. There no doubt would have been talk of his trip to the Stanley Cup final with the Canucks in 1982, riding the crest of Neilson's Towel Power.

And then his life as a coach. Five years as an assistant in Detroit, where, amongst other things, he tried to be Bob Probert's sober companion and watchdog to keep the troubled player from going astray; three years in New York as a Ranger assistant coach, first to his mentor and dear friend Neilson and then during the tumultuous Mike Keenan regime that ultimately led to the first Ranger Stanley Cup championship since 1940, followed by a four-year stint for himself as head coach of the Mark Messier–Wayne Gretzky-era Blueshirts that ended the way most coaching appointments end—by being fired.

There would be discussion of his move to the NHL executive suite, how the old-school hockey guy took over as NHL commissioner Gary Bettman's right-hand hockey operations man, administering all on-ice discipline, and how, like Brian Burke before him and Brendan Shanahan after him, he suffered the slings and arrows of public criticism and ridicule for unwaveringly doing what he thought was best.

And yet, for all he accomplished in his hockey life, his true measure would be as a family man: his marriage in 1976 to his Tillsonburg sweetheart, Heather, the subsequent birth of their three children and two grandchildren and his involvement with their lives and their own families—daughters Lauren, the teacher, and Courtney, the lawyer, as well as son Gregory, the hockey player who went on to win the Stanley Cup in 2011 with the Boston Bruins.

But the eulogies would have to wait. January 8, 2010, wasn't Colie Campbell's day to die.

The morning of what could've been Colie Campbell's last day on earth was much the same as the night before: busy and problematic.

In his job as senior executive vice-president of the NHL and head of hockey operations, there was almost always a fire to put out somewhere, and the slate of games on Thursday, January 7 that year was no exception.

There was major controversy in a game between Pittsburgh and Philadelphia when the producer of the Penguins' home-team broadcast intentionally held back—from the broadcast, and from the NHL's hockey-operations crew—a video replay that conclusively showed Philadelphia's Simon Gagne had scored a shorthanded goal. After a lengthy video review by Campbell's staff in Toronto, the goal was disallowed for lack of conclusive proof the puck crossed the line. Once the Flyer goal had been disallowed, the Pens' home-team producer then showed the replay.

And all hell broke loose.

Another night in the NHL, another firestorm.

So Campbell awoke early that Friday morning and knew it was going to be busy dealing with the fallout from the night before, not to mention the overnight snow that had fallen in southwestern Ontario, and who knows what else that might be on the horizon.

He also was already well behind on his list of chores around the farm. A week into 2008, Campbell still hadn't disposed of the family Christmas trees, one from his home and one from his mother-in-law's place next door. Now there was snow to plow on the long driveways connecting the two homes situated on a scenic tract of land just southeast of Tillsonburg. There's a forested ravine behind the houses. In front, there's the county road that separates both residences from the sprawling 140 acres of prime southwestern Ontario farmland that, once upon time, used to be a thriving tobacco farm. Today, though, most of it is rented out to local farmers who grow corn and beans. Campbell might have a farmer's sensibilities in life, but he had neither the time nor the inclination to be an actual farmer.

So he got up that Friday morning and knew there was plenty on his plate.

He debated whether to wear his sneakers or put on his "Roots boots," as he calls them; because of the snow, he opted for the latter, a decision he thinks about now as perhaps life-saving. He went outside, walked over to the barn and climbed up into the spacious cab of the big orange Kubota tractor, a massive, modern beast of farming technology with a fully enclosed glass cab boasting all the amenities (including heat and stereo), a big shovel/bucket on the front and a blade on the side for plowing.

And off he went. Campbell started plowing the driveways, but, as so often happened when he was doing anything at the farm, his BlackBerry was constantly buzzing. He'd plow a bit, stop, take a call, make a call, read some emails, send some emails and handle the fallout from the Gagne goal (by the way, the Pittsburgh TV producer was suspended for the balance of the season but was reinstated the following season). That scene played itself out over the next couple of hours and, with the driveways plowed, Campbell was finally going to dispose of those Christmas trees he'd been meaning to get rid of.

He tossed them into the big front bucket of the tractor and off he went, down the long driveway, out onto the county road in front of his house, crossing over it and proceeding south into the frozen farm field. A kilometre or two away, on his property, there's a berm, a natural break in the otherwise flat landscape, an ideal spot to dispose of the Christmas trees. It was a bright, beautiful, but cold winter's day and Campbell drove the tractor across the field, navigating around the irrigation pond set squarely in the middle of the field en route to the berm.

Campbell looked at the pond as he drove by. A week earlier, on New Year's Day, he and much of the hockey world had been in Boston at historic Fenway Park for the annual NHL Winter Classic outdoor game between the Bruins and Flyers. For a kid who grew up in a small town, playing pond hockey was a winter way of life. So, just a week removed from the Winter Classic, Campbell mused how much fun it might be have his very own version of the Winter Classic right on his own property, maybe play a little shinny himself, maybe get the kids and the whole family out there.

As he headed towards the berm to dump the trees, he decided that, on his way back to the farmhouse, he'd stop and plow the snow off the pond. And why not? As ponds go, this one was pretty much idyllic. Although it's located smack in the middle of flat farmland and half a kilometre from the farmhouse, two of the pond's four sides, the entire southern and western edges, are framed with a thicket of beautiful evergreens and stand of trees and bushes. The northern and eastern sides of the pond are lined with reeds and bulrushes on a short slope down from the field. With the fresh snow that just had fallen, it looked like a Canadian picture postcard, or maybe even the perfect setting for a Tim Hortons commercial starring Sidney Crosby. For an old hockey player and country boy who'd just been to the Winter Classic, the idea was too inviting to pass up. Even the shape (more or less rectangular) and size (almost 150 feet long and 90 feet wide) were darn close to the standard 200-by-85-foot NHL ice surface. And if you're sitting behind the wheel of what amounts to the farm version of a Zamboni, on a clear and cold Canadian winter day, why the hell not?

So Campbell pulled the tractor up to the northwest corner of the pond. He's not a reckless man by nature. So he climbed down from the tractor and walked out onto the pond to check it out. But he knew it had been a really cold winter and that the irrigation pond should be fully frozen, easily able to take the weight of the tractor. He climbed back in. Just to be sure, he pulled the wheels up to the edge and, without actually venturing onto the pond, used the fully extended tractor bucket to tamp up and down on the ice to make sure it was solid.

Convinced it was, he drove the tractor onto the pond and turned it so it was facing due east. And in the midst of his very first plow pass across the pond, he suddenly felt the tractor crack through the ice. But it dropped no more than, by his guess, four to five feet, not really submerged as much as it was just stuck. He was still high and dry. Campbell's first thought was that the big tractor was resting on the pond's shallow bottom. His overriding emotion was more aggravation than fear. He was not happy at being stuck and figured he'd have to walk all the way back to the farmhouse to call his brother-in-law to tow the tractor out of the pond.

In the time that followed—no more than 30 seconds—as he contemplated his salvage options and cursed at how much busier and more aggravating his day had just become, the tractor suddenly plunged entirely through the ice to the actual bottom of the pond. And the bottom was deep enough to fully submerge the entire tractor. The top of its roof was visible just a few inches below the surface.

It had been warm in the tractor cab while he was plowing, so Campbell had taken off his coat. He was sitting there in his T-shirt, sweat pants and boots as the icy water started to seep into the floor of the fully enclosed tractor cab.

"I was sitting there, with it stuck the first time, and I'm kind of shaking my head, thinking how stupid this is when the whole thing suddenly crashed to the bottom," Campbell said. "When I saw the water coming in on the floor, I thought, 'Shit, this could be serious.' But I wasn't panicked at that point. I figured I'd be able to get out somehow. So I tried to open the door, but it was shut tight. There was, I guess, too much water pressure on the outside and it wouldn't open. So I put my gloves back on and tried to punch out the window, but it didn't budge. The water was starting to fill up a lot faster now. It was up to my knees and I realized, 'I could be in real trouble here.' I tried punching out the door and windows again. All of them. Really hard. I tried kicking them out. I don't think I had time to physically panic, but now I was really panicking on the inside. Once the water started to come in, it was really rushing up quickly. It wasn't long before it was over my head. I'm trying to lift my head to get the last bit of air that was left at the top of the cab. Then it was filled up completely. That's when I thought, 'I'm going to die in here.'"

With his lungs literally ready to burst and a most horrific death seemingly imminent, floating on his side, that was when Campbell experienced the dual visions—of his wife, Heather, watching the morbid salvage operation from the edge of the pond and his own funeral procession up on the county road.

Even now, Campbell's a little unnerved by them; how lifelike they both seemed, how it was an almost out-of-body experience for him at the precise moment he was drowning, but there's no doubt those visions inspired him to give one last kick for freedom.

A kick that saved his life.

"I've been told since then that the window probably popped out when I kicked it the last time because, once the cab filled up with the water, there was equal pressure on both sides of the glass," Campbell said. "That makes sense. Still, I'm glad I wore those big Roots boots, because I had thought about wearing running shoes instead, and I don't know if I would have been able to kick [the window] out with shoes on."

Once out of the cab, Campbell bobbed up to the surface, but the jagged edges of the hole in the ice the tractor had fallen through cut his head in numerous places. He was able to grab onto the just barely submerged tractor arm that led him onto the big bucket, which he crawled over to get to solid ground.

The weird thing, Campbell said, was that at no time during the entire ordeal did he ever feel cold or think about the cold. Not when the icy water was rushing over him in the cab, not when he was swimming up to the surface, and not even when he scrambled up to the field in his water-soaked clothing on a below-freezing day and walked the better part of half a kilometre to the house.

"I was probably in shock, but the cold never registered, not in or out of the water," he said. Yeah, it was probably shock. Or the fact that, as a hockey player, Campbell was tougher than a two-buck steak. Don't forget, we're talking about the father whose son, Gregory, had gained NHL-wide acclaim and universal respect for playing a shift on a broken leg suffered when he blocked a shot against Pittsburgh in the 2013 Stanley Cup playoffs, still managing to leave the ice under his own power. So perhaps we shouldn't be too surprised when the father, after a near-death experience, plodded across that frozen field to his home with nothing on his mind but an overwhelming sense of relief at still being alive.

"That's all I thought about," Campbell said. "I was alive. It was kind of exciting. I was just happy to be alive."

Campbell walked up to his house—to the side garage door, actually. He was standing there, now trembling, soaking wet and frozen, vainly trying to recall and punch in the security code to open the garage door. As he fumbled with the keypad, he could hear Heather, who was putting garbage in the garage from an inside door leading to the house. Campbell started banging on the garage door and yelling to get her attention. She came over, hit the automatic opener and couldn't believe what she saw when the door opened: her husband standing there, rivulets of blood all over his head and face, wet and frozen.

"At first, because of the blood, she thought I had been attacked by coyotes," Campbell said.

Many a man, having been through such a traumatic physical ordeal with exposure to ice-cold water, bitterly cold winter weather and quite likely hypothermia, to say nothing of nearly drowning with dirty pond water filling his lungs, would have gone to the hospital for medical attention. But Campbell possessed a hockey player's mentality and farmer's stubborn streak. Besides, it was a workday.

All he wanted, once he got into the house, was a long—very long—

hot shower. And, practical man that he is, he wanted to make arrangements to get the tractor hauled out of the pond.

Campbell spent a good half hour in a steaming hot shower, doing nothing, he said, but luxuriating in the "sheer joy of breathing." A doctor friend who lived in the area did drop by the house later that day, but aside from taking some Advil, Campbell seemed to be okay. Mind you, as the day wore on, he lost his voice, leaving him with just a hoarse whisper. And by that evening, he had tremendous lower-back and rib pain, which turned out to be a nasty kidney infection from ingesting the dirty pond water.

But the NHL schedule waits for no man, not even one who almost drowned at lunchtime on a Friday afternoon. By seven o'clock that night, NHL games were being played. And in Campbell's world, that meant the next issue or controversy was only a puck drop away.

Right on cue, in the second period of the New Jersey Devils–Tampa Bay Lightning game at the Prudential Center in Newark that night, the lights unexpectedly went out. A circuit breaker blew, and the computers controlling the lights in the arena were damaged and couldn't be repaired. There was a delay of more than an hour and 40 minutes.

For much of that time, there was great uncertainty as to how the league could, would or should proceed, all initially exacerbated by the inability of many to get hold of the league's senior executive VP and director of hockey operations. Campbell's cell phone was still at the bottom of the pond in the big, orange Kubota. (As an aside, Campbell said when the tractor was pulled out of the pond, he got the cell phone back, dried it out for a day or two, and it worked like a charm. Even his cell phone had a knack for survival.)

No rest for the weary. Campbell had no choice but to be back at work, using his landline to consult with his right-hand man, Mike Murphy, in Toronto.

"We felt the teams could not continue playing," Colin Campbell was later quoted as saying in the newspapers in New York City and northern New Jersey. "We tried for an hour and [42] minutes to restore power and appropriate lighting but were left with no alternative but to postpone further play for the evening."

Campbell could have added: "Oh, I came within a breath of dying today." He didn't, of course.

After the fact, it bothered Campbell that his tractor had crashed through the ice at all. He'd been careful, he thought. With the extended frigid temperatures that winter, he was convinced the ice in the man-made irrigation pond was plenty thick enough to take the weight of the tractor. Campbell even asked the NHL's ice expert, Dan Craig, about the thickness and weight ratios and couldn't, for the life of him, figure out why he'd almost met a most untimely end.

It was later, long after the ice had melted that spring, that Campbell discovered, to his surprise, that the man-made irrigation pond they often needed to top up with water in the summer was, in fact, also fed by either a very small underground spring or underground runoff through the tiling. The water entered the pond at the northeast corner, mere feet from where his tractor crashed through the ice.

"The ice all over that pond was more than thick enough to take the weight of the tractor," Campbell said. "It was just at that one point, where the spring or the runoff feeds into the pond, there was a little bit of current. That's why I went through the ice right there. It wasn't as frozen."

Campbell was comforted somewhat to get the answer to that question. He had so many more, though.

"Sure, you wonder why, you wonder about a lot of things," Campbell said in November 2012, standing at the edge of the pond where his tractor plunged through the ice almost three years earlier, the first time he was prepared to discuss for the record what happened that day.

It's not as though he had gone out of his way to keep what happened a secret. His family, friends and co-workers obviously were aware of it shortly after it happened, and in the weeks that followed, word did filter out to others. But when asked if he wanted to discuss it in any public fashion, Campbell had always declined.

Even three years after the fact, it was difficult for him to put into words the range of emotions he'd had since his brush with death.

"I'd say—for the first year afterwards, anyway—not a day would go by that I wouldn't think about it," Campbell said. "As more time goes by, you don't ever completely forget about it, but it's not like you wake up every day and it dominates your thoughts. It's not like I put together a bucket list and said to myself, 'I have to do this or that before I go,' but, yeah, it changes you in some ways. It's a cliché, but probably the biggest difference is you don't sweat the small stuff as much."

Campbell knows he's not the same man he was before he almost drowned. He can't go past that pond, or even look at it from afar, without an involuntary shudder that reaches deep into his soul.

Truth be told, Campbell said he's much more cognizant of potential danger now than ever before, that before he begins any task on the farm, he thinks about what could go wrong, about the inherent risk.

"I don't just do something now," he said. "I try to be more careful, a little more cautious."

If he ever forgets that, there's no shortage of reminders. When Campbell is doing any work around the farm, especially anything involving machinery, his wife or daughters are much more likely to monitor it. And if he's doing anything on the farm that includes having one of his grandkids with him, he said, the scrutiny from his wife and daughters is even greater.

It wasn't just crashing through the ice that January day that had an impact on Campbell's view of life and death. The following April, in 2011, Campbell's friend and co-worker E.J. McGuire—the director of the NHL's Central Scouting Bureau—succumbed to a five-month battle with a rare and incurable form of cancer, leaving behind his wife and two teenaged daughters. McGuire, one year older than Campbell, was 58 when he died.

"Those two incidents really hit home for me," Campbell said. "E.J. was a healthy guy with a young family, and just like that, no warning, everything changes. It could have been the same thing for me. But, you know, E.J.'s death was just so unfair. He's healthy, he didn't do anything to get the cancer. He just got it. If I had died, that was on me. I was the one who caused it by going out on the pond and falling through the ice. So between what happened to E.J. and me, it hit me pretty good.

"I realized you don't get any guarantees on how long you live. I tell my kids, I tell Gregory, if he's going through a tough stretch [in hockey], you can't get too upset with little things you think are big things because, well, you never know . . . which is funny me saying that, because when I coached, [like] any coach, we all get so goofy about a loss or a losing streak, but it's really not life-altering stuff, even if we think it is when it's happening."

Campbell has since dabbled a little in trying to understand the hereafter. He's read material about people with near-death experiences, in particular Dr. Eben Alexander's *Proof of Heaven*, a bestselling non-fiction book that chronicles the story of the atheist neurosurgeon who came out of a week-long coma believing he had come in contact with heaven.

Campbell's own near-death experience didn't leave him with any deep or abiding knowledge of what happens, or doesn't, after you die, but he was unquestionably curious about those two visions that had come to him so vividly at the precise moment when he thought he was about to die.

"Who knows what it all means?" he said. "Is [life and death] just fate? Are you just lucky to live or unlucky to die? Is your time just up? I don't honestly know the answers to those questions, but I've thought about them. I don't really talk too much about [the visions] because I think people look at you like you're a bit crazy. It's not like I saw myself at the gates of heaven with Roger [Neilson], my dad, my grandfather, all there waiting for me, waving at me. That's not it.

"I'm no more religious now than I was before [the near-death experience]. You know, I've always believed in God, gone to church, so you do kind of wonder about it all. I mean, was it something more than dumb luck that got me through it? I think maybe it was. I guess I really wonder about that moment in time, those seconds, when you think you're dying. I know I went from being anxious to panic-stricken to 'I'm done,' and I won't forget that scary feeling of thinking my life was over.

"I think of those poor people who jumped from the World Trade Center on 9/11, and as they were falling to their death, however many seconds it was that they were still alive while they were falling, what must have been going through their minds? There was a story I saw of a construction worker who fell off a 70-storey building and died when he landed on top of a 15-storey building, so for 55 storeys and however long it takes to fall that far, he was alive. What was he thinking? What was that like for him? Because I can tell you, for the last 30 to 40 seconds I was underwater, I was certain I was dying. But I didn't, and I'm not sure exactly why."

Campbell is wholly certain of only two things, really.

One, after coming so close to dying, he's happy to be alive; he cherishes each and every day.

Two—and he isn't being flippant about it—he hopes others will think twice before they venture out like he did: "I'll never go out on another pond. Growing up, I'd play pond hockey all the time. There wasn't a day went by when I was a kid that I didn't walk across the frozen pond in town and never thought twice about it. But I can't do it now. Those days are over."

CHAPTER 2

Magic Hands, Healing Hands

Mark Lindsay's ART Form and Desire to
"Stay Hungry, Hidden and Humble"

———————

The best hands in the National Hockey League do not belong to Sidney Crosby, Patrick Kane or Pavel Datsyuk.

In fact, the guy with the best hands in the NHL also has the best hands in the National Football League, Major League Baseball, the Professional Golfers Association and the Association of Tennis Professionals (ATP), as well as the Olympic Games—summer and winter, in case you were wondering.

His name is Dr. Mark Lindsay. If you haven't heard of him, don't feel bad. He is the first to tell you his friends sometimes call him "The Ghost." It's been said by some that it's easier to track down Keyser Soze, the mythical underworld figure from the movie *The Usual Suspects*, than it is to reach Lindsay, whose personal motto in life (which he borrowed from a famous athlete) is: "Stay hungry, hidden and humble."

So who, precisely, is this international man of mystery with the gifted, magic hands?

Mark Lindsay is a Canadian chiropractor, born in 1963 near the little Ottawa Valley town of Arnprior, Ontario (population 8,114).

Mind you, calling Lindsay a chiropractor is like saying Picasso was a painter or Sinatra was a singer. He's a star in his field who treats athletes to allow them to excel in theirs.

That would include the NHL's pre-eminent superstar, Sidney Crosby, and upwards of 100 active NHL players, not to mention countless retired NHLers. Modesty, as well as the bond of confidentiality he shares with his world-famous clients, prevents him from even acknowledging who he treats.

"The people I treat value their privacy and so do I," Lindsay says of his clientele. "They trust me to work on them; they also trust me to not talk about it. That's sacred, and rightfully so."

U.S. publications have reported he's worked with Tiger Woods and Alex Rodriguez. There's talk within the sporting community that Lindsay may have, at one time or another, worked with tennis ace Maria Sharapova and Canadian/world figure-skating champion Patrick Chan, amongst so many others who are world class in their respective disciplines. Suffice it to say he's worked with the best of the best and won't discuss any of it.

To know Lindsay—and what he can accomplish with his healing hands as well as a wealth of practical experience on how the human body should optimally function—is to want him to treat you. He's a man in great demand, even though the most devoted sports fan likely wouldn't be able to pick him out of a lineup or recognize him if he were standing next to the stars he looks after. But in the eyes of the athletes he treats, and those of his peers, Lindsay is also a superstar.

"Between the tactile, his incredible ability with his hands, and his thirst for learning, to be current and innovative and ahead of the curve, Mark is the best at what he does," said Ottawa-based high-performance chiropractor Dr. Duane Smith, who also treats elite athletes.

"Mark has that X factor and it's his hands," said highly regarded Toronto sport chiropractor Dr. Mike Prebeg, another star in the field who works with the Toronto Blue Jays as well as myriad other elite athletes in all sports. "In our field, Mark is a stud. When Mark puts his hands on an athlete, they immediately know it's special, that he's special. He has the touch."

"He has the gift of touch, no doubt about that," said former NHL player Gary Roberts—who would know, since Lindsay has probably treated him, quite literally, thousands of times. "But with Mark, when you combine his touch with his incredible experience, to have treated so many great athletes in so many sports and be able to apply all that he has learned when he's treating you, that's what makes him special."

Lindsay is humbled by his station in life. He's blown away that sports' best and brightest athletes, the *crème de la crème*, seek him out for injury treatment or rehab or to maximize athletic performance. And that they are willing to put their faith and trust in him to the point where their bodies, careers and entire futures are in his hands. Literally.

"It is like playing an instrument," Lindsay said. "You can be super-bright, super-intelligent, but it has to translate to tactile, to the hands. I mean, you're working on someone's body. You have to feel it. From my own experiences, getting treatments, you can tell right away when someone gets it, when someone has the touch. . . . It's like watching Wayne Gretzky or Connor McDavid play hockey and you say, 'How do they know to do that?' What they do isn't easy, they just make it look that way. . . . I shake my head a lot at how things have gone for me. I grew up in a small town. Never in a million years did I imagine I'd be doing this. Sometimes I think, 'This is cool—this is my job.'"

Imagine a 39-year-old Mark Lindsay being called into the office of the notorious Oakland Raiders boss Al Davis and being given his marching orders for the 2002–03 NFL season: keep the aging core of Raider veterans healthy enough to stay on the field and make plays.

That veteran core included Rich Gannon, Tim Brown, Charlie

Garner, Rod Woodson, Charles Woodson, Bill Romanowski and Jerry Rice, amongst others.

Every Friday during the season, Lindsay would fly from Toronto to Oakland or wherever the Raiders were playing. He'd treat the star veterans the day before the game, the day of the game, and on the sidelines *during* the game. On Monday, he'd fly back to Toronto and his regular, and thriving, chiropractic practice.

"It almost killed me," Lindsay said, laughing. And all that separated Lindsay and the Raiders from fulfilling Davis's Super Bowl dream were the Tampa Bay Buccaneers, the revenge of former Raider coach Jon Gruden and the bizarre disappearance of Raider all-pro centre Barrett Robbins, who went AWOL from San Diego the day before the Super Bowl to party in nearby Tijuana, Mexico. (Robbins was later diagnosed as bipolar and has suffered from mental, emotional and legal issues since then.)

Word travelled fast about the skilled young Canadian chiropractor with healing hands. There's no better calling card than word of mouth, and whether it was athletes from one sport talking to those in other sports or their agents talking amongst themselves, it wasn't long before the biggest names in football, baseball, tennis and golf were clamouring for Lindsay to rehab their injuries or treat them on an ongoing basis. With a thriving practice back home in Ontario, there were occasions when Lindsay actually had no choice but turn down some of the invitations from some of the world's pre-eminent athletes. No sooner would one door close, though, than another two would open.

"It was an unbelievable experience," Lindsay said. "This was all happening in a period of a few years between 2008 and 2011 when I was working with some incredible athletes in so many different sports. I had, in my profession . . . I can honestly say I reached the pinnacle."

Maybe Mark Lindsay was always destined to be a healer of high-performance athletes. As a teenager growing up in White Lake, near Arnprior, he dreamed one day of going to medical school. And he always loved and played sports himself. He ran track—400-metre hurdles—and was a wide receiver in football in high school. He was good enough to get an NCAA Division I football and track scholarship to Ball State in Indiana, a school he chose in large part because of its strong exercise physiology department and the presence of Dr. David Costill, who did work in the 1980s with distance runners Mary Decker and Alberto Salazar.

Two years in, Lindsay realized Ball State and Division I football weren't for him. He came home to Canada, ended up being a receiver and punt returner with the University of Guelph Gryphons, coached by the late Tom Dimitroff, and won the Vanier Cup—the national university football championship—in 1984. His roommate then was Parri Ceci, who was named MVP of that championship game and whose son Cody was the Ottawa Senators' first-round pick in 2012.

Lindsay graduated from Guelph with a degree in kinesiology and was planning on going to medical school at McMaster University in Hamilton. Until, that is, he suffered a herniated disc in a bad waterskiing fall in Muskoka. He was in back-pain hell until treated by a noted Scarborough, Ontario, chiropractor, Dr. Keith Innes, who was at that time treating, amongst others, sprinter Ben Johnson.

Innes did such an amazing job of easing Lindsay's back pain and healing him without surgery that it made a tremendous impact on the young would-be medical doctor.

"I was like, 'Wow, I can't believe what he did,'" Lindsay said. "I was totally fixed. That's when I decided I wanted to be a chiropractor."

It was too late to apply to chiropractic college in Toronto, so Lindsay went to Palmer College of Chiropractic, which is the founding college for the science, in Davenport, Iowa. He graduated from Palmer

in 1989 and did a one-year residency in Texas before finally returning
home to Ottawa to set up his practice there. In 1991, Lindsay hooked
up with chiropractic pioneer Dr. Michael Leahy to get in on the ground
floor of Leahy's brainchild: Active Release Technique (ART). It's aptly
named because it is as much an art form as a science.

Leahy, a chiropractor from Colorado Springs, Colorado, graduated from the United States Air Force Academy and served as a fighter
and test pilot. In 1985, he discovered ART, a hands-on manipulation
of soft tissue for the treatment of injuries. In 1991, Leahy taught his
first ART class to other chiropractors. There were two Canadians in
Leahy's first class of six: Lindsay and Mark Scappaticci, another highly
regarded Toronto-area chiropractor whose resumé is strikingly similar to Lindsay's. Each of those six "students" in Leahy's first class has
gone on to become an ART instructor, teaching and registering the
ever-increasing number of chiropractors who have embraced ART
not only as a treatment for trauma and injuries, but as a systemic
approach to prevent injury and enhance athletic performance. It's a
much more commonly known procedure now than it was then, but
like all young sciences, its boundaries and applications are constantly
being redefined, and Lindsay is at the forefront of that movement. And
Toronto, Lindsay said, has become a mecca of sorts for practitioners
of ART.

"There are more good ART chiropractors in the Toronto area, in
Ontario, than anywhere in North America," Lindsay said.

And if he had to explain to a layperson exactly what ART is and
its benefits?

"Every muscle has a wrapping of fascia, like Saran wrap, and every
vein, artery and nerve that goes into a muscle is also encased in fascia—
it all really floats in fascia," Lindsay said. "The muscles glide over each
other in these fascia casings. What happens when you have an injury
or overuse or trauma, [is] it creates an inhibition of the gliding. ART is

the manual manipulation to restore that glide. It's like you have a hard-shell suitcase and you want to make it a soft shell. It's not like you're trying to make spaghetti out of the muscle; you're just trying to create gliding, create space . . . does that make sense?"

Around the same time Lindsay was embracing the brave new world of Leahy's ART, all the while working at his chiropractic practice in Ottawa, he got hooked up with the Canadian bobsleigh team that was preparing for the 1992 Winter Olympics in Albertville, France. Lindsay had run track with some of the bobsleigh athletes. Noted strength and conditioning coach Charles Poliquin was looking for a chiropractor to treat his Canadian Olympians. So Lindsay started working with the bobsleigh team and the short-track speed skaters (Marc Gagnon and Nathalie Lambert, amongst others). He had found his calling, not to mention his wife.

In 1994, while at the Winter Games in Lillehammer, Norway, Lindsay met Canadian and world champion downhill skier Kate Pace, who in 1993 was ranked No. 1 in the world. In 1995, the two were married in Ottawa, and their reception was held in the Hall of Honour in the Centre Block of the Parliament Buildings.

It was around that time that Lindsay's career path took a meteoric rise. The newly minted Kate Pace-Lindsay wanted to compete in one more Olympics—Nagano, Japan, in 1998—so Lindsay sold his Ottawa practice after getting married and, amongst other things, became the Canadian Alpine Ski Team's therapist between 1996 and 1998. It was a great way to spend time with his wife while continuing to expand his professional horizons, treating Olympic athletes. The real turning point, though, came in 1995 and 1996, when Lindsay became part of trainer Dan Pfaff's team overseeing the training and treatment of Canadian sprinter Donovan Bailey.

Mark and Kate would spend their summers with the Pfaff–Bailey crew working and training in Texas, working not only with Bailey but with his Olympic sprinting teammates, Bruny Surin, Glenroy Gilbert and Robert Esmie. Mark and Kate's winters were spent on the ski circuit, effectively living the life of athletic nomads for the first three years of their marriage.

But when Bailey won gold and set a world record in the 100 metres at the 1996 Summer Games in Atlanta, and then Bailey, Surin, Gilbert and Esmie teamed up to upset the Americans on their home turf to win gold in the 4 x 100-metre relay, it was a major turning point in Lindsay's career. Bailey was golden and so were all those who were part of his team.

"Donovan was successful on the biggest stage," Lindsay said. "And we had had a lot of success with the short-track speed skaters in the '90s, so a lot of doors got opened for me after that. That really paved the way for everything else—the football, all the other pro sports."

In 1998, at his wife's final Olympics, Lindsay began working with Dr. Tony Galea, the Toronto sports doctor who was doing cutting-edge work with injury treatment, specifically PRP (platelet-rich plasma) injections. It was the beginning of an ongoing and successful partnership, though one that didn't lack for controversy along the way. Lindsay worked out of Galea's sports medicine clinic in Toronto's west end until 2007, when Lindsay and his wife escaped the hustle and bustle of city life to build their dream home on White Lake.

PRP is the legal (with a letter of consent from a sport's governing body and approval from the International Olympic Committee) injury-treatment process that involves taking blood from the injured athlete, spinning it in a centrifuge, taking the condensed elements of the centrifuged blood and reinjecting it into the injured athlete's precise muscle tear or tendon damage. It is not, when done as specified, considered to be blood doping or performance-enhancing.

"It's very effective," Lindsay said. "It's legal so long as you're fixing a legitimate injury. There are growth factors in the platelets—it's basically a form of stem cell, but it's autologous. It's your own tissue—no drugs, no foreign substances. It causes protein synthesis, healing power. It can fix the injured area—it doesn't mask the thing like cortisone [does]. It works best for hamstring tears, Achilles tears and groin tears.

"You have to fix the lesion and then you need to fix the 'system.' That's why Tony and I worked so well together. Tony would treat the specific injury and I'd work on the [body] system."

But in 2009, Dr. Galea ran afoul of the law. His assistant was stopped at the U.S.–Canada border in Buffalo with a small quantity of human growth hormone (HGH), Actovegin (a derivative of calf's blood used to accelerate healing of injuries that isn't approved in Canada), and vials of foreign homeopathic drugs. Because all this happened not long after Galea was administering PRP injections to Tiger Woods, which was a matter of public record, it generated international headlines. PRP, when performed as specified, may be legal, but if, for example, HGH was added to the syringe cocktail, the process would cross the line into the realm of illegal performance enhancement. Galea claimed he had been using HGH on himself and other older, non-athletic patients.

Dr. Galea initially faced charges in both the United States and Canada relating to selling an unapproved drug, conspiring to import an unapproved drug, exporting a drug and smuggling goods into Canada. But in 2011, Galea pleaded guilty to a much lesser charge of illegally transporting "misbranded" drugs, including HGH. In 2012, Canadian authorities dropped all charges against Galea.

As of 2013, the College of Physicians and Surgeons of Ontario, which regulates all doctors in the province, had never brought any charges against Galea and he continued to practise medicine in his Toronto clinic, with many professional athletes from all sports continuing to make their way to him for PRP treatments. But *The Globe and Mail* reported in the summer of 2013 that the College of Physicians and Surgeons had an open investigation concerning Galea, though no other details were provided.

"What can I say?" Lindsay said. "I treat athletes for injuries. I'm trying to heal them. It's all about healing, not cheating."

Lindsay's wealth of experience has made him wise to the ways of the world, the highs and lows that are so much a part of athletics, but it's interesting that one of the people who had the greatest impact on Lindsay isn't an athlete at all.

Isadore (Izzy) Sharp is the octogenarian Canadian hotelier from Toronto, the founder and chairman of Four Seasons Hotels and Resorts. Getting to know a businessman like Sharp had as big an impact on Lindsay's approach to the "business" of healing.

"I tell this story all the time. I'm in Mr. Sharp's office and he's at the window. He says, 'Come over here, I want to show you something. What do you see out there?' I said, 'I dunno . . . traffic?'" Lindsay recounted, laughing. "He said, 'Those people out there are too busy working to make money.' I didn't get it, so he told me: 'You're providing a service, but you can't treat 100 people a day. Take your top 20 per cent of your clients and *really* look after them.'

"I'd never thought of it that way. The traditional thing for a chiropractor is you work in a clinic or an office and you adjust and treat as many people as you can in a day. I was obviously in a different situation. What [Sharp] said changed my life."

Lindsay didn't work with only athletes. There were entertainers and captains of industry, too. The late tap dancer and actor Gregory Hines would regularly fly from Los Angeles to Toronto just to be treated by Lindsay.

But there's always going to be that phone call from an athlete or an agent, asking Lindsay for help. And some of his favourite clients and stories with the happiest endings come from those out-of-the-blue calls, where a young athlete is on hard times not only because of a specific injury but maybe due to messed-up biomechanics or a lack of strength and conditioning. Lindsay will assemble a team and apply his comprehensive approach.

"You need the right physical trainer, the right therapist, the right medical doctor . . . you need it all, a whole team of people, and you need it all working together in harmony," Lindsay said. "That's how it's supposed to fit together, and when it all comes together like that, it's great."

He's got lots of stories of like that. He just can't share them.

Mark Lindsay only played minor hockey to midget age as a kid growing up in White Lake, and most of his first 10 years in the business didn't give him much involvement with hockey, but Gary Roberts ultimately changed all that, though in a somewhat circuitous fashion.

The Calgary Flames forward had to retire from the NHL in 1996 because of ongoing issues with his surgically repaired neck. He had nerve damage, bilateral stingers, and simply could no longer play the game at age 30.

Roberts's strength and conditioning coach, Lorne Goldenberg of Ottawa, called Lindsay to see if there were any unexplored treatment options for Roberts. Lindsay referred Goldenberg and Roberts to ART founder Michael Leahy in Colorado Springs. Leahy put Roberts back together. Roberts's soft tissue and neck flexors had all pinched around the nerve roots, causing the numbness and stingers. Leahy freed Roberts from the pain and numbness, Charles Poliquin rehabbed him on the strength and conditioning front and Roberts went on to play another 12 years in the NHL. It was a miraculous recovery and it was primarily due to ART. Roberts became fanatical about nutrition, training and treatment, so much so that he's become a highly respected strength and conditioning coach himself now, right there on the cutting edge of the industry and a huge advocate of ART science as an everyday part of the game.

"Mike Leahy and Gary Roberts created a revolution in hockey," Lindsay said. "They brought ART to hockey."

"ART, Mike Leahy and Mark Lindsay," Roberts said. "Between them, they saved my career. It would have been over without them."

When Roberts went from Carolina to Toronto in 2000, Lindsay began doing almost daily ART on the Maple Leaf winger, and it wasn't long before he was working on pretty much the whole team of that era—Mats Sundin, Joe Nieuwendyk, Bryan McCabe, Alex Mogilny, Tie Domi, Eddie Belfour and Curtis Joseph. With the blessing of the Leafs' medical and training staff—which is often unusual when it comes to the sometimes strained relationship between pro teams' staffs and outside chiropractors and/or practitioners of ART—Lindsay would go to the players' individual homes, often spending a full hour treating each. Lindsay estimates that in one calendar year alone, he probably laid hands on Roberts as many as 200 times.

"The real value of ART for me is prevention of injuries and freeing up athletes' bodies to be at their best," Lindsay said. "At that time, with those Toronto guys, I didn't know of anyone using ART in a maintenance, preventative paradigm as opposed to specific injury treatment. When an athlete gets ART, he feels so much better, they're all freed up, everything feels more effortless, but they want to be treated all the time."

It's almost addictive.

Yet treatments can be time-consuming—expensive, too, in many instances, because ART is most effective when it's done over and over again.

"It's worth every dollar," Roberts said. "I think it's actually an undervalued investment. Sure, it cost me a lot of money, but not when you measure how much I spent on ART versus how much I made in the 12 years I played (after ART revived his career). It's a drop in the bucket. For a player today, I don't think there's any better investment."

In some ways, it's actually surprising NHL teams don't employ full-time chiropractors whose specialize in ART, because if ever there were a sport tailor-made for the benefits of ART, it's hockey.

Skating, in and of itself (putting aside for the moment the potential for trauma), goes completely against normal human posture, which is upright and open. Skating causes a player to be hunched over and closed. Hockey players skate virtually every day, so the body becomes trained to be in a position that is anything but "normal." The wear and tear of simply skating every day can break down an athletes' soft tissue. The same thing applies to off-season strength training for hockey players. Matt Nichol, a top strength and conditioning coach in Toronto, not only trains and conditions his hockey players all summer, he regularly has ART chiropractor Mike Prebeg and his staff on site to treat the athletes. It's foolish to think a high level of maintenance isn't required to keep a hockey player healthy and functioning optimally.

"It's like tuning a guitar—I don't know how else to explain it," Lindsay said. "You tune a string, play it, tune it some more, play it some more. You never stop tuning or playing. If you don't ever tune the strings of that guitar, it won't play music like it's supposed to."

Yet there are many times when an NHL club or player's first call to an ART chiropractor, if they make the call at all, is only to treat a specific injury or trauma. Yet it could very well be that the injury itself was a direct result of not using ART as preventive maintenance.

The human body is an amazing machine. The muscles and tendons are designed to fire in a very specific sequence. The action of one muscle triggers the action of another. When's it's unfolding as it should, it's like a beautiful symphony orchestra. But if there's just one instrument out of tune . . . simple wear and tear, or any traumatic incident—let's say, a blocked shot taken on the player's ankle—can set off an unnatural and potentially destructive deviated sequence for the athlete.

The ankle is sore, not broken or fractured—not anything that would prevent a hockey player from playing through the pain. But maybe that pain hinders the athlete—very subtly, without him even recognizing it—causing him to maybe not flex his ankle to the same degree he normally would. Suddenly, the muscle-firing sequence that starts in skating with the flexion of the ankle is "off" ever so slightly, and that alters every muscle movement up the leg and into the hips and core, which is where a hockey player ultimately derives his dynamic speed and power. When that sequence is off, it can cause muscles to break down or shut down, and one problem leads to another. Maybe two months after blocking a shot that didn't cause the player to miss so much as a shift, never mind a game, he's plagued with a hip problem or sports hernia that requires season-ending surgery. It all started because of a sore ankle.

"You learn the patterns of a sport when you treat its athletes," Lindsay said. "Hockey is all about ankle flexion; you have to be able to dorsiflex. The degree of that flexion changes the action of your knee and hip, and then you can't activate your glutes, you get too far forward . . . when you have a joint that doesn't move right or soft tissue is tight, it's the equivalent of being in the wrong place at the wrong time, and that's when you get injured. ART is releasing everything so it can all go back into its normal sequence."

Which is why, after treating hundreds of NHL players thousands of times, Lindsay says with dead certainty: an ankle sprain or other ankle injury, if not treated properly, leads to hip problems. Every time.

Every time?

"One hundred per cent," Lindsay said.

One hundred per cent? Really?

"Non-negotiable, 100 per cent," Lindsay said. "It's ankle, knee, hip . . . every time."

And yet Lindsay is in the most demand when there's been an injury. It could be Sidney Crosby's high-ankle sprain, Steve Moore's neck trauma and post-concussion syndrome—you name it, Lindsay has likely experienced it with the more than 100 current NHLers he's treated. Sometimes the work is done with the blessing of the club's medical and training staffs; sometimes it's strictly hush-hush, on the side. There isn't a chiropractor practising ART who hasn't gone through that dance over territorial turf wars and issues of control.

Lindsay is convinced that "friction" between the disciplines—team doctors vs. team athletic therapists vs. outside chiropractors—isn't as prevalent as it once was, though it still most certainly exists. The fact that so many ex-NHL players who received ART during their playing days are now in management or coaching, he believes, should open more doors to outside treatment without conflict. Yet ART chiropractors will still tell you stories of NHL players sneaking off to see them because they fear their NHL club won't approve.

Lindsay said most of today's elite athletes, especially the new breed of young stars in the NHL, have already figured out the global approach to high performance and wellness. He notes the young guns in the NHL have assembled "teams" of experts running the gamut from strength training to nutrition, to power skating, to chiropractic treatments, to soft-tissue treatments, to medical treatments.

The evolution of his own career, Lindsay said, has been nothing short of amazing. ART started as a way for him to heal a specific injury to a specific piece of soft tissue, and then developed into overall injury prevention and wellness, but has gone to a whole new level as injuries in sports have become more complex and complicated.

Professional sports' modern-day plague—concussions—has absorbed a huge amount of Lindsay's time and effort over the last decade. Lindsay has helped many a concussed athlete—soft-tissue neck trauma is almost always part of any significant blow to the head—but the science and complexity of it goes way beyond that.

"It's not about sport, it's about life," Lindsay said of concussions. "The work that's being done in Boston with Dr. [Robert] Cantu and Dr. [Ann] McKee is unbelievable; the research is showing more and more how much trauma and havoc is created in the brain with a concussion . . . I get calls every day from people who have kids suffering from it, eight, nine, 10 years old, they can't concentrate in school, they can't sleep. I don't want to be known as a concussion guy, but you want to do as much as you can to help. I most certainly don't have all the answers. Now you've got [Atlanta-based] Dr. Ted Carrick [who treated Crosby, amongst others] looking at neurology from a functional point of view—eye movements and vestibular and inner ear functions—but it's just one piece of a really big, difficult puzzle. For the future of hockey, all these specialties have to come together to work more."

As much as Mike Leahy's ART gave Lindsay the foundation for what he does with his hands, he's constantly trying to broaden those horizons. He's studying the work of and working with noted French osteopath Dr. Guy Voyer as well as learning from and working with Carrick, for the past seven years working towards earning his status as a Board Certified Diplomate with the American Chiropractic Neurology Board, making him one of only a handful of Canadian chiropractors who have attained that status. He feels treating the human body is now all about interrelating a variety of disciplines and the way the brain processes movement of muscles and joints.

"Guy Voyer has changed my whole perception of the body as a complete system. I'll always be thankful for the touch that Mike Leahy taught us, and Ted Carrick is looking at the brain as a processor—eye movement, inner ear, balance—as something that dictates what the joints and soft tissue do. I've spent all these years doing peripheral treatments; I'm just now starting to understand the integration of it all, and let me tell you, the results are crazy. ART, for me, it's a lifetime course."

It's the summer of 2013 and Lindsay, just shy of his 50th birthday, is in Kingston, Ontario, dissecting human cadavers at Queen's University, trying to learn even more about the fascia he's been manipulating for more than 20 years. His thirst for knowledge and new information and techniques is insatiable. As much as he still enjoys the practical part of his work, using his hands to treat a world-class athlete, he can see himself doing more academic work in the future, more studies, more clinical research. For example, he's absolutely convinced there's a correlation between players who get concussed and suffer soft-tissue neck trauma and those who end up subsequently needing hip surgery, but as he says, "The medical world won't listen to you unless you can quantify it, so I want to go back into the academic world and quantify some of these things I believe I know from my experiences."

But the small-town guy who estimates he spends at least 150 days a year on the road knows he'll never stop treating athletes.

"That's the rush," he said. "You get a call from a great athlete and he needs your help. Those are the ones you remember. It's been a privilege for me to work with these athletes. I've learned so much from them. You watch them train, it's no joke. Their level of preparation is incredible, they're all in. The best athletes still prepare the best and they make it look easy and it's not easy. I also love working with these young kids in hockey today, to see the change in the attitude of these young guys, how they understand the big picture. They just get it.

"I'd like to have that mix—do some academic work, treat some athletes who need it. I'm trying to travel less, pick my spots more, get home for four- or five-day stretches. It's a good thing [wife] Kate is so understanding. She knows—she was in three Olympics, she's an elite athlete—and the only reason she puts up with me is because she understands what I'm doing and who I'm doing it for. Along the way, after 20-plus years, it's all about evolving, deciding what to add to your arsenal. It's just not possible to stop learning; I'm perpetually learning. I don't have the answers. I want to get better and help as many athletes as possible."

In the meantime, though, as he sorts through it all, Mark Lindsay tries every day to take to heart the advice his wife, Kate, passed along to him years ago, when he was treating a tennis superstar at a tournament. Kate was on another court, chatting with Rafael Nadal and his famous coach, his uncle Toni Nadal.

"It was an impromptu thing, very casual, and Kate was talking to Rafa and Uncle Toni. They talked to her about their philosophy; they said it included three things, and we've really tried to adopt them: stay hungry, hidden and humble. You have to be humble because you realize you can't fix everyone—there are going to be people you just can't help. You have to stay hungry because there's so much to learn, it's constantly changing and evolving, and you have to try to stay up on it. And hidden . . . well, most times I can walk into a room full of people and no one knows who I am."

If the face goes unrecognized, the hands do not.

CHAPTER 3

Uncle John, Young John

*Sharing the Tavares Name, and Phenomenal Skill, to Become
Elite in Both of Canada's National Games*

———

Joe Tavares is not the type of man to wonder what might
have been. He's economical with his words, projecting equal parts
stoicism and strength. If he were being cast in a movie, he'd be the
strong, silent type.

So as much as a nine-year-old boy, brand new to Canada, desperately wanted to join the other boys his age and play the sports they
were playing—soccer and baseball in the summer, hockey in the winter—Joe Tavares knew it was not to be.

"I wanted to play so badly," he said, "but I couldn't."

Tavares said he had to deal with "reality," and this was his: when
Manuel and Dorotea Tavares left the harsh life of the Azores (a string
of volcanic islands off the coast of their native Portugal in the Atlantic
Ocean) behind them in 1967, emigrating to Toronto in Canada's cen-
tennial year for the promise of a better life, there was neither time nor
money for sports or recreation—certainly not at first, not for their eldest son, Joe, or his younger siblings seven-year-old Rita and five-year-
old Danny.

Even as a nine-year-old, when his grade school day was over at Ryerson Public School in the Alexandra Park neighbourhood located on the western fringe of downtown Toronto, Joe had to hustle to his part-time job to help support the family, hucking dry goods in Kensington Market. But that didn't mean there weren't times when Joe was still sorely tempted to be a kid, one with a passion for sports.

"One day, instead of going to my job at the market after school, I played for the school baseball team," Joe recalled. "I was pitching. I was on the mound when I saw my mother coming across the [baseball] field towards me. I dropped the ball and ran right to work. My teacher was mad. He didn't understand why I left. I ran because I knew what was coming next if I didn't."

Not only was there no time for Joe to play sports, it wasn't long before there was no time for school at all. His reality was work, not education. With the Tavares patriarch, Manuel, working as a labourer and matriarch Dorotea staying at home to look after the family, there were soon more Tavares mouths to feed. Another brother, John, the first of the family to be born in Canada, arrived in 1968, and the youngest brother, Peter, in 1976.

By the age of 15, Joe was no longer going to school; instead, he was working two jobs that allowed younger siblings like John to play the games Joe couldn't. And even though Joe was able to play some soccer and hockey once he got into his twenties, getting married and having a family of his own meant that reality would at times trump sports once again. Joe's own son John would be given every chance to play the sports he loved, but Joe was often too busy in the sheet metal and structural steel business, supporting his family, to fully partake in his son's sporting endeavours.

"I didn't really have that chance to play [sports], but I did what I could so [brother John and son John] could play," Joe Tavares said. "If [son John] wanted it, the opportunity was there for him. I would tell him, 'It's there if you want it. Go for it.'"

Go for it, they did. Both of them. Like you wouldn't believe. Joe's little brother John, the lacrosse player; Joe's son John, the hockey player; an uncle and a nephew; the same name, but a different game.

Little did Joe Tavares realize, when he dropped the ball on the pitcher's mound to run to work that day with his mother in hot pursuit, it would help to spawn two of the country's greatest athletes, each of whom would not only play one of Canada's two national games, but, quite remarkably, dominate them.

If you hear the name John Tavares and automatically think of the 1990-born centre with the New York Islanders of the National Hockey League, it's understandable. The eldest son of Joe and Barb Tavares of Oakville, Ontario, has been a national headliner since he became, at age 15, the first player to be granted "exceptional" status in the Ontario Hockey League, gaining admission to the league a year earlier than normal. He broke Wayne Gretzky's OHL record for goals by a 16-year-old, starred for Canada in back-to-back gold-medal performances at the World Junior Championship in 2008 and 2009, and was the first-overall selection in the 2009 NHL Entry Draft. At age 23, he lined up with the *crème de la crème* and played for Team Canada at the 2014 Winter Olympics in Sochi, Russia. Five seasons into his pro career, he was already an NHL superstar in every sense of the word, and if he plays his way into the Hockey Hall of Fame, it will come as a surprise to no one.

So, yes, it's perfectly understandable if he's who you thought of when you heard the name John Tavares.

But that would only mean you haven't met Uncle John—or Johnny T or the original J.T., as he's known (with apologies to his nephew and

Justin Timberlake), the 1968-born, mild-mannered high school math teacher by day, who on summer nights and winter weekends becomes the ageless wonder and Canadian box lacrosse phenom. If there were a prize for the sports personality who epitomizes Canadian athleticism while garnering the least national recognition, Johnny T would win it in a walk.

"Put it this way," says Hockey Hall of Fame player Brendan Shanahan, who played minor lacrosse with J.T., "John Tavares the hockey player has a long way to go to accomplish what John Tavares the lacrosse player has done."

Young John would be the first to agree, if only Uncle John would slow down long enough to let anyone catch up. Every time he stepped on the floor for the National Lacrosse League's Buffalo Bandits, he was setting NLL records. His statistical dominance in the NLL has been Wayne Gretzky–like. Going into the 2014 season, Tavares had played more games than anyone else (280), scored more goals (779—142 more than the next best), assists (887—109 more No. 2) and points (1,666—404 more than the nearest competition).

If his offensive prowess is Gretzkyesque, his longevity brings to mind Gordie Howe. The NLL was originally known as the Major Indoor Lacrosse League (MILL). It opened its doors in 1986, but it was in 1992 that a 23-year-old Tavares burst onto the scene with the Bandits, winning three MILL championships in his first five seasons. In 1998, the MILL became the NLL, and while Tavares led the Bandits to three appearances in NLL championship games, there was just one more title, in 2008. At the age of 45, in his 23rd consecutive season, he was still at it, one of Buffalo's most revered athletes, a big reason why the Bandits, first at the old Memorial Auditorium and then at its replacement, First Niagara Center, have been the NLL's marquee franchise.

J.T.'s an institution in Western New York. Every time he scored a goal, the P.A. announcer would say: "Bandit goal scored by Johnny Who?" And the crowd would roar "Tavares" in response.

His impact in the summer lacrosse leagues of Ontario and British Columbia is the stuff of legend. In 1992, at the age of 24, he helped lead the Brampton Excelsiors to the national championship, the Mann Cup. They did it again in 1993. In 1994, he moved to the Six Nations Chiefs and won three consecutive Mann Cups.

But merely recounting his championships or MVP awards or all the goals or points can't begin to paint the true picture of the artistry and athleticism of the five-foot-11, 185-pound Tavares. Lacrosse is a hard game, especially the summer variety, played in hot, steamy, sauna-like arenas. Just running up and down the hard concrete floors can break down a man's body, never mind that there are big men— mean ones, too—using the legal lacrosse cross-check and other more violent illegal tactics to physically punish whomever has the ball. And in any game played by J.T., he has the ball. A lot.

There's no place to hide in lacrosse. Ask any hockey player who has played lacrosse, and there are many, and they'll tell you how much tougher and rugged a sport lacrosse can be than hockey, especially in front of the net, where a goal scorer takes his life into his hands while cutting through the middle.

Lacrosse fans are no different than hockey fans in that they like to debate who is the greatest player of all time. In hockey, some will cite the statistical dominance of Gretzky, the longevity of Howe, the game-changing dynamic of Bobby Orr, Mario Lemieux's unheard-of size, speed and skill, or the fire in the eyes of Maurice (Rocket) Richard.

It's no different in lacrosse. Old-timers will say the greatest of all time is Gaylord Powless or John Davis. In the modern era, many would say it has to be Victoria's Gary Gait, or his twin brother, Paul—big men who excelled in field lacrosse at Syracuse before dominating any box game they played anywhere. Peterborough's John Grant Jr., six years younger than Tavares, was making his own case to be considered the greatest of all time. But there's never any shortage of lacrosse people who'll tell you Johnny T. is No. 1.

"I think he's the best who ever played," said Brian Shanahan, the older brother of ex-NHLer Brendan and a stalwart lacrosse defender who won five Mann Cups alongside Tavares with Brampton and Six Nations. "It's not just that he's played the game at the highest level possible, it's how long he's done it. It's incredible. Gary Gait is amazing, he's a lot like Mario Lemieux, that's a good comparison. There'll be lots of people who say Gary or Paul Gait are best. There's always going to be that debate. But, for me, J.T. is Wayne Gretzky *and* Gordie Howe all in one. Like Gretzky, he's not the biggest or the fastest or the strongest, but he is the smartest and the most skilful. He just thinks the game on another level from everyone else. He's dominated for such a long time, so he's like Gordie Howe that way. He's 45 years old and he's still playing. It's incredible. He's so competitive. He'd slit your throat to beat you, but he's a tremendous teammate and a great guy, a really good person."

Troy Cordingley would take it a step further.

"Not only do I think he's the greatest lacrosse player of all time," said the head coach of the 2014 Buffalo Bandits and a four-time Mann Cup teammate of Tavares, "I think you could make a case for him being the one of the greatest Canadian athletes, if not *the* greatest, in any sport. To do what he's doing at age 45, in as physically a demanding game as lacrosse is, to have done it year in and year out—yeah, I think he's one of the best Canadian athletes ever in any sport."

Scoff if you like, and many will, but I'm going to tell you a story.

Since the early 1980s, I've had a front-row seat to the greatest professional hockey performances of all time. I was in Hamilton's Copps Coliseum when Wayne Gretzky and Mario Lemieux teamed up to win the 1987 Canada Cup. I was there at Maple Leaf Gardens when Gretzky played what he said was the greatest single game of his career, Game 7 of the Western Conference final against Toronto in 1993. I was maybe 50 feet away from Sidney Crosby when he yelled "Iggy" and scored the Golden Goal to give Canada the gold medal at the 2010 Vancouver Winter Olympics. All of those performances, and so many more, are burned into my memory as extraordinary athletic accomplishments, but then there's the hot, summer night in July 1992, when I first saw John Tavares play lacrosse.

It was an athletic display I'll never forget, a seminal sporting moment for me that I couldn't help but think about when Cordingley made a claim many would say is outlandish.

It was a midweek regular-season game in the Ontario Lacrosse Association Major Series, between the visiting Brampton Excelsiors and the Brooklin Redmen at tiny Luther Vipond Memorial Arena in Brooklin, Ontario. There couldn't have been more than 50 to 75 people there. I stood in the corner, at the glass, near the dressing rooms on the far side from the stands where everyone else sat to watch the game. It could not have been further removed from Copps Coliseum, Maple Leaf Gardens or the Winter Olympics.

It was Tavares's third year of senior men's lacrosse, but his first in Ontario after having played two seasons in B.C. I went to the game never having heard of John Tavares, and I left the arena that summer night feeling as though I had witnessed one of the most incredible feats of athleticism ever, bar none.

I was totally captivated. He seemed so much smaller than the other players, yet he was so dynamic and explosive, so graceful and cerebral. He ran the floor with a fluidity that's difficult to put into words, but his game was also so visceral. He was so lean, especially his legs, but they were like coiled steel. His swarthy skin glistened with sweat, his hawkish features evident under the wire face mask, his eyes bright like white-hot lights.

To the best of my recollection, he probably scored five or six goals that night, but it wasn't how many he scored as much as *how* he scored them, how he played the game, demonstrating an uncanny blend of intelligence, athleticism and extraordinary skill.

His passing and shooting were on another level from virtually every player on the floor. You could seem him process the game like no other, with Gretzky-like vision and creativity. The things he could do with the ball in his stick cannot even be described. He shot the ball overhand, underhand, sidearm, over the shoulder, behind the back, between the legs. He juked and jived all over the floor, faking and feinting, creating open spaces for himself, but he also carried big, aggressive defenders on his back through heavy traffic. He absorbed more physical punishment—cross-checks, big hits, blatant attempts at intimidation, both physical and verbal—than I'd seen any star hockey player take. Ever. He gave as good as he got, too, figuratively baring his teeth, literally getting his stick into the faces of opponents taking liberties, protecting himself, creating space for himself. He used trickery to sneak off the bench and score on a breakaway. He scored a goal diving through the air like Superman. He scored in tight and from far out. From behind the net and in front of it. He beat opponents one on one, he beat them one on three. He played with unbelievable passion, yet there was a calmness and sense of control and purpose to everything he did. Boundless energy, not an ounce of it wasted.

I clearly remember thinking I was seeing someone and something truly extraordinary, an athlete who was every bit as gifted in his discipline as Wayne Gretzky was in his. I remember going into the parking lot outside the arena between periods and seeing him sitting on a curbstone minus his equipment, quietly gathering himself, sipping on a Gatorade, performing the intermission cool-down ritual that is standard practice at any lacrosse game on a hot summer's night (the dressing rooms are, as a rule, stifling hot, and it's not uncommon for both teams to be out there in the parking lot). I recall thinking how Gretzky-like his body type was, and that anything No. 99 could do in hockey, John Tavares could do in lacrosse.

I was fascinated by him, captivated by what he'd done. I asked the lacrosse fans, "Who is this guy?" John Tavares, they told me. A rising star, a phenom, they added. And they were right.

Tavares led Brampton to the first of his five straight Mann Cups that season. Twenty years later, in the summer of 2012, having played summer box lacrosse with Vancouver, Brampton, Six Nations, Akwesasne (twice), Victoria and St. Regis, J.T. played for the Peterborough Lakers and hoisted the Mann Cup for a record eighth time. Laker captain Scott Self received the trophy, and instead of being the first to lift it over his head, as is the custom for the winning captain, he immediately handed it over to 43-year-old Tavares, who lifted it, quite likely, for the final time. A year later, in 2013, he didn't play summer lacrosse for the first time since he picked up a stick as a young boy, resting his body for what he thought might be his final NLL season in 2014.

Unlike his older brother Joe, 10 years his senior, the first Canadian-born member of the Portuguese Tavares family wasn't obliged to work one job as a kid, never mind two. So as a young boy, John Tavares was able to pursue his passion for sports. That didn't mean his parents were thrilled with John's sporting life. Money was still hard to come by, and sports cost money. So when John borrowed his older brother Danny's lacrosse stick and wanted to play for St. Christopher's at nearby Alexandra Park—the registration fee was $20—it was tolerated rather than embraced.

"My father didn't dislike sports. He actually liked them," John said. "He just felt playing sports was taking away from potential income for our family. So, me playing lacrosse, they didn't really want me to play."

Maybe they would have looked more favourably on it had it been a sport they knew, like soccer, but John played a single game of European "football," never touched the ball and had no desire to ever do it again.

Lacrosse, though, he took to instantly. It just felt right. Dorotea couldn't always see John from their house on Ryerson Avenue when he went to Alex Park, but she could certainly hear him. For hours at a time, he'd be there, shooting the Indian rubber lacrosse ball against the boards. It wasn't long before he was scoring goals, lots of them, and thrilling the rowdy, enthusiastic neighbourhood crowds who would come out on summer nights to cheer on St. Christopher's at the outdoor box.

He also gave hockey a try. More ball hockey than organized ice hockey, which wasn't readily available at Alexandra Park. But he'd try skating in the winter when the lacrosse box became the community hockey rink.

"I was a real ankle burner," he said. "I had a pair of old Orbit skates we bought from Honest Ed's. But hockey was never my game."

In fact, if winter and hockey season were holding on too long, John the lacrosse player would hurry them along.

"I was so impatient for lacrosse season to start, I'd go over once the ice started to melt and I'd chip away the ice with my boots, break it up, help it along so the box would be clear for lacrosse," Tavares said. "I couldn't wait for lacrosse season to start."

Tavares loved playing for St. Christopher's at Alexandra Park. It felt like home. It wasn't easy for him when his family left the area near Bathurst and Queen Streets for the suburbs in Mississauga, where he wound up playing minor lacrosse as well as Junior B and Junior A.

Even when he played midget lacrosse, alongside future NHLer Brendan Shanahan, everyone knew J.T. had that special something.

"What I always remember about him is that he was working on his [lacrosse] stick," Shanahan said. "Constantly. The other thing about him is that he was so smart, so tricky. He was always working on trick plays, hiding the ball, pretending to leave the floor on a line change but then racing back into the play to score a goal. I can't tell you how many times he would score a goal and the game would be delayed because the refs would have to consult and figure out what they just saw and whether it was legal. He was always pushing the envelope on rules, finding loopholes, getting creative.

"He was in minor lacrosse what Pavel Datsyuk is now, a guy you just like to watch practise to see all the creative things he would try."

Shanahan loved lacrosse, too, but knew he would have to give it up to focus on hockey. Tavares, though, was a pure lacrosse player, although Shanahan laughed at what might have been had Tavares been inclined to skate or play hockey.

"John Purves, who was a very good hockey player, played lacrosse with us too and [he] would rent ice in the summer," Shanahan recalled. "John [Tavares] would come out for fun. He couldn't skate very well at all, but you could see he was taking everything in, sizing up what everyone was doing, where they were on the ice. It was like he was studying us. So even though he couldn't skate, it wasn't long before he was starting to dangle guys and make plays. [Purves] always said, 'If [Tavares] ever decided he wanted to be a hockey player, he'd be better than all of us.' He had that kind of mind to really process things."

Tavares won a Founder's Cup national Junior B championship with Mississauga in 1986. Statistically, he ripped up Junior B (scoring 132 goals in 17 games in one season) and Junior A lacrosse. He played and starred in high school football and wound up going to Wilfrid Laurier University in Waterloo, Ontario, playing defensive back on the varsity football team.

He graduated from Laurier with a desire to become a teacher. He wanted to go to teacher's college, but didn't have the money. He found work at the high school he attended as a student, Philip Pocock

Catholic Secondary School in Mississauga. He was hired as an educational research worker with special-needs kids and did that for a couple of years. It was while he was playing for the Buffalo Bandits that he got hooked up with D'Youville College in Buffalo, where he got his teaching certificate. Ultimately, he landed a full-time teaching job at Pocock.

Technically, one of Canada's most gifted athletes is a high-school math teacher.

It wouldn't be accurate to say Tavares made no money playing lacrosse, but it's never been nearly enough to call it a livelihood. In 2014, he was getting the maximum NLL salary of close to $40,000 for the five-month season. Officially, the summer leagues in Ontario and B.C. are amateur loops, though everyone knows there's a little cash to be made—"expenses" to be paid. But even for a superstar like Tavares, a 14-game regular season, and maybe that many more playoff games, might yield around $500 a game, if that. By anyone's best guess, the most Tavares has ever made in one year from lacrosse would be around $50,000, and keep in mind, when he started playing in the MILL in 1992, he got $125 per game for the eight-game season.

"Yeah, but it went up to $150 a game in my second year," he said with a laugh.

If such an extraordinary athlete ever felt bitter about his career lacrosse earnings being a mere fraction of what the lowest-paid NHL player would get for one season, never mind what superstar athletes of Tavares's ilk earn in other sports, he doesn't show it. Or that he had to spend hours in rush-hour traffic, driving the 160 kilometres from Mississauga to Peterborough for summer games rather than travelling in style on an NHL charter.

"It would have been nice to make more money, but lacrosse has brought a lot of good things to my life," Tavares said. "It would have been great to make a livelihood at it, but that wasn't possible. I am a math teacher. When I was growing up, I played lacrosse because I loved it. There was no pro league to aspire to. I never set out to be a lacrosse player, so I can't be disappointed. I'm fortunate to have been able to play at the level I've played."

Now he takes great pride in being a father. He and his wife, Katrina, had son Justin in 2006 and daughter Breanne in 2007. J.T. coached Justin in tyke lacrosse, but Justin suggested he might want to play baseball.

"If he likes [baseball] better," Tavares said, "I don't mind."

But when Justin suggested he's interested in being a goalie, the father had to put his foot down.

"I told him when he can afford to buy goalie equipment, he can play goal," Tavares said. "I've never liked goalies."

As he prepared for the 2014 NLL season, he knew there was a good chance it would be his last. His body had been breaking down. His 2012 summer season and 2013 NLL year were marred by injury, micro-tears of his calf muscles that made it difficult to run. If it turns out 2014 was his final season, he's at peace with it.

"When you're old, you can't be playing hurt," he said late in the summer of 2013. "[Injuries] caused me to struggle the last few years. [The Bandits] still seem to think I can help out, and I'm still loving to play. I'm not sure why they want a 45-year-old on the team. I look at it that there are stages of being retired. Like, when you're at home and you don't want to go to the arena, but once you get to the arena, you like being there. That's when you know you're near retirement, but not there yet. That's me [going into 2014]. I've still got some fire left. But the next stage, the one where you know it's time to retire, you just don't want to go to the arena at all. That's when you know it's time. I'll know. That won't be a problem for me."

If the 2014 season was his last, Tavares enjoyed it. The Bandits lost to eventual NLL champion Rochester in the semifinal, and that was disappointing. But he played and produced well early in the season, battled through a midseason lull and rallied for a strong individual finish. In July 2014, he sounded like a man who was leaning towards retiring but wasn't quite prepared to make it official. He wanted to wait a bit longer before committing.

As for his place in the game, his legacy as the greatest player of all time, the comparisons to Gretzky, he doesn't get too caught up in any of it, his humility shining through it all.

"I've got numbers others don't, but the numbers don't tell the whole story," he said. "That doesn't make you the best player.

"Gretzky?" he said with a grin. "I was dirtier than Gretzky. I'd stick guys or fight. Wayne was a Lady Byng guy. Me, not so much. For me, hands down, Gary Gait is [the best lacrosse player of all time]. Paul was no slouch, either. John Grant's name should be in there, too. There are so many great players. I'm just fortunate to have played for as long as I did.

"You know what I'll remember more than any championships, any accomplishments or goals I scored? My early years, my minor lacrosse, just playing in the box at Alexandra Park, with the rowdy crowd, just looking forward to go there with my stick. I wanted to play lacrosse because my brother Danny played and I'd take his stick. That's what I'll remember most."

John Tavares the lacrosse player was never going to be a hockey player, but John Tavares the hockey player most definitely could have been a lacrosse player.

Young John's mother, Barb, remembered her brother-in-law Danny suggesting she put four-year-old John in peanut lacrosse, which she did. Uncle Danny took little John to his first game, brought him home and told Barb they would have to put John in an older age group with his Danny's six-year-old son Ryan.

"In John's first lacrosse game, his team won 17–1," Barb Tavares said. "John scored all 17 goals."

As natural as John was with a lacrosse stick in his hand, hockey was his first and enduring love. He first skated at Clarkson Arena when he was two and a half years old.

"At any given time, it was hard for me to say what I enjoyed more, hockey or lacrosse, but I know I fell in love with hockey first," the NHL star said. "I can still vividly remember learning to skate, not wanting to use the boards, going to the middle and trying to not fall down. I had a hockey stick in my hand when I was two years old. My first connection was to hockey, but as I got older, I wanted to be [Uncle] J.T."

Uncle John remembered a Young John who was crazy for hockey. "He'd rather watch Wayne Gretzky videos than cartoons," J.T. said. "I'd come over to his house and we'd play hockey in the basement. If I didn't let him be the commentator, he would cry. I wouldn't let him beat me, either."

But seeing Uncle John play for the Bandits had a huge impact on Young John, who, with his collection of cousins, would make the drive on Friday nights to see the Bandits play at the old Aud in Buffalo.

"I was only three or four years old and it was so loud," Young John said. "What I remember is how steep the seats were in the Aud."

"His mom [Barb] would tell you [Young John] would just stare at the game, even as a four-year-old, and take it all in where a lot of kids would be running around all over the place," J.T. said.

In the summer months, Young John would go to the old Memorial Arena in Brampton and watch Uncle John in the OLA Major Series. That, too, left an indelible imprint on him.

"It was such a great atmosphere in a real old barn," Young John said. "The lacrosse was so good. I would watch it and say, 'Wow, I can't believe I play this game.' It was fantastic. I loved it."

It didn't matter which sport Young John was playing, he filled the net in both, always playing up one age group in hockey, but since lacrosse age groupings span two years, he was even more advanced—in peewee, for example, he was a ten-year-old playing against 12-year-olds. It just didn't matter. In the highly competitive peewee, bantam and midget provincial qualifiers and championships, the underage kid would still dominate and often lead everyone in the province in scoring. In hockey, he was the kid the other teams would go to extraordinary lengths to stop.

"I loved playing both sports," Young John said. "I really looked up to [J.T.], and until I was 13 years old, I really thought I could just keep on playing both sports. I played lacrosse with my cousins and we had a lot of good friends. It was how we bonded. My lacrosse highlight was winning the provincial championship in bantam. Our Oakville team started out as kids and we were getting beat by Whitby by 15 or 16 goals, and in bantam, we won it all. That was a really tight group of guys that grew up together. We beat Whitby in the final. I had the game-winning goal in the semifinal and the final."

In midget lacrosse, at the Ontario Summer Games in London, Tavares's Oakville team finished third, but his lacrosse game really took off. He was named tournament MVP. He played a year of Junior A lacrosse for Mississauga the summer before he was granted early admission to the OHL. And even after he finished his rookie season in the OHL with the Oshawa Generals, he played one more season of Junior A with the Tomahawks.

It was only after he played his second OHL season that he knew, as difficult as it was for him, he'd have to stop playing lacrosse to focus on his hockey career.

"I went to the [Junior A lacrosse] tryouts that summer, and for the first time, I knew that was it for lacrosse," he said. "I ran in that practice, and when it was over, I told them I was done, that I had to put more time into my off-season hockey conditioning. You just can't train for hockey and play lacrosse at the same time. I'd get home at one in the morning from Peterborough or St. Catharines and then have to get up and work out in the morning. I just couldn't do it. It was time."

Joe Tavares never imagined that the two Johns—his brother the lacrosse superstar and his son the hockey superstar—would make the impact they have on their respective worlds, so there's plenty of family pride to go around.

"We're all very proud, our whole family," Joe said. "They're phenomenal athletes and they're very proud of each other. You can see that."

Proud, and thankful as well, especially to the man who never got the same athletic opportunities as they did, which allowed them to chase their sporting dreams and scale the greatest of heights in their respective games.

Older John is eternally grateful that Joe sacrificed his own youth to work and support the family so he was able to play lacrosse. Younger John feels the same way about his dad doing everything he did to allow him to play both hockey and lacrosse.

And maybe, just maybe, this J.T.–John Tavares story could turn out to be a trilogy. Peter Tavares, 18 years Joe's junior, is the youngest of Manuel's and Dorotea's children. On September 14, 2012—six days after Lacrosse John's 44th birthday and six days before Hockey John's 22nd birthday—Peter Tavares became a father for the first time. He and his wife Misty had a little boy.

They named him Jonathan.

Jonathan Tavares.

• • •

In an effort to unearth the secrets of goal-scoring success,
we didn't need to go around the world. We needed only to invite two
of the greatest natural goal scorers in two sports—the lacrosse J.T. and
the hockey John Tavares—to a coffee shop in Mississauga, Ontario.
Here's the transcript of an interview conducted in August 2013:

BM: First goal you ever scored, do you remember it?

Uncle John: I was five or six. I zigzagged through the whole Mimico
team and scored. It's funny, I don't remember the ball actually going in
the net. What I remember is what I felt after I scored: confident. I knew
I could get through everyone and score.

Young John: I don't remember my first goal, but it's weird, I remember not being able to score. I was at a hockey camp, I was really young
and I had six or seven breakaways in a scrimmage at the end, and I
didn't score on any of them. I didn't start off too well. My mom took
video of it. I remember watching it a few years ago—maybe that's why
I remember it.

BM: From an artistic point of view, what's the best goal you've ever
scored?

Uncle John: Hmmm, I'm like [Young] John: I remember more of my
errors than my goals. There was a goal I scored, and my part of it, that
was the easy part. It was the most artistic because of the whole play. It
was in Brampton. Darris Kilgour won the faceoff and he passed it to
Jim Veltman, and Veltman backhanded a beautiful pass to me and I
just shot it in the net. It was like *boom-boom-boom.* What I did wasn't
anything special, but the whole play, the flow, the simplicity of it . . . it
was just beautiful. But I think you're looking for something else, more
individual.

Okay, I came down my wrong side, which I did a lot. I would normally bring the ball across myself, cross my arms and dive through the
air and just push it in on the far side where I was diving. But goalies

would catch on to what I was doing, and the goalie this time—it was Anthony Cosmo—he knew me really well, so I started doing it and then I realized he knew exactly what I was doing. So while I was in the air, diving across the crease, instead of shooting it into the net far side, I somehow wrapped the stick around behind my back and twisted my body while I was in the air and shot it back to the other side and it went in. I don't think there's any video of it, it was Buffalo vs. Toronto. I would like to see that one again.

Young John: I can't believe you didn't say the one that was on the ESPN Top 10.

Uncle John: Oh yeah, that was a good one, too. [*He grins.*]

Young John: Look it up on YouTube. It was on ESPN. Buffalo against Portland. He went through three guys and made, like, eight fakes. It was an incredible goal, one of the best I've ever seen.

A few stand out for me. There was a minor hockey game, they were checking me all game. I got hauled down on a breakaway. Laying on my back, I somehow shot it, the goalie was down and I just sort of chipped it over him. The other one I think of, it was my first goal in the OHL, against Kingston. We were shorthanded—I'm not sure why a 15-year-old was on the ice, killing a penalty, in his first OHL game. [*He laughs.*] I just let a snap shot go from top of circle, one of the best shots I've ever taken. It went far side, top corner. I don't normally shoot it like that.

BM: What about your most important goal?

Uncle John: It was 1992 [Tavares's rookie season in the NLL], Buffalo versus Philly at the Spectrum—a great game, sudden-death overtime, sold-out crowd. The atmosphere was unreal. It was a broken play. Philly's goaltenders were Dallas Eliuk and Dwight Maetche, who I played with in Vancouver. Dwight was a great goalie, I really respected him, and I never say a goalie is good, but he was good. In practice, he would never let me score. I hated that. So Dwight got into the game and I didn't want to shoot on him—he was in my head a bit. So there's a broken play and the ball comes to me in overtime, and I decide I'm going to take a backhand [over the shoulder]—and I don't take a lot of backhands. I see the top corner open and I take the shot. It went straight into the ground and between Dwight's legs and in. [*He laughs.*] Nice shot. But it won the NLL championship.

Young John: For me, it's probably the [2009] World Junior Championship. It was New Year's Eve, we're down 3–0, like that, against the Americans. I scored three goals, but it was the second goal that was the big one. I drove wide, shot it into the top corner. That goal really turned things around for us in that game and the tournament. But I would have to say the shootout goal I scored against Russia in the semifinals that year was really important, too. We all remember the [miraculous tying goal by Jordan Eberle], but I knew I couldn't miss on the shootout. What I remember is I didn't hear anything—*nothing*—when I skated in on the goalie, and the place was going crazy, but that's the most focused I've ever been on a shot. I almost lost the puck, but the goalie went down and I scored.

BM: This may be repetitive, because you've talked about a lot of goals already, but what about, for any reason you see fit, the most memorable goal you've scored?

Uncle John: That would be the game-winning goal in the Founders Cup Junior B championship or the 1992 NLL [overtime game-winning goal] against Philly.

Young John: For me, that would be when I broke Wayne Gretzky's record for most goals by a 16-year-old in the OHL. I tried to pass the puck to Cal Clutterbuck on the back door, Logan Couture went down to block it, the puck went off his skate and back to me. The goalie anticipated the pass, went down, and I shot it low blocker. I didn't even celebrate the goal; I just went and got the puck. The guys gave me a hard time about that one.

BM: How about this one: the most vindictive, suck-on-that, in-your-face goal you scored?

Uncle John: I don't have one like that.

Young John: Oh, I do. There were tons in minor hockey. Kids would follow me and slash me and stick me and I'd score and be so pumped . . .

Uncle John: Yeah, I probably have a few like that, but not one I remember any more than another. I'd be in Peterborough or Boston, and I'm tired, and some guy is yipping at me from the bench, saying, "You're too old," and I'm thinking, "You don't really want to wake me up. I'm an old man now." [*He laughs.*] So I'd take the ball, I'd have a look up at the 30-second shot clock and I'd just shoot it in and look over the bench, like, "Really?"

Young John: I know when I played in minor atom, a guy was shadowing me, being really dirty with me. My dad thought it was coming from their coach, and he would tell me to protect myself. They would butt-end or stick me in the nuts. I scored a hat trick in this game. The guy who was sticking me, after I scored, he faked like he was going to slash me in the head. He got a penalty. I didn't even move, never flinched. I scored again and I said, "What are you going to do now, fake slash me in the head again?"

BM: How about a goal someone else scored that you wish you scored? Do you have any goal envy?

Uncle John: I played some minor lacrosse with Brendan Shanahan and he'd say to me, "Show me a fancy goal." I didn't score fancy goals; I'd just try to do things the right way. Gary Gait, now there's a guy who scored some fancy goals. He'd rip a backhand from the top of the power play into the top corner. I wouldn't even have the guts to try that, especially on the power play. So I'd like to score a Gary Gait backhand from the top of the power play.

Young John: For me, it would be a goal with great meaning. Maybe because it's coming up, the Olympics—I would have loved to score

Sid's goal in Vancouver, in Canada, to win Olympic gold for Canada. Either that or Brett Hull scoring a game-winning goal in overtime to win the Stanley Cup. Those are the kinds of goals I dream of scoring.

Uncle John: I've been trying to convince [Young] John to pick up the puck on the blade of his stick and whip it around and bounce it in, like Robbie Schremp did. As a fan, that's what I'd like to see John do on a shootout shot. What's the percentage on scoring on a penalty shot or shootout—maybe 20 per cent? I'm surprised you don't do that.

Young John: I do it in practice.

Uncle John: Do you score?

Young John: Yeah, sometimes.

Uncle John: See, it's easy. I've seen high school kids do it. Easy. Do it.

Young John: Now you sound like my dad. My dad can shoot right or left in hockey, both ways, and he always says to me, "Shoot both ways, it's easy."

BM: Most goals you've ever scored in one game?

Uncle John: I think in junior, I once had 12 or 13. In pro, I think the most I ever had was seven. My manager in Buffalo told me that if I get a few goals early and the game is in hand, I really back off and don't try to score as much. He's probably right.

Young John: Once in lacrosse, I had 13 or 14 points, but I don't recall how many goals. In minor hockey, I've scored six or seven goals. That would be the most for me in hockey.

BM: Outside of your contract that pays you, did anyone—a family member—ever give you money to score a goal?

Uncle John: Nope, never any money. Maybe a shot in the head if I didn't score. [*He laughs.*]

Young John: My dad would just say, "If you don't get a hat trick, don't come home." After the game, we'd pull up and he'd open the door a crack and peek out and say, "How many did you get? Okay, c'mon in, then."

BM: Let's talk celebrations. Do you guys have a go-to celebration?

Uncle John: I don't celebrate goals too much. More in practice. I joke around that I'm going to jump up on the glass and really go crazy, and then I score and I just raise my arms. Honestly, excessive celebrating just stirs up the other team. Why would you want to do that?

Young John: I go through stages. I don't mind celebrating a goal—nothing too crazy, though. I'll do the same thing for 20 or 30 games and then switch it up a bit.

BM: I went through a lot of [Young John's] goals on video, and you're right: you stick with the basics, but there are little variations that you throw in there. You're mostly a two-arms-straight-in-the-air guy, but sometimes you'll throw in a little something extra—

Young John: Fist pump, usually. I don't mind a little fist pump.

BM: Yes, sometimes it's down low from your midsection, but sometimes you like to go upstairs and give the overhead, overhand fist pump to the crowd with a look into the stands. But you're right, it's all relatively subdued.

Young John: My dad always told me, "Don't ever celebrate, it's like saying the F word." So when I was young, I'd put my hands in the air and then take them down. Actually, there probably was one for me: the World Juniors in Ottawa, against the Americans. When they went up on us 3–0, one of their players went by our bench and taunted us, with his hand to his ear. When I scored my second goal to make it 3–2, I did it back to them. I probably would like to take that one back, but it was a really emotional game. I try not to be too obnoxious.

BM: I ask this question, and I already know the answer, but is it easier to score goals in hockey or lacrosse? The answer, in theory, should be hockey, because the net in lacrosse is a lot smaller and the goalie equipment is much bigger, but it's obvious by the number of goals scored in a game, it's lacrosse.

Young John: In lacrosse, you have more control where the ball is going. It's *in* your stick, you're not on skates.

Uncle John: In hockey, they have only one angle: up. In lacrosse, you can move the ball from high to low and shoot up or down. [*To Young John.*] By the way, you should use your backhand more than you do.

Young John: He always tells me that. It's the only move he ever had in the basement when he would come over to play hockey with me. Forehand, backhand, deke, same move every time.

BM: Where's it more dangerous in front of the net: in hockey or lacrosse?

Young John: Lacrosse.

Uncle John: Really?

Young John: For sure. You can legally cross-check in lacrosse. Guys would cross-check you in the hips. And in lacrosse, you have to go through the middle, and that's where you can see the kids who are afraid. You have to have balls to cut through the middle in lacrosse, because you're taking your life into your hands.

Uncle John: There's cross-checking off the ball in lacrosse, too. If your team has the ball, the other team can start cross-checking anyone who doesn't have the ball. That's intense

Young John: I remember playing against Six Nations. Every defender had a wooden stick. When you went to set a pick, you know you were going to get destroyed. I would wear all sorts of extra equipment. I was a lot younger, I was 20 to 30 pounds lighter than them, and they'd just give it to you even if you didn't have the ball.

Uncle John: I like a tough game, always have, but I don't know much [physical] intimidation should exist in sport. I've got a kid playing now. Do I really want him playing lacrosse and hockey and taking shots to the head with barely any penalties?

BM: I'm sure you guys have heard the term "natural" or "pure" goal scorer, which on one level is counterintuitive because I think you guys would be the first to admit it takes a lot of hard work and practice to score, but there's no denying some guys simply have the knack, and that would be both of you.

Uncle John: Positioning is everything for me in scoring goals. I think I put myself in a good spot to score. My skill level maybe isn't the highest in the game, but my sense of where to be—I just try to put people to sleep and then, when they least expect it . . .

BM: Brett Hull used to subscribe to that theory. He would say he liked to be invisible until he got the puck on his stick in the right spot on the ice.

Uncle John: In lacrosse, I would try to set up the guy playing defence against me. I would show him routine, same thing over and over again, do routine, do routine and let him think he was getting the better of me for a while, and when I could see he was relaxing, getting comfortable with my routine, that's when I'd break the routine, do something different and beat him for a goal. . . . I asked [Young John] once whether he considers himself a playmaker or a goal scorer. He said he's a goal scorer, which surprised me a bit. I kind of think of myself as a playmaker first, although when the game is on the line, I guess I like to be a goal scorer.

Young John: When you talk about a natural or pure goal scorer, I think you're talking about some guys who don't look like they have the greatest skill set—they don't have a real hard shot or they're not fast or big—but when you talk about a guy like my linemate, Matt Moulson, or someone like Luc Robitaille, they have great scoring instincts and an ability to put the puck in the net. That's my definition of a natural goal scorer. Some guys have the skill set to be great goal scorers, some guys just have the knack; some have both, and those are the really great ones.

BM: That precise moment when the puck or ball goes into the net, how does that feel? Can you put it into words?

Uncle John: For me, it's the exact same feeling every time. It's satisfaction and gratification that all the hard work has paid off. Now when I score, I'm so happy inside. When you're older, you *need* that goal, really need it. At age 28, if you go two games without scoring a goal, it's called a slump. When you're 40, you go two games without a goal and you're washed up. I need those goals now for confidence. It makes me believe I still belong.

Young John: I can't describe it. As a kid, I knew the objective is to score, and I felt if I could do that better than anyone else, it would help my team win and help me become the best at it. There's no emotion like it, nothing like scoring a goal. I'm driven by it.

BM: Goal scorers get into the zone. How do you know when you're "in the zone"?

Uncle John: In lacrosse, your stick has to be on. In lacrosse, the stick is everything. If your stick feels great, it seems like the game is so easy. Then things just seem to happen so naturally.

Young John: Those moments are hard to explain because it's hard to stay at that level for any length of time, and when you are "in the zone," you often can't figure out why you are. Usually, it means something good happened early. I remember a Belleville–Oshawa game—I wasn't feeling well at all, I slept only two hours the night before, and yet I scored a power-play goal, an even-strength goal, two shorthanded goals, had an assist and scored on the shootout to win the game. I didn't think I was going to play well in that game because I didn't feel good. But you start, things go your way, and it's as if some unseen thing is taking your skill to the next level. Why? No idea, none.

BM: What about the flip side: the dreaded slump, when you can't do anything right?

Uncle John: Superstitions get made on those times. You start thinking, "What did I do when I was playing really well?" If I'm struggling, I just ask myself, "Am I getting chances?" If not, I'll go do something else—make a defensive play, help the team in some way. You can't let it bring you down.

Young John: I always grew up scoring goals, and I obviously don't like it when I'm not. So like a lot of guys, if I'm not scoring, I try to do other things. My first year in the NHL, I wasn't getting many chances, was not scoring. It's tough mentally; it can play with your mind. I learned a lot from that experience. I went 15 or 16 games without scoring—longest I've ever gone. It was good for me, but I didn't like it.

BM: You mentioned superstitions. You have any?

Uncle John: I like a pre-game nap. Is that a superstition? I don't think so. I don't have any.

Young John: Not anything wacky. My superstitions are based more on preparation. There's no excuse to not play well, so it's more routine than superstition, I think. The one superstition I guess I have is that in junior, at the old [Oshawa] Civic Auditorium, there's small room, a medical room, and all the players would put their stick on the wall outside that room. But I would put my stick inside [trainer] Brian Boyes's medical room. I still do it now, always put my stick in the medical room. But that's about it.

Uncle John: No intimacy the night before . . . for most of my career, anyway. [*He laughs.*]

BM: Okay, guys, most important question: What's the deepest, darkest secret to your goal-scoring success?

Young John: I just feel like I want it more than anyone else. Whether it's lacrosse or hockey, I always wanted to score. I feel like I wanted it more than anyone else. I still feel that way. I know everyone likes to score, but I just have this feeling that there's no one in the world who wants to score a goal more than me.

Uncle John: I never went into a game saying I want to score. I just wanted to make the right play. That's how I got my opportunities to score. If you make the right play, you're going to get scoring chances for not just [yourself] but your team. Is there an actual secret to it? I don't know, but I can tell you I don't respect any goalies. I refuse to show them any respect. I think they're no good, because if you say a goalie is good, then you're giving that goalie an edge over you. I won't do that.

It's a mindset, I guess. I hated stats, too. I hated milestones—you know, 500th goal or whatever. I hate that stuff, I didn't like the attention being on me.

Young John: I'm not a big stats guy, either. I won't look at them, I won't look at league leaders. I just want to focus on playing well. That's where I'm focused.

BM: Can you guys imagine what it'll be like when you're finished playing and there's no more goals to be scored?

Uncle John: I'm okay with not scoring any more goals. If I don't play, if I retire, I'll be fine. I've scored my share. I was golfing with [ex–Buffalo Sabre] Rene Robert and someone asked him if he still plays any hockey. He said, "What kind of question is that? I'm retired." I'll be the same way; you won't see me playing masters' lacrosse, I can tell you that. [*To Young John.*] You, on the other hand, you've got lots more goals to score. Lots.

Young John: I'd like to play as long as he has. [*He points to Uncle John.*]

Uncle John: [Young John] is a great player, but—and I tell him this all the time—he's at his best when he just puts his nose down and just goes to the net, when he doesn't get too cute and just goes for it. So do what I tell you. [*He laughs.*]

CHAPTER 4

#fancystats

Colliding Worlds and the Surprising Real Story of Corsi,
Fenwick and PDO

———

All these years later, I owe my high school math teacher an
apology, because I'm about to break a long-standing promise.

Sorry about that, Mrs. Uyenaka.

It was the final week of my Grade 12 year, June 1974, at Woburn
Collegiate Institute in Scarborough, Ontario. As I recall, I was in a state
of high anxiety because the list of students who would be obliged to
take the year-end final exam was soon to be posted. In order to be
exempt from taking the exam, a student required a mark of at least 55
per cent.

It was going to be touch and go for me.

Math—or science, for that matter—had never been my strong
suit. The written or spoken word? Write an essay or make a speech?
Bring it on. An equation or formula? Find a solution? Get out of here.
My brain is not wired to deal with it.

I approached Mrs. Uyenaka the day before the list was to be posted
and asked her if I was going to make the cut at 55. She looked it up in
her book, looked at me and shook her head.

"No, I'm sorry," she said. "You have 53 per cent. You have to write the exam."

I might not have known what a logarithm was—still don't, actually—but I damn sure knew if I had to write that final exam, I was not going to pass it. If I didn't pass the exam, I would fail Grade 12 math. If I didn't pass Grade 12 math, I wouldn't get the required credit for my high school diploma. If I didn't get my diploma—well, if you knew my mother, that was not an option.

I'd already chosen my six courses for Grade 13—two English, two history, French and family studies—so it wasn't as if I actually needed Grade 12 math as a prerequisite for anything, other than getting my diploma and graduating in good standing.

I showed Mrs. Uyenaka my option sheet for the next year, explained to her my innate inability to process numerical data, guaranteed her I could not pass the exam, told her there was no benefit to anyone—least of all me—to my writing that final exam, and then made her a solemn promise in the form of an offer I was fearful she *could* refuse.

"If you bump up my mark to 55 and exempt me from the final exam," I pleaded, "I'll never, not ever, have anything to do with numbers or math for the rest of my life. I promise."

She said she would think about it. The next day, she posted the class list with our marks alongside our names: Bob McKenzie 55.

Exempt.

I've never forgotten what Mrs. Uyenaka did for me that day, nor have I forgotten or broken the promise I made to her back then.

Until now.

Damn you, #fancystats!

We will likely look back one day on the 2013–14 NHL regular season as the proverbial turning point, the year in which advanced statistics in hockey—a.k.a. #fancystats or analytics (Corsi, Fenwick, PDO, etc.)—went mainstream. Maybe "mainstream" is a bit of a stretch, but there most definitely was an awakening. A line was crossed. Advanced hockey stats became more of a talking point, started showing up more often in more prominent places. The debate over their merits, or lack thereof, became louder and longer and more spirited, waged in newspapers and on television, radio and the Internet and social media.

For that, we can thank the Toronto Maple Leafs.

The Leafs, and many of their fans, believed their 2013 playoff appearance—the historic third-period-and-overtime Game 7 meltdown against the Boston Bruins notwithstanding, to say nothing of the team's first playoff date since 2004 coming on the basis of a lockout-shortened 48-game regular season—was a portent of good things to come, a launching pad for a team headed in the right direction. But the purveyors of #fancystats said it before the 2013–14 season even began: the Leafs were cruisin' for a bruisin'. Their "puck possession" numbers (as measured by tools such as Corsi and Fenwick) were way too low; their save percentage and shooting percentage (PDO) was unsustainably high. It was, the hockey eggheads maintained, a perfect statistical storm.

The battle lines were clearly drawn. The Leaf season, for better or worse, was going to put #fancystats on trial.

That this was playing out in Toronto, of all places, only raised the stakes. Next to Mayor Rob Ford (no comment), Corsi and the Leafs might have been the hot-button topic in Canada's largest city in 2013–14.

"I don't think there's any question about that, the [Maple Leaf angle] pulled [advanced statistics] into the spotlight," said Tyler Dellow, a Toronto-based lawyer and blogger (his blog can be found at www.mc79hockey.com) who has emerged as one of the foremost authorities on the use of analytics in hockey. "The Leafs are a big deal and Toronto is the centre of the [hockey and hockey media] universe. They raised the profile of the debate to a level that couldn't have happened anywhere else."

The mercurial Maple Leafs, meanwhile, cooperated by providing a dramatic, season-long script. They went 11–6 in their first 17 games. Maple Leaf general manager Dave Nonis, speaking at a sports business management conference at that point in the schedule, made a remark along the lines of having had teams in the past that outshot their opponents and lost, but now the Leafs' Corsi—in his word—"sucks," yet the team was winning.

For many in the mainstream media who either didn't like the creeping presence of #fancystats or perhaps just didn't like their zealous proponents, it was open season on the newfangled numbers. As the season wore on, the Leafs certainly looked like a playoff team. With less than a month to go, they had 80 points in 68 games. They sat third in the Eastern Conference and ninth overall in the 30-team NHL.

Critics of #fancystats were giddy with delight. They started doing their touchdown dance at the 10-yard line. We all know what happened next.

Incredibly, the Leafs lost eight straight games in regulation time, and then briefly stopped the bleeding with a pair of wins, before closing out the regular season with another four straight losses in regulation. They lost 12 of their final 14, all in regulation time, falling from third in the Eastern Conference to 12th in the span of less than a month. The Leafs' playoff hopes were incinerated into a mushroom cloud.

It was one of the most epic collapses in NHL history. It was also taken as vindication and massive victory for the #fancystats gang.

"As a person with some investment in seeing hockey analytics become more widely accepted, watching the Leafs collapse in slow motion after a season of taunting from the more traditional corners of the game was exceedingly gratifying," Dellow said. "As a fan of irony, it might have been even better."

Dellow said the Leafs were exceedingly fortunate to have piled up 80 points in their first 68 games; still, it was reasonable to expect they would have played well enough in the remaining 14 games to make the playoffs. That they didn't, Dellow said, was as much bad luck as anything else.

"They died as they lived—on the bounces," Dellow said. "While the numbers guys were vindicated, in that we'd correctly identified the Leafs as a team that wouldn't make the playoffs, it also served as a reminder that you can't say *when* the luck will run out, just that it will."

It mattered little that similar #fancystats forecasts of doom and gloom for the 2013–14 Colorado Avalanche never came to pass, that the Avalanche posted terrible Corsi, Fenwick and PDO numbers but dodged all the bullets and still finished with 112 points, second in the powerful Western Conference, third in the entire league. In advanced stats, as in any sport, you win some, you lose some. Some victories, though, end up having a greater impact than just another two points in the standings. Toronto's collapse, the fulfilment of the Leafs' #fancystats prophecy, was the analytics equivalent of a franchise-defining, we-walk-together-forever, last-second win for the ages.

The truth about advanced stats in hockey is that they're not really all that advanced. (This from the guy who had to beg his way out of a Grade 12 math exam).

Advanced is more a relative term, given that goals, assists, points, penalty minutes and, more recently, plus-minus, have always been the standard currencies by which individual players were evaluated. Wins and losses, meanwhile, were always the norms by which teams are judged.

But if advanced stats in hockey aren't really all that advanced, they are most certainly new to the game—at least, relatively speaking.

Many proponents of #fancystats point to the advent of Corsi, the puck-possession metric, as perhaps the dawn, or at least the big breakthrough, of modern-day hockey analytics. There was no specific date when Corsi was born, though Dellow recalled the concept might have come up on message board chatter (on sites like the HF Boards at hfboards.hockeysfuture.com) amongst the number-crunching community as early as the NHL lockout of 2004.

Perhaps the first documented evidence of the actual statistic now known as Corsi—arguably *the* seminal moment in #fancystats history— appeared in 2006. Legend has it that Edmonton Oiler fan and blogger Vic Ferrari—the man, the myth, the legend— heard Buffalo Sabre goalie coach Jim Corsi explain in a radio interview how he counted shot *attempts* (totalling shots on goal, missed shots and blocked shots) instead of the conventional (and official) measurement of shots on goal. The story goes that Ferrari took that notion, worked with it and *voilà*: Corsi—the concept, not the man—was born. It's believed Ferrari first wrote about it in any length on March 5, 2006, on his *Irreverent Oiler Fans* blog.

Gabe Desjardins, a native Winnipegger, lifelong Jets fan and electrical engineer who graduated from Queen's University in Kingston, Ontario, but moved to California's Silicon Valley to work in high tech, believes the #fancystats movement had much deeper roots, starting in almost prehistoric hockey times. As in the 1950s. Desjardins would know: he is, for all intents and purposes, one of the godfathers of hockey analytics, the individual (along with Corsi creator Ferrari) who has done the most groundbreaking work to pioneer the cause. He started writing about hockey analytics in 2003. In 2006, as Ferrari was writing about Corsi, Desjardins established *Behind the Net* (www. behindthenet.ca), the hardcore hockey analytics website. There isn't anyone today within the advanced stats community who doesn't pay homage to Desjardins as a master.

"We know the Montreal Canadiens of the 1950s were tracking plus-minus as a statistic long before it came into existence [in the NHL]," Desjardins said. "Some scorecards from the 1972 Summit Series have been found that showed [Team Canada coach] Harry Sinden was having someone [Ron Andrews, then the NHL's statistician] count shots in a 'Corsi way.' We know Roger Neilson was scoring his players using shots for and shots against, so it's been going on for a long time."

Incredibly, it appears at least one man, a true visionary, was looking at hockey in a complex, analytical, statistical way as far back as the early 1950s. Lloyd Percival—the man who pioneered everything from cutting-edge athletic training to injury treatment, to nutrition, to coaching methods, and the author of *The Hockey Handbook*, which Anatoly Tarasov, the godfather of Soviet hockey, credited as the blueprint for the development of Russian hockey—was doing work for the Detroit Red Wings in the early 1950s, but also for the St. Michael's Majors Junior A hockey club. In Gary Mossman's fine biography *Lloyd Percival: Coach and Visionary,* there is evidence that Percival was breaking down hockey games in a truly advanced analytical way. Not relatively advanced for the 1950s; advanced by even today's standards.

Of Percival's work with St. Mike's, Mossman wrote:

Percival was able to do things for [St. Mike's] that he was denied in Detroit. For example, he produced a seven-page "Hockey Survey Analysis" of a playoff game between St. Michael's and St. Catharines on March 19, 1952, in which body checks for both teams are recorded, categorized, counted according to location on the ice and the level of success, and connected to

*scoring chances. Shoot-ins and recovery rates are also totaled,
positional play is analyzed and passes are tabulated according
to their locations, their success rate and the reasons for their
success. Furthermore, shots at and on goal are counted and
the location from which they were directed is analyzed, and
the time of puck possession inside the blue line is recorded for
each team. Along with conclusions in each section, Percival presented [St. Mike's] with a summary of twelve "General" comments and recommendations for tactics and improved play for
the next game in the series.*

Not only was Percival apparently embracing rudimentary Corsi in
1952, he was light years ahead of his time on zone entries and recovery
rates, to say nothing of coming up with tangible tactical changes for the
next game based on stats compiled from the previous game. Percival's
level of statistical sophistication was nothing short of incredible.

In more modern times, Desjardins also cited the pioneering concepts and written work of people such as Tom Awad and Alan Ryder,
from the 1990s through to the present, as ample evidence of thinking-
outside-the-box hockey statistics that pre-date Corsi. Also, the NHL's
move to real-time stats around 1997 was a factor, as was Desjardins's
own involvement in an advanced sports stats/analytics site—Protrade,
which later became Citizen Sports, formed in late 2003 and early 2004,
where Desjardins was the lone hockey "expert" amongst others doing
the same work for baseball, basketball and football.

Still, Desjardins, like most everyone else involved in hockey analytics, points to the arrival of Corsi by way of Ferrari as a watershed
moment.

Whatever you think of advanced stats in hockey, the story of
Ferrari and how Corsi came to be is a mindblower that most of the
#fancystats community would not believe.

Ferrari and some fellow "hockey nerds" (as he affectionately termed them) were discussing, in or around 2005, the concept of how one might efficiently measure puck possession, lamenting the absence of stats (blocked and missed shots) that would permit data to be collected. Then Ferrari heard Buffalo Sabre general manager Darcy Regier—not Jim Corsi, as legend has it—talk in a radio interview about missed and blocked shots, precisely the path Ferrari and his pals were interested in following.

In a rare—if not unheard-of—telephone interview with me in April 2014, Ferrari explained publicly (for the first time) what happened after that:

> I heard Regier on the radio. He had all these great stats about missed and blocked shots that we just didn't have at the time, although they became available [from the NHL] not too long after that. There was a small group of us that had been talking about [the concept] for a while.
>
> I was going to call [Corsi] the Regier number. But it didn't sound good; it didn't seem right. Then I was going to call it the Ruff number [after Sabres coach Lindy], but that obviously sounded bad. So I went to the Buffalo Sabre website and looked at a picture of a guy on their website, and Jim Corsi kind of fit the bill. So I called it a "Corsi number," and then I pretended it was him I heard him on the radio talking about it—that's what I told people. That's basically [how Corsi got named].

Wait a minute. Pump the brakes. This qualifies as breaking #fancystats news.

Was Ferrari actually saying Jim Corsi's only connection to the statistic was that Ferrari liked the look of his photo on the Sabres' website, especially his moustache, and the sound of his name?

From Ferrari's perspective at the time, yes, that's entirely accurate.

"I always prepared myself [that if the stat ever became well known]—hey, it was just a small group of nerds talking hockey—that eventually Corsi or someone would come to me and say, 'What the hell are you guys talking about and why are you [using my name]?' I figured if it happened, I would apologize and carry on. I was really surprised a few years ago when I read a story in *USA Today* where Corsi talked about how the inspiration [for the numbers] came to him when he was skiing in the Alps, and I thought, '[Expletive deleted], it came to me when I saw your picture on a website, because I liked your moustache.'"

But the story gets even better.

Ferrari had no idea at the time—nor even when he gave this interview in 2014—that the metric's name turned out to be fortuitously labelled. One of the reasons Regier was on the radio talking about shot attempts in the first place was that Corsi was, in fact, a believer in measuring a goalie's workload not by just shots on goal but by blocked and missed shots as well.

"Oh, I had no idea of that," Ferrari said. "I just liked his moustache."

Seriously, you can't make this stuff up.

But it's true, all of it.

Regier was an NHL general manager who was in on the ground floor of analytics, and his goalie coach, Corsi, was a thoughtful, deep thinker, a former algebra teacher.

"I always kidded Jim that he was the self-proclaimed protector of all goalies," Regier said. "He was always looking for a stat that would give his goalies their due. [Adding up shots on goal, blocked shots and missed shots] was something along those lines. Jim was always charting shots—where they came from, that stuff. In all the years I've known him, Jim never tried to take credit for [the Corsi metric as it's more sophisticatedly applied now]. He was just interested in tracking shots for his goalies."

Regier said there was other outside-the-box thinking going on within the Sabres organization at that time, mostly out of necessity.

"Our scouting budget had been really slashed," Regier said, "so we hired a bunch of young kids to track things [from games] on video. I can assure you, if I was on the radio talking about that sort of [statistical] stuff, it would have come from Jim and those kids and the work they were doing."

If the story of how Corsi came to be named is fascinating, what are we to make of the story of the mysterious, international man of mystery, Vic Ferrari?

If you happened to be a fan of the 1980s TV sitcom *Taxi*, you'll recognize the Vic Ferrari moniker. A character on the show, Latka Gravas—played by eccentric actor Andy Kaufman—created a suave but obnoxious alter ego who went by that name.

The Oiler-loving, stat-creating Ferrari, though, had two simple rationales for the *nom de plume*.

"I liked Andy Kaufman," Ferrari said, "and at the time, no one used their real name on the Internet. I still generally don't. Being a bit older [Ferrari was born in 1967], I guess I'm not comfortable with how kids pour out their whole lives on Facebook and put everything about themselves on the Internet. It's a terrible idea, I think. I'm a private person. I also had a professional life and I didn't want people I was working with to know I was a hockey nerd. It's not something you're proud of."

Ferrari always loved hockey. He played it growing up. He had a deep and abiding passion for the Edmonton Oilers—still does, although the Oilers' streak of missing the playoffs, eight straight years and counting, has pretty much mutilated his heart. It was originally his fascination with gambling and sports betting, though, that got him into blogging and analytics. That was also, in part, what led him to depart—at least in the public sense.

"I came from a sports betting background, that was my initial interest," he said. "I loved hockey, played it, coached it, but until I got into the [sports betting] industry and saw how they looked at the game, I realized I really knew nothing about hockey. All the stuff I thought I knew was wrong. That changed my life."

Eventually, though, as much as he enjoyed being a "nerd" and trying, through his site, to come up with ways of understanding how the outcomes of games were determined, it was in his best interest to go underground, to lower his profile.

"I was hurting myself," he said. "I was helping to make other people smarter, which is good, but not if you make them too smart. Not if you come from my [sports betting] background."

If Ferrari did any media interviews, other than comments he made or dialogue he had on stats-related websites, there's no record of them. He's been like a ghost to most. So why do an interview with me in 2014, a few years after he'd stopped blogging regularly and mostly dropped out of sight?

"I guess I've become a bit less concerned about [putting myself out there] because lately, everyone seems to be more open about it [on the Internet]," Ferrari said, noting that he still has no interest in revealing his true identity, other than being comfortable in saying that, as of 2014, he was living in Chicago and working as a trader in the stock market there.

The man is something of a #fancystats legend, primarily as a bright mind and innovator, but also because of a well-known salty disposition, acerbic online attitude and, of course, his shadowy, anonymous existence. Even a fellow analytics legend like Gabe Desjardins didn't know Ferrari's real surname or that Ferrari had moved from Edmonton to Chicago.

"I think I know Vic's real first name and I think I've got an idea of where near Edmonton he lives, assuming he still lives there," Desjardins said before Ferrari gave the interview for this book. "I honestly don't know his last name or if he still lives where I think he lived or what he's doing or what he does for a living. He once told me, 'I don't do interviews. I'm from a different generation.' He's a mysterious man."

Mysterious, yes. Some would say even mythical.

"Mythical?" Ferrari said, laughing. "People can imagine all sorts of shit. I am pretty special, though, don't kid yourself."

That last part was a joke. He laughed hard.

But when the history of hockey analytics is written, it's no joke: Ferrari and his *Irreverent Oiler Fans* website will almost certainly be identified as the cradle of #fancystats civilization.

This new Corsi concept didn't exactly take the entire hockey world by storm right out of the gate. It was, however, a topic of much discussion on Ferrari's website. One of the commenters who frequented the site was Calgary native Matt Fenwick, a mechanical engineer with a passion for hockey and the Flames who, at that time, was living in Lethbridge. He had an ongoing Internet debate with another fan, Cameron Thomson (known by the handle RiversQ), on Ferrari's site because Fenwick felt strongly that blocked shots should *not* be included in the Corsi calculation. The two of them would go back and forth on the merits of each other's argument.

Ferrari was posting the Corsi numbers of Oiler players on his site at the time, but in November 2007, he started posting a second column of numbers beside Corsi, simply calling the new column "Fenwick": shots on goal plus missed shots, but not blocked shots.

"I just liked Matt Fenwick; he's smart and he's a really nice guy,"

Ferrari said of why he started posting Fenwick numbers. "I had already made Corsi famous; I wanted to make Matt Fenwick famous. That was pretty much it. I'm not sure it really matters whether blocked shots are counted or not—it's still basically the same thing. It's which way the puck is going. It's all about possession. It was at times, I thought, a nonsensical argument in some ways, but I thought Matt should have his own stat. I really like Matt.

"I named all the stats after people. I was criticized for that—people said they're stupid names. But I think hockey stats get more talk in regular [non-hockey] circles than any other statistics. I live with nerds, I live in the trading world, I know people who know metrics inside and out and only casually follow hockey, but they know the [hockey] stats by name. That's because they're cool [names]."

So Fenwick, the engineer who fancied himself more a fan of the game than a numbers geek—"I'm not really very mathy," he said—ended up with his very own stat with his very own name. How cool is that?

"Well," Fenwick said in April 2014, "it's getting a lot more interesting all the time. It was one thing to see it on the web, on a stats site, but when]Edmonton Oiler left winger] Taylor Hall is dropping references to Fenwick in his postgame comments or Brendan Shanahan is talking about it on his first day on the job with the Toronto Maple Leafs [as team president], that's not really something I ever could have imagined."

Again, that 2013–14 NHL season, when Hall and Shanahan dropped Fenwick references will be remembered as #fancystats' coming-out party.

Ferrari's *Irreverent Oiler Fans* site turned out to be Ground Zero not only for Corsi and Fenwick, but also what has become the third element of the advanced hockey stats trilogy: PDO.

PDO stands for . . . well, it doesn't really stand for anything. At least not anything that relates to the statistic, which adds shooting percentage to save percentage to get a numerical value that appears to have great predictive powers. PDO was the Internet name Oiler fan Brian King used when he commented or posted on Ferrari's site. King played a video game on the old Nintendo 64 system, called Perfect Dark. That's where the PD part came from. And the O, to make it PDO?

"It had no meaning," King said. "I just put down PDO, it means nothing, it has no significance."

Seriously.

First Vic Ferrari, and now PDO?

Again, you can't make up this stuff.

In late August 2008, the then 20-year-old King and a bunch of Oiler fans, including Ferrari, were batting around Corsi and Fenwick talk as it related to the Oilers when King—I mean, PDO—posted the following: "Let's pretend there was a stat called 'blind luck.' Said stat was simply adding shooting percentage and save percentage together. I know there's a way to check what this number should generally be, but I hate math, so let's just say 100 per cent for shits and giggles."

King maybe didn't fully realize it at that precise moment, but he had stumbled upon the embryonic form of what is now widely regarded as the most tried-and-true advanced stat in hockey, PDO: the one number that, in all probability, tells you whether a player or a team is either incredibly lucky or unbelievably unlucky, and in which direction the player's or team's performance is highly likely to trend in the future.

"PDO is great," said Ferrari, who further advanced King's initial concept. "It's about the role of chance in the game, it's about understanding that relationship with chance."

In a span of less than two and a half years—from March 5, 2006, when Ferrari first publicly documented his Corsi revelation, to August 29, 2008, when King, "for shits and giggles," stumbled upon PDO, with the creation of Fenwick's Fenwick tucked in between—hockey's advanced statistics community had been given three building blocks with which to launch an offensive on the sleepy, non-numerical hockey world that had no idea what was coming.

Ferrari, Fenwick and King. Corsi, Fenwick and PDO. The Big Three—the hockey analytics equivalent of Larry Robinson, Serge Savard and Guy Lapointe.

Okay, it's the moment of truth. It's time for a Grade 12 math fraud to try to explain Corsi, Fenwick and PDO to many who, I suspect, are as numerically challenged as myself.

Remember when I said advanced stats aren't all that advanced? It's true—sort of.

Let's start with Corsi, which is the difference between two teams' shot attempts while playing even-strength, five-on-five hockey: shots on goal plus missed shots plus blocked shots, minus the same items for the opposition.

Let's assume your team had 10 shots on goal, missed five shots and took five shots that were blocked. That's 20 shot attempts for you.

Let's assume my team had eight shots on goal, missed four and took four more that were blocked. That's 16 shot attempts for me.

Corsi is the difference between the two. It can be expressed in a number of ways. We could say you are plus-four (the difference between your 20 and my 16) or I'm minus-four. But it's most often, and best, expressed as a percentage. That is, of the 36 total shots taken by both teams in the game, you had 55.5 per cent. I had 44.5 per cent. There's your Corsi.

So, obviously, any number over 50 per cent is better than a number under 50. It doesn't get much more basic than that.

"The thinking behind it," Ferrari said, "is that the more you have the puck, the more likely you are to win."

You might ask, why count shot attempts? Wouldn't counting goals make more sense?

Fair enough. A team's goal differential—the number of five-on-five goals it scores minus those given up—can be a valuable metric, but statistics tend to be more effective the larger the sample size. In an NHL season, teams usually score between 200 and 300 goals. They often take more than 2,400 shots, plus all those missed shots and blocked shots. So the sample size for attempted shots is so much greater than that for goals scored—maybe 10 times as great. Many goals are scored as a result of skill and artistry, but most involve a great amount of luck or random bounces. Corsi gives you a volume of events that helps to offset the high degree of luck when using a smaller sample size.

You may also ask, Why even bother tracking Corsi? What's the point of it?

Corsi's value is that it has been proven, time and again, to provide a reasonably accurate representation of puck possession. That makes total sense. The more shots you attempt, it stands to reason, the more you have the puck on your stick. Just to be sure, researchers have used a stopwatch to actually measure puck possession in specific games, and the corresponding possession ratios inevitably correlated to the Corsi numbers. This is not fiction.

Now, positive puck possession doesn't absolutely guarantee victory—as noted earlier, the 2013–14 Colorado Avalanche were 25th in the NHL (47.4 per cent) in Corsi rankings, but finished with the third most points in the entire league. But the *probability* of a team's success is greatly enhanced with positive puck possession. Intuitively, I think we can all agree that makes sense.

That's not exactly an advanced notion, if you think about it, although the non-believers remain dubious of Corsi's usefulness and/or validity as a predictive number because, well, the numbers don't *always* add up.

It is by no means perfect, not even close.

In 2013–14, for example, three of the NHL's top 10 Corsi teams—New Jersey at No. 4 (54.6 per cent), Ottawa at No. 8 (52.2 per cent) and Vancouver at No. 9 (52 per cent)—didn't make the playoffs. And, of course, there was the glaring case of the Avalanche, who became to the #fancystats skeptics what the Leafs were to the numbers crowd.

"Each [exception] is different," Desjardins said.

The Devils, for example, went an incredible 0-for-13 in shootouts.

"I think we can agree that is just bad luck," Desjardins said. "With average luck in the shootout, the Devils make the playoffs."

This is also where that line about advanced stats not being that advanced falls apart. Guys like Desjardins and Dellow can, and will, explain in great and complicated detail the whys and wherefores of Ottawa and/or Vancouver's misleading Corsi numbers. If I let them do that here, trust me, you'd get as lost in the numbers as I did with logarithms in Grade 12.

That, of course, infuriates the anti-numbers advocates, who believe the #fancystats guys trumpet the validity of their numbers when they're proven to be "right," but find ways rationalize the hell out of them when they're perceived to be "wrong."

The reality is that the stats guys know there's no one magic number that is right all the time; there will always be outliers and exceptions. They will be the first to tell you luck, or sheer randomness, is a big part of hockey and no metric can actually measure or forecast all the bounces. They'll also note Corsi is a five-on-five, even-strength stat that doesn't take into account special teams or goaltenders or a host of other factors that help determine the outcomes of hockey games. Therefore, while using Corsi, the #fancystats disciples will often apply it in conjunction with other metrics. But that's not something non-numerically inclined fans can always get their heads around. It starts to get complicated, putting the "advanced" in advanced stats.

When all is said and done, though, whatever frailties, real or imagined, exist within Corsi, the #fancystats crowd will tell you the data makes them right a lot more than they're wrong, that the probability of a good Corsi equalling a good hockey team is far greater than not.

Of course, we could make all of this even more complicated. But we won't do that now, other than to note there are myriad derivatives from basic Corsi.

Corsi can be a team metric or it can be applied individually to any player. Also, you can factor in whether faceoffs originate in the offensive or defensive zone, the quality of opposition a player faces, even the quality of teammates he plays with. You can measure a player's Corsi when he's on the ice in relation to his team's Corsi when he's not on the ice (a metric called Corsi Relative). It goes on and on . . .

There is, however, one further aspect of Corsi that can't be glossed over: the "close" factor.

Most Corsi references you see are what are termed "close," which simply means the shot attempt calculations are made based on when the score is either tied or the teams are separated by only one goal in the first two periods. What the stats guys quickly figured out is that, once a team is ahead or behind by two or more goals, there is either a conscious (through coach's orders) or unconscious (through players instinctively "protecting" a lead) decision to alter behaviour to play a more conservative, defensive-minded game. If there were no distinction between "close" games and the others, Corsi's integrity would be severely compromised because of a radical change in mindset affecting how the game is played, depending on the score.

This concept is known as "score effects."

"There is an almost universal tendency for NHL teams to get a greater share of the shot attempts when they are behind than they do when they're tied," Dellow said. "They also get a greater share of the shot attempts when they're tied than they do when they're leading. For example, the 2013–14 Bruins had a five-on-five Corsi percentage, when leading by one, of 50.3 per cent. With the score tied, their Corsi was 55.7. When the Bruins were trailing by a goal, their Corsi was 59.3.

"One of the funny things about this is the 'If we just started the game like we played the third period' postgame quote, which so many fans of bad teams have heard. It's funny to hear these quotes from people who have spent years in the NHL, seeing this phenomenon play out over and over. They aren't going to start games like that unless they start with a one-goal deficit, which isn't going to help them win games."

Still with us?

Good, that's as far as we'll go with Corsi.

Now, on to Fenwick, which is going to be really easy because everything you read about Corsi still applies. The only exception is that Fenwick doesn't include blocked shots. Otherwise, all the equations, standards and terms of reference are identical.

So, you ask, why bother with it if it's so closely aligned with Corsi?

Well, Matt Fenwick was of the opinion that, while Corsi was a very good proxy for puck possession, if you wanted a metric to more accurately reflect scoring chances, blocked shots should be removed from the equation. A blocked shot, after all, is not a scoring chance. Neither is a shot from the blue line, but that gets counted in Fenwick, as it does in Corsi. Again, as was the case with a researcher actually timing puck possession to ensure Corsi was a good proxy, the same thing has been done with scoring chances and Fenwick. They match, more or less. Fenwick is, therefore, considered a valid proxy for scoring chances. Again, this is not fiction.

The difference between the two for #fancystats aficionados may be no different than your preference for Coke or Pepsi.

Corsi has perhaps better brand recognition. Because Corsi tracks more events, it tends to illustrate puck-possession trends more quickly than Fenwick. Stats guys will tell you that, in the short run, Corsi may be a preferable metric. But because Fenwick is perceived as a little more accurate than Corsi as a proxy for scoring chances, over the long haul, many feel it's superior to Corsi. My sense is the #fancystats cognoscenti tend to slightly prefer Fenwick, but will utilize both, since multiple studies have shown puck possession and scoring chances to be linked anyway. For the most part, Corsi and Fenwick tend to mirror each other pretty well, and on those rare occasions of marked differences, the nod seems to go to Fenwick.

As an aside, from a strictly neutral observer trying to grasp #fancystats, having two metrics so close in nature is more confusing than helpful and, therefore, hinders the "marketing" of new-age numbers. But that's just me.

Which brings us, finally, to PDO.

"A brilliant number," Desjardins said of PDO.

Hockey's advanced number crunchers use all three metrics in concert with each other, as well as other, more complicated calculations, but you get the sense that if they could have only one of them, it would be PDO.

That's because it's perceived to be the most "predictive" of the Big Three.

"Saying that guys or teams with a really high PDO will regress is sort of the ultimate shooting fish in a barrel of hockey analytics," Dellow said.

Here's how PDO works, or at least what intrigued Brian King enough to come up with the initial concept.

King figured if you take a team's shooting percentage with a given player on the ice (his "on-ice shooting percentage," not to be confused with his individual shooting percentage, which is calculated only on his own shots and goals) and add it to his team's five-on-five save percentage when he is on the ice, there should be a total number that represents the baseline for any player who is neither extremely lucky or unlucky. As he said, "for shits and giggles," he chose 100 per cent, which turned out to be pretty much perfect. When King calculated the PDOs for individual Oiler players at the time, he discovered those with PDOs of greater than 101 tended to get contract extensions, while those below 99 tended to get shipped out of town.

The more research that was done on PDO, the more it became clear that players or teams (PDO works well for both) with exceptionally high or low numbers were often experiencing really good luck or wallowing in the misery of bad luck. It was determined that the outliers would, over time, regress to meet somewhere in the middle.

Five-on-five team shooting percentage, for example, tends to run between 6 and 10 per cent, but the average is around 8 per cent. Five-on-five team save percentage generally ranges from .900 to .940, but the average is around .920. So, add the on-ice shooting percentage of .08 to the save percentage of .92, and there you have it: your midpoint of one—or 100, depending on how you want to present it. Players and teams can post PDOs much higher or lower than 100, but over time, that's roughly where they'll end up.

King couldn't possibly have known what an incredibly predictive tool PDO would become, both for players and team. Non-believers in #fancystats often don't like PDO because its core concept can really rain on a hockey fan's parade.

Take Edmonton's Jordan Eberle, for example.

In 2011–12, his second NHL season, Eberle had a breakout year, scoring 34 goals and 76 points in 78 games. The widespread sense at the time was that it was a hint of things to come, that Eberle might be on the cusp of becoming an elite-level point producer who was only going to get better, to put up bigger numbers. The sky was the limit. It was exciting, so hopeful and optimistic.

Dellow—like Ferrari, a passionate Oiler fan—looked at Eberle's underlying numbers (as measured by PDO) from that season and didn't like what he saw. The Oilers shot 12.7 per cent in five-on-five situations when Eberle was on the ice and had a .909 save percentage, making Eberle's PDO 103.7. If Oiler fan Dellow didn't believe so firmly in the power of PDO, perhaps he could have joined the cheery chorus predicting Eberle was on the launching pad to become a perennial point-a-game player (or better).

But he didn't. Or couldn't. The numbers wouldn't allow him, and the numbers, Dellow believed, don't lie. He wasn't shy about saying so, either. He didn't say Eberle wasn't—or couldn't become—a good hockey player; he just said Eberle's numbers that year were much more likely to be an aberration than the norm and that Eberle was likely to score less, not more, in coming seasons. A PDO of 103.7, Dellow told anyone who would listen, was unsustainable.

And it was.

Eberle scored 16 goals and 37 points the following year in the lockout-shortened 48-game season; he had 28 goals and 65 points in 80 games in 2013–14. His PDOs for those two seasons regressed from 103.7 to 98.9 and 100.5.

The same principles of PDO apply to teams.

That was, in large part, the rationale for the infamous #fancystats Maple Leaf Prophecy of 2013–14. Toronto had a PDO of 103.0 in 2012–13, which was viewed as unsustainable. Sure enough, in 2013–14, it dropped to 101.2.

That mean of 100.0, for most teams, is like a magnet. The teams with PDOs significantly above or below 100.0 tend to regress towards it. Again, though, as with Corsi and Fenwick, it's not inviolable. You can find exceptions to the rule. Pittsburgh posted back-to-back PDO seasons of 102.2 in 2007–08 and 2008–09 (regressing to 99.5 in 2009–10). Anaheim went from 101.7 in 2012–13 to 102.3 in 2013–14. Teams with chronically poor goaltending (bad save-percentage teams) can get mired in the range between 97.5 and 99.5 and not drift towards 100. Teams with really extraordinary goaltending can stay above 100 longer than they should.

Dellow conceded PDO is not infallible, but in a game where luck plays such a huge factor, PDO is, relatively speaking, as good as it gets for identifying teams and players whose results are likely to change, for better or worse.

Dellow reviewed team PDOs for six NHL seasons, from 2006–07 to 2012–13. During that time, only 32 of 180 teams posted a PDO of 101.0 or better. Of those 32 teams, only three didn't regress the following season. Two of them—the Vancouver Canucks (from 2009–10 to 2010–11) and the Penguins (from 2007–08 to 2008–09)—stayed the same. The only team with a PDO of 101.0 or greater that improved the next season were the Ducks, from 2012–13 (in the 48-game lockout-shortened season) to 2013–14. Twenty-nine of the 32 teams with a PDO of 101.0 or more regressed.

The trend is clear. One might call it overwhelmingly clear.

That's why the Ducks (102.3 in 2013–14) and the Avalanche (101.7) were the #fancystats gang's picks to take a step back in 2014–15. One of them could prove to be the exception to the rule, but probability suggested otherwise.

"Everyone [eventually] crashes towards 100," Dellow said. "The best tend to stay a little higher than 100, but it's by a small amount. So when I say Colorado is going to crash next year, I'm really saying, 'Historically, teams with a PDO like Colorado's do not repeat that PDO the following season. If Colorado doesn't get a high PDO, they can't win unless they improve their possession game.' It's very rare that the same team posts a high PDO two years in a row, so I'm comfortable saying Colorado probably won't. In that sense, PDO is very easy to predict: just assume a team will be close to 100, even if it was significantly above or below 100 in the previous year."

If there's a final exam on this at the end of the chapter, I'm going to ask to be exempt.

Many more NHL teams than not are into analytics.

That's not a real news flash. The number grows each day. The real questions are, to what degree, for what particular purpose and to what end are analytics being used by these teams?

That would qualify as difficult to quantify. NHL clubs are secretive at the best of times. When it comes to what new-age data they're using, how they collect it, who's collecting it, what specifically it's being used for . . . well, suffice it to say they're not too forthcoming.

Again, though, that 2013–14 NHL season seemed to be, at least in terms of public perception, the year in which the profile of hockey analytics was greatly heightened.

The New Jersey Devils, for example, have long been known as one of the most secretive organizations in the NHL. In January 2014, lo and behold, the Devils advertised on their own website a job posting for a director of hockey analytics.

"We've had . . . I don't know how many applicants," Devils president and GM Lou Lamoriello told espn.com.

If Lamoriello wouldn't share how many people applied, I don't like anyone's chances of getting the godfather of NHL GMs to explain what metrics the Devils would like to track and how they would use that information.

On May 1, 2014, the *Chicago Sun-Times* published a feature on how Blackhawks' GM Stan Bowman had fully embraced analytics.

Also in the 2013–14 season, Oiler winger Hall, as Matt Fenwick noted, dropped some #fancystats knowledge in a pre-game interview on TSN: "Whether they're use useful or not, I do think they are for sure, but the thing for a hockey player, if you're an advanced-stats guy and you're describing to a hockey player, you have to have, like, some kind of end point. Like, what does he have to do better to get this stat better? That's the thing I'm lost on with Corsi and Fenwick and all this stuff—how do you improve a player by it, what do you tell him [to do]?"

I would suggest the closer to ice level you get in the NHL, the further away you get in terms of an understanding and/or appreciation of analytics. The further up the food chain you go, the greater it is.

That is, players are the least likely to know or care about them. Most of them just want to play. That's challenging enough without bringing analytics into the mix. But for players who do understand new-age stats, they're not easy to embrace because there often is, as Hall noted, a disconnect between knowing what a stat is and knowing what to do to improve the stat, assuming that improving it would make a positive difference on the player's or team's play on ice.

NHL coaches are all over the map in terms of their views on analytics. Some do embrace them to some degree; others not at all. Mostly, though, I think you could safely say coaches are so focused on their own team, they tend to use two tools in particular: their eyes, while standing behind the bench; and expansive video, to draw conclusions on how the team is playing and how it would be better served to play. Don't get the wrong idea: a lot of NHL coaching staffs are well aware of Corsi and Fenwick, and many get supplied with that information (or perhaps, for teams really into analytics, something unique and/or more advanced) period by period, but I'd wager the vast majority are more likely to trust what they see themselves or what the video coach gives them.

Video is such a huge part of NHL coaching. The video programs have become so sophisticated that a single player's entire game can be viewed with the push of a button. In the age-old battle between #fancystats non-believers ("I watch the games") and believers ("The numbers don't lie"), an NHL coach has the advantage of being responsible for only one team, and watching every second that team plays, with the added benefit of rewatching every or any aspect of it any time he likes.

Dellow is a big believer that the onus is on hockey analytics people to answer Hall's question—that it's not enough to come up with the numbers, that there's another step in terms of it being actionable. In other words, a player or coach needs to be told, "If you do this, this and this on the ice, it may better than what you're currently doing."

Much of Dellow's published work is in that vein, taking actual game occurrences, measuring and quantifying things, and suggesting tactics or different approaches to improve the results.

Gabe Desjardins said the cost of one really good analytics expert working for a team would be saved with one good decision from that individual—that using analytics for the acquisition of one good player, or not overpaying on one contract extension for another, would be the wisest investment a team could ever make.

All of these guys—Desjardins, Ferrari, Dellow and their growing legion—have, in one manner or another at some time, worked for or consulted with NHL clubs or have been asked to.

In fact, for a relatively brief period of time, during or sometime around the 2010–11 NHL season, Desjardins, Ferrari, Dellow, Tom Awad and Sunny Mehta, a former pro poker player who was also a notable contributor to Ferrari's website, worked as consultants for the Phoenix Coyotes. They were among a group of analysts who were known within the Coyotes' organization as "the Quants," named for Scott Patterson's bestselling 2010 book that looked at quantitative analysis of Wall Street hedge funds and the men who operated them.

This hockey statistics equivalent of the Dream Team, in a manner of speaking, was put together by prospective Coyotes' owner Matthew

Hulsizer, the financier who seemed to be on the verge, at that time, of gaining control of the bankrupt NHL franchise. The hockey ops people in Phoenix did utilize the Quants for some input on statistical analyses, but the Quants didn't last long and neither did Hulsizer, who ultimately pulled out of the running to purchase the Coyotes in 2011.

More and more teams now have full-time directors of analytics, applying their work not only to the team's play on the ice but everything from contract negotiations to the drafting of players.

Well-respected advanced stats blogger Eric Tulsky wrote a piece, an effective NHL status report, on October 21, 2013, chronicling just how many teams are hopping on the analytics bandwagon, but it's well known in hockey circles that some teams—Boston, Los Angeles, San Jose and Chicago, for example—have been at it for years, and likely at relatively high levels of sophistication.

Each year, more and more NHL personnel are turning up at the renowned MIT Sloan Sports Analytics Conference in Boston, which used to be the almost exclusive preserve of baseball, basketball and football executives.

In the summer of 2013, the Edmonton Oilers hosted the Oilers' "Hackathon 2.0," where the club invited any citizen with an idea for a metric or statistical analysis to submit it for consideration. The written submissions were then winnowed down to allow a few of the very best to make their case in person before Oiler management personnel. Also, in August of that year, Dellow and others were part of organizational meetings with Oiler management and coaching staffs.

The Oilers, for years, have had an interest in analytics, employing Dan Haight, who is the chief operating officer of Edmonton-based Darkhorse Analytics and managing director of the Centre for Excellence in Operations at the University of Alberta.

There's no doubt the Oilers' acquisition of David Perron from the St. Louis Blues on July 10, 2013, for Magnus Paajarvi and a second-round pick, was driven in no small part by the team's advanced-stats analysis.

Haight's work with the Oilers has been applicable on numerous platforms throughout the organization, but perhaps most noteworthy—at least from a public or measurable way—was Haight's involvement in the Oilers' 2013 NHL draft.

Remember the name Marc-Olivier Roy.

The Oilers made the six-foot-one, 182-pound forward the 56th-overall pick in the 2013 draft. Oilers head scout Stu MacGregor and his staff had liked the 1994-born forward with Blainville-Boisbriand of the Quebec Major Junior Hockey League as a potential Oiler draftee, a prospect they had some interest in. But Haight, using an advanced statistical evaluation of draft-eligible prospects, had flagged Roy as a high-priority target.

"A lot of data gets put into the hopper and this particular player, with his statistics, the team that he plays on, the league he plays in, the numbers he put up, all of those factors and others, his profile was one that was identified as having a very good chance of being successful in the NHL," Edmonton GM Craig MacTavish said in September 2013, when Roy was playing for the Oilers' prospects in a rookie tournament in Penticton, British Columbia. "So we made drafting [Roy] a priority."

The Oilers selected Roy late in the second round, though they used their interest in him to employ another draft metric, the relatively common practice of parlaying a higher second-round pick into multiple lower picks. In fact, Oilers' senior vice-president Scott Howson has his own metric or formula to determine the value of specific picks, when it makes sense to trade a higher pick for multiple lower picks and how all those numbers should add up.

The Oilers were scheduled to pick 37th overall in the second round of 2013. The Oilers could have taken their primary target, Roy, at that point, but knew he would likely still be available later in the second round, when they were scheduled to pick again (56th). The Los Angeles Kings, meanwhile, had a particular prospect they were after—Valentin Zykov of the Baie-Comeau Drakkar—and recognized he likely would not stay on the board until the Kings picked at No. 57 overall.

So, reasonably certain Roy could be had at No. 56, the Oilers traded the 37th pick to the Kings, who took Zykov. In exchange for that pick, Los Angeles traded to Edmonton the 57th, 88th and 96th picks. Edmonton then traded that 57th pick to St. Louis (who took William Carrier) in exchange for the 83rd, 94th and 113th picks.

Edmonton selected Roy with their existing No. 56 pick, but the knowledge they would get him there allowed them to parlay that 37th pick into a total of five more picks that became prospects: Russian forward Bogdan Yakimov (83rd), Russian forward Anton Slepyshev (88th), Vancouver Giant forward Jackson Houck (94th), London Knight forward Kyle Platzer (96th) and forward Aidan Muir of Victory Honda (a Detroit-area midget team).

Even within the Oiler organization, how Roy fares as a prospect—to say nothing of the additional five prospects who came to be Oilers mostly because of the analytics-driven desire to draft him—was being viewed as a noteworthy test of the analytics process, and the application of #fancystats to the evaluation of draft prospects.

One suspects this is, in various forms, an exercise repeating itself throughout the NHL. For every NHL club that rejects #fancystats, I would wager there are two or three more clubs that are far beyond debating Corsi and are working on far more sophisticated concepts and metrics tailored to their individual needs and preferences.

If there is a battle between the traditionalists in hockey who eschew #fancystats and the growing legion that embrace them, I have bad news for the old guard.

The fight is over. In truth, it's no contest and probably never was.

It never is. Not in a society like ours, where there's such a premium placed on more information, more science, more technology or anything that helps to promote greater understanding and/or knowledge.

This same so-called advanced-statistics fight took place in baseball and basketball. The outcome was predictable there; it is in hockey, too.

Corsi, Fenwick, PDO—they're here to stay. Unless, of course, they're replaced by some other new innovative number or metric that is deemed to be better or more useful. Which is always a possibility, but it's always going to be more, never less.

I know the argument against that. Hockey is different. It's not baseball. It doesn't lend itself to numerical evaluations because there's a flow and unpredictability to it that doesn't exist in any other sport. There's some truth to that.

On that note, actually, the traditionalists and new-wave number guys do agree, in a manner of speaking. As analytics expert Gabe Desjardins freely admitted, "There is no Holy Grail number in hockey," no one metric that singularly defines success, whether individually or as a team. For mathematicians, scientists, deep thinkers or whatever these #fancystats guys ultimately are, it was surprising to learn how much they do ascribe to, or write off as, old-fashioned puck luck. So much of what they try to quantify is set against the backdrop of hockey's intrinsic randomness, which makes their pursuits all the more challenging.

Now, no one is forcing anyone to subscribe to their work. If you're a fan, a member of the mainstream media, a blogger, an agent, a player, a coach, a manager, an owner or whatever, you're free to go about your hockey business or pleasure as you see fit. Watch, play or coach the games through whatever lens you choose.

Numbers aren't for everyone. I get that people may not want

to embrace Corsi or Fenwick or PDO, but for the life of me, I don't understand mocking or dismissing them, either.

Part of the problem, I think, is that critics of #fancystats may have as much or more animosity towards the individuals putting out the numbers as the numbers themselves. It's a fascinating dynamic, as are all conflicts.

It's fashionable to portray the advanced-stats crowd as geeky or nerdish, especially in a sport that is as macho as hockey, and quite a few them actually seem to embrace that in a humorous yet prideful sort of way. I mean, the #fancystats label is almost an embodiment of that. Ferrari joked often about being a "hockey nerd." But you have to understand that these guys also see themselves as pioneers in a new field, that they've come up with some information that, in their minds, is incredibly revealing and relevant—groundbreaking, if you will. And for a time, maybe even still, no one wanted to listen or recognize their work. Worse still, they were dismissed out of hand; they were mocked.

As they made some inroads—information is power—they did become more empowered and confident. Where once they might have had a raging sense of insecurity about any role in the hockey world, in some instances that insecurity has morphed into an air of superiority. Their numbers add up, they will tell you, and if you're going to be disrespectful to them—well, then, they might just call you on it. The ridiculees have become the ridiculers; they're the smartest guys in the room, and if you don't believe them, just ask (some of) them. That said, though, it's been my experience that so many of those who are "into the numbers" are welcoming and receptive to sharing or explaining their craft to anyone who is interested or doesn't understand it.

I shake my head sometimes at the trading of barbs between the #fancystats believers and non-believers. At times, it reminds me of the dynamic in society between creationists and the scientific community, though obviously on a much lower, more secular level. I understand the backlash coming from the stats guys, but there are times when I think they'd be far better off just letting their work speak for itself than antagonizing those who choose not to see it as they do. But I also understand their frustration at those within the hockey establishment who are not only wilfully ignorant but derisive of them and mocking of their work.

As usual, I always see the world in shades of grey when, it seems, most everyone else has it as black and white.

"Corsi is the best."

"Corsi sucks."

I can't believe some colleagues in the media who are totally dismissive of advanced stats, who treat them with contempt, finding zero practical application for them. I'm equally miffed at how some in the advanced-stats community feel like the numbers are all that matters and how little time they have for the so-called intangibles.

Now, the mere mention of "intangibles" is a sore spot for many numbers guys. Rightly, they cite a lot of really bad decisions (that don't add up statistically) being made because a certain player "is good in the room." Fair enough on that. But there are still elements of hockey, which is an incredibly visceral team game, that can't always be quantified. A player may have a fantastic set of advanced metrics, but he may also have personality traits that, in the context of a team sport, work against him or serve to discount his numbers in some way. Maybe he's a bad teammate. Maybe he's creating negative energy on the bench. Maybe he's a coach killer. Or maybe he's needy, in spite of his great numbers. Teams, like individual players, are living, breathing things. There's no equation to measure that positive or negative energy.

Again, it seems like—some of the time, anyway—there are too many extreme viewpoints. Some guys believe in nothing but the magic and wonder of the game; some guys believe in nothing but what the numbers tell them. Each individual instinctively knows which side of the intangible/tangible side of the coin is more appealing to them, but I've always thought they shouldn't be mutually exclusive.

At the end of the day, though, we all have to do what works best for each of us. As someone who's not predisposed to enjoying working with numbers, that means challenging myself to keep an open mind on this relatively new information, embracing the parts of it I think make sense in terms of giving me a better understanding of the game and how I do my job. What metrics or numbers I can't understand or choose not to use, I just set aside.

I look at so-called traditional hockey stats now, like plus-minus and conventional shots on goal, and I see virtually no value in them. From my perspective, keeping in mind my sterling math background, they seem antiquated.

Quite frankly, I'm incredulous that anyone could find more value in those numbers than Corsi or Fenwick or PDO. I don't need to equate Corsi rankings to who will win or lose a game, or the Stanley Cup, but riddle me this: How could anyone think simple SOG is better than knowing how many shots were attempted (Corsi)?

Some of the advanced stats give me a better, clearer picture of what's happening. It's a big league. You can't watch every game. I don't need Corsi or Fenwick or PDO to be anything more than one tool in the belt. It's just information, subjectively better in my mind than what's currently being released as official by the NHL in their real-time stats.

One of the reasons advanced hockey stats are going to become more mainstream is better packaging. The traditional websites—Desjardins's *Behind the Net,* for example, but there are countless others—have been a boon to the cause since their inception, but many of them were or still are decidedly user unfriendly, unless you're a real numbers guy with a natural inclination for this stuff.

As you know, I'm not.

But along came, as an example, *Extra Skater* (www.extraskater. com), and suddenly #fancystats have a shiny, new user-friendly package that isn't overly intimidating for a neophyte. When I'm watching an NHL game at work now, I've got the NHL website open to all the real-time stats for that game, and that's great, but I'll also have *Extra Skater* open as well, as a companion, for all that useful information I can't get anywhere else.

When it came time for me to fill out my official NHL awards ballot in 2014, I got as much or more relevant information from *Extra Skater* as the official NHL stats package. Between Corsi, Fenwick, PDO and a plethora of derivative metrics, it's possible to get an incredible amount of detailed information on any player or any team. At a glance, you can see which players are being used in which situations, who's matching up with whom, who's playing with whom.

What's not to like about having more information?

If there's a day when I just want to put my feet up and watch a game, forget about the numbers, just soak up the wonder and magic of sport, that's fine, too. There's so much more to the game than math or science; there's no quantifying emotion, drama, joy and heartbreak. The numbers are always there if I want or need them; they're not going anywhere.

It's funny, actually. While we think there's this battle going on for mainstream acceptance of Corsi, Fenwick and PDO, and superficially I suppose there is, the reality is that next-generation numbers and principles are being worked on like never before.

Gabe Desjardins has, more or less, hung it up as a hockey analytics innovator. In 2014, he got an offer from an NHL club to jump on board and do some extensive research work. He thought about it, but ultimately took a pass, "because there are other things I want to do with my life now."

Desjardins knows, though, there is still going to be a surge in the movement. He said chip technology exists right now (in 2014) that would allow sophisticated tracking of the detailed movements and actions of NHL players while on the ice, that it's only a matter of time until that's how new groundbreaking data will be collected.

For every pioneer like Gabe Desjardins or Vic Ferrari, who take a step back or drop out of sight entirely, there are more bright, young guys committed to the cause, always moving it forward because there's no going back. Tulsky, the San Francisco–based Philadelphia Flyer fan (his *Outnumbered* blog can be found at www.sbnation.com/outnumbered), is known for doing groundbreaking work on zone entries and countless other intriguing concepts; Dellow is churning out novel looks at what happens from offensive-zone faceoffs and myriad other subjects.

"No one is writing better stuff in hockey right now than Tyler Dellow," Ferrari said, a sentiment echoed by Desjardins. "Eric Tulsky's work is fantastic, too. Those two guys are really good. There are some others too. My time is past. I'm happy to have played some small part in it. I take pride in that. I hope people listen now to guys like Tyler and Eric."

Who knows what other nameless, faceless individuals are out there, who may one day find themselves working for an NHL team on some concept or metric we can't even begin to imagine today, a measurement that could change the way we look at the game tomorrow.

"People need to understand, it's not about the math," Ferrari said of next-generation analytics. "It's about thinking. The math Fs people up. A lot of what's written now is way over the top with numbers. It's crazy—kids with graduate degrees in stats or math, and they're always looking for raw numbers and they want to throw them in the regression hopper and say, 'Your answer is this.' Hockey fans, people in general, don't know what this shit means. So they're either impressed or they say, 'This is shit. You're a nerd.' Neither is a good thing. The kid with the PhD is probably a good person but he's f---ing up really bad. The conversation doesn't move forward. At some point, you don't want the conversation to move forward. You want to move forward ahead of the conversation."

It's endless, really. The possibilities are infinite. What's that old saw about putting 100 monkeys in front of 100 typewriters? One of them is going to come up with a masterpiece?

Or maybe just explain PDO.

The #fancystats battles will, to varying degrees, always exist in hockey—conflict is the nature of our game—but there's going to be more mainstream acceptance of them with each passing day.

Count on it.

This, of course, coming from a guy decidedly lacking in numerical acumen; smart enough, though, to talk his way from a grade of 53 to a 55 to get out of a final math exam and still know either one of those numbers would pass for a damn fine Fenwick.

Note from the author:

If the premise of this chapter was to prove the 2013–14 NHL season was the turning point for hockey analytics, the events of the summer of 2014 validated that supposition, over and over again.

In the first few months after this chapter was written and put to bed, in May 2014, the magnitude of #fancystats developments was mind boggling. It was so great, in fact, that it was difficult if not impossible to rewrite the chapter to reflect those changes.

Instead, here is a brief summary of those noteworthy developments that made 2014 the Summer of Hockey Analytics. It's yet even more compelling evidence of the rapidly evolving world of hockey #fancystats.

• In mid-June, the New Jersey Devils hired their analytics expert. It was Sunny Mehta, the former pro poker player and Ferrari protégé from Irreverent Oilers fame.

• In July, renowned stats blogger Eric Tulsky was hired on a part-time basis by an NHL club, calling into question what, if any, blogging he would be able to do on his site in the future.

• On July 22, the Maple Leafs, of all NHL teams, fired two assistant GMs (Dave Poulin and Claude Loiselle) and hired 28-year-old Kyle Dubas, the Sault Ste. Marie Greyhound general manager who is a huge proponent of advanced statistics and was to oversee that department as assistant GM of the Leafs. He was hired by team president Brendan Shanahan to work in concert with Toronto GM Dave Nonis.

• On August 5, stats blogger Tyler Dellow, who was interviewed extensively for this book's #fancystats chapter, was hired by the Edmonton Oilers to work as a consultant to the hockey operations department, notably head coach Dallas Eakins. Upon his hiring, he took down his website.

• On August 6, the day after Dellow was hired in Edmonton, *Hockey Night in Canada*'s Elliotte Friedman wrote an excellent feature on www.cbc.ca that not only included an interview with the mythical Vic Ferrari, but also identified the mystery man as 47-year-old Tim Barnes, an engineer turned financial analyst from Alberta who had studied at the University of Calgary and had lived in England, Toronto and Edmonton before settling in Chicago. Friedman's interview with Ferrari was the first ever published and his unmasking of Ferrari was groundbreaking within the hockey statistical community. Ferrari's interview for this book was conducted three months before Friedman's story was published.

• In mid-August, Dubas hired a "team" of analysts for the Maple Leafs. Two of them—Cam Charron and Rob Pettapiece—were #fancystats proponents from the blogging/writing community. The third was Darryl Metcalf, who created the Extra Skater website, which (sadly for those of us who used it) was taken down once he was hired by Toronto.

By any standard, the volume, rate and significance of 2014 off-season analytics-oriented developments were staggering, only reinforcing it as the year of #fancystats. But while two NHL teams gained analytics expertise in Tulsky and Dellow, the #fancystats blogging community also lost its two most noteworthy and original voices, to say nothing of the demise of Extra Skater, advanced hockey stats' most user-friendly site.

CHAPTER 5

Grapes, Unplugged

Father and Son Cherish Precious Moments Watching
"The Best Hockey in the World"

"I hope we have a good referee for you. I don't know this guy.
If the ref calls lots of penalties at the beginning, the game will be chaos.
If the ref is good, he lets the boys play."—Don Cherry

———

It's a blistering-cold Tuesday night in mid-December, and there's pretty much just family and friends inside icy Victoria Village Arena. The utilitarian rink is tucked into an industrial section of the Don Mills area of Toronto, and the small group of fans sparsely dotting the stands are there for the 9 p.m. Greater Toronto Hockey League minor midget game between the middle-of-the-pack Don Mills Flyers and the lower-end Toronto Young Nationals. It's not exactly a marquee matchup. While some of the 15-year-old boys on both teams will get drafted into the Ontario Hockey League the following spring, and a couple may even play there as soon as the next season, there are no superstars on either team, no can't-miss kids.

A veteran scout of more than 13 years, who works for the OHL Central Scouting Bureau, is in the house tonight. It's his job. This is one of anywhere between two and four games he normally sees each week, and, as is their custom, his soon-to-be-80-year-old father has joined him on the drive from their Mississauga homes.

"I go with him all the time," the father says. "If he goes, I go. He'll phone me in the morning, and on the days I know we're going to a game, that's what I'll look forward to all day. It's joy—pure joy. I'd rather do this than anything. I'd rather be here than anywhere."

The father and son walk to the far end of the rink, away from the arena entrance and past the few people who are there. They stand in the far corner, noses pressed right up to the glass, inches away from the action. There's no thought given to sitting in the stands, even for the man whose 80th birthday (February 5) is less than two months away.

"Best place to watch a game," the scout says. "You get a real feel for the speed and the size of the players. You can really see and hear everything here, too. It's a little colder here, but it could be worse. In some rinks, when you stand in the corner, you're actually standing on ice. Sometimes we'll sit—maybe if it's a doubleheader—but we like standing in the corner. That's our spot."

The father is wearing a black toque emblazoned with a red maple leaf, pulled down over his ears, tight to his eyes, to ward off the cold and dampness. The toque matches his all-black melton and leather jacket, which is also adorned with large red maple leaves, black sweat pants and black boots.

"I'd rather watch these games than the NHL," Don Cherry tells his guest for the evening. "This is the best hockey in the world when you get a good referee that lets them play. It never stops; it's hockey like it used to be played. No bullshit—you know what I mean?"

Tim Cherry, his son, nods his approval.

Game on.

"This is a good referee . . . he's letting them play."

Welcome to Don Cherry, unplugged.

Grapes is Grapes, of course. What you see on "Coach's Corner"
during the first intermission of *Hockey Night in Canada* is what you
get. It's no act. He believes what he says, say what he believes. But anyone who actually knows Don Cherry understands that when the lights
go down, when the colourful suits and ties are exchanged for black
sweat pants and a winter coat and hat, and he's standing alongside
his son, Tim, in a cold suburban rink instead of sitting next to Ron
MacLean in the *HNIC* studio, there is a difference. Noticeably so.

"He's basically the same guy; he's just a lot more amped up when
you see him on TV and a lot less amped up when he's not on TV,"
Tim says.

It's such an apt description.

On TV, Cherry's voice fairly booms, and in a segment that lasts six
or seven minutes, he seldom stops talking. It's not so much a dialogue
with MacLean as it is a performance, though no one would suggest for
a moment Cherry isn't true to his core values every Saturday night.
That's him. But get him in a rink watching 15-year-olds play hockey,
or see him hanging with Bobby Orr at his hero's summer golf tourney
in Parry Sound, Ontario, and it's striking how many decibels his voice
comes down, how he's perfectly comfortable saying little or nothing for
stretches at a time, happy as a clam to listen to others and how, when he
does speak, there's a subdued, understated, almost soft-spoken quality to
it. It's so . . . how can one put it . . . conversational? Endearing, too.

It's almost like there's a degree of serenity or wonderment eman-
ating from him that you rarely see for the confidence and swagger on
Saturday night, when he's liable to be calling someone a "a rat" or getting himself in hot water with someone, oftentimes his bosses. Maybe

that's because he truly does love this level of hockey and feels so at home standing at the glass. Or perhaps it's the natural warmth—the love. really—that comes with one of these regular father-son outings that he looks forward to more than anything on this earth. Told he's lucky he gets to share so much quality time with his son doing what they both enjoy, that others would be envious of this relationship with Tim and vice versa, Don Cherry considers that momentarily and says softly: "You're right . . . I am lucky, I am, eh?"

> **"What I don't understand is icing the puck for a change.
> It's been drilled into these kids to stay out for only 30 seconds, so they ice
> it to get off. We would stay on the ice and hope the whistle never went.
> Now they get yelled at if they don't ice it. Icing used to be a bad thing."**

Tim Cherry was born in Hershey, Pennsylvania, in 1963. The story of his family, and especially his father's rise through the professional hockey ranks to Canadian icon status, has been well documented. In fact, it was Tim who told it as a producer-writer for two made-for-television movies: *Keep Your Head Up, Kid: The Don Cherry Story* (2010) and *Wrath of Grapes: The Don Cherry Story II* (2012). Tim also produced and oversaw Don Cherry's *Rock'em Sock'em Hockey* videos, including getting all 25 years of them compiled for a silver-anniversary boxed DVD set that was released just two weeks prior to the game at Victoria Village Arena.

"You're a pretty talented guy," the guest says to Tim.

"I don't know about that," Tim replies, "but it's been really busy with the release of the DVDs."

"Well, Tim, you must have something going for you," Don adds, chuckling, "because good looks and charm will only carry you so far."

The first impression upon meeting Tim Cherry is that he seems a kind and gentle soul, the same as what anyone would say about his mother, Rose, who passed away in 1997 after battling cancer. Rose was a lovely woman, the love of Don's life, and while there are most certainly similarities in look and manner between Don and Tim, it seems obvious there's a lot more of Rose in Tim.

"There's no doubt," Tim says, "I've got my mom's temperament."

It's a close-knit family, certainly close in the literal sense. Tim's older sister, Cindy, and her family live in a house on the same street as Don—right across the road, in fact. Tim's house is a literal stone's throw away from both, just around the corner. Don and his wife, Luba—they were married in 1999—live in the same suburban Mississauga home that's always been the Cherry family home. It's Don's sanctuary. He's a homebody at heart, and loves nothing more than puttering around the house, reading books or watching television. On the nights when isn't out at games with Tim, he'll be at home, having a few "cold ones" and watching NHL games on TV until the western games are over at 1 a.m.

"I'm glad I'm down in my basement," Cherry says. "I can yell at the screen. 'You [expletive deleted].' I hate when refs make phantom calls. Drives me crazy."

Imagine for a moment what it's like to have Don Cherry as your father.

Tim Cherry ponders that one for a moment.

"You know, it's good," Tim says. "He's a good dad. He was obviously busy, and there were times he wasn't around, but I played hockey in Boston and Dad would get out to games and practices when he could. I'd get to go to Bruin practices and Dad would have me on the ice before practice, giving me tips. We'd go fishing together."

Don recalls how, as coach of the Bruins, he used to wear a long, blue leather coat that had a fur collar, not unlike the one Reggie Dunlop (played by Paul Newman) wore in *Slap Shot*, which led to his players calling Grapes "Reggie."

Tim laughs at the memory of it: "Dad took me to *Slap Shot*. I was 10 years old. He walks up, 'Two for *Slap Shot*.' The lady looked at us and she didn't say anything, but you could tell what she was thinking, 'You're taking your 10-year-old kid to *Slap Shot*?'"

The time Don and Tim spend together now is precious because they're both well aware of how fleeting it can be. There was a time when they both wondered what quality of life Tim would be able to lead.

When Tim was 12, he had a tonsillectomy and ran into infection complications (strep) that resulted in severe kidney damage. Tim was hospitalized in September of the year he turned 13. Doctors told Don and Rose that his kidneys would never function properly and that he would have to live with dialysis, but would eventually require a kidney transplant.

"Rose took charge of the whole thing," Don recalls. "I was a coward. Training camp was on and I went off to the [pre-season] games. Rose said Tim was too young a boy to have dialysis his whole life, so we had to find a donor. It turned out that Cindy [who was then 21, eight years older than Tim] might as well have been Tim's twin [in terms of] a match. The hospital Tim was in was the first hospital to ever do a kidney transplant, so he was in good hands. I didn't know anything about dialysis or kidneys or transplants, but we all found out in a hurry. Everyone in Boston rallied around it. The Bruin players and their wives all gave blood."

What Tim remembers most, though, about his two-and-a-half-week stint in the hospital is that his mom was urging him after to get out of his hospital room and go for a walk. On the day he finally left his room for the first time, some of the Boston Red Sox—Johnny Pesky, Dwight Evans and Carl Yastrzemski, to name a few—came to visit him. They left him an autographed bat.

"I came back and the nurses were all excited," Tim says. "I couldn't believe I missed them. I still can't believe it. Now Cindy works for the

Kidney Foundation, and that all started with her donating her kidney to me. Mom did a lot of volunteer work for them, too. That all started with me getting sick."

Tim first started scouting junior hockey in the years after his dad purchased the OHL's Mississauga Ice Dogs in 1998, following the team's scouts to Junior A, Junior B, midget and minor midget games all over the province. He enjoyed seeing the games and evaluating the players, and eventually wound up working with the OHL Central Scouting Bureau.

"It's easier now," he says. "All the kids are playing at one level, minor midget. But you still have to see each team a bunch of times to really get to know them. I'm amazed how much better the kids get from the start of the season to the end."

On this particular night, Don was chauffeured to the game in Tim's Ford Fusion Hybrid, but it's not uncommon for Tim to drive one of Don's vehicles to the game. Don owns two 1993 Ford F-150 Flareside pickup trucks, both jet black, but they both were in the shop being reconditioned. Don also owns two 1983 Lincoln Continental Mark VI sedans. One of them was originally owned by Toronto Maple Leaf owner Harold Ballard, though the late Pal Hal wouldn't recognize the custom-made Maple Leaf blue vehicle with the distinctive white roof, since Cherry has had it totally reconditioned. It's now all black. His other Lincoln is white.

Black and white—seems an appropriate colour scheme for Cherry.

"As my father used to say of me," Don says with a grin, "'Don is very fond of what he likes.' And he was right about that!"

As much time as Tim spends with his dad scouting or being involved in the family *Rock'em Sock'em* franchise, there's more to his life than hockey. Tim has a 15-year-old daughter, Grace. Tim's divorced, but he and his wife adopted Grace from China in 2000, when she was just two years old. While Don was preparing for his trip to the 2014 Sochi Olympics—he celebrated his 80th birthday there—Tim was planning for a visit back to China with Grace in March 2014 to see her orphanage.

"She never really got into hockey," Tim says of his daughter. "She skated for a bit when she was younger, but where she's from in China, it's far south, almost subtropical, and I think she's got warm-blooded genes. We always kind of played down who Dad is anyway, but when she was in grade school, she never fully grasped who Dad is. So one time, Dad went to one of her [grade school] recitals and he got mobbed there. She said to me, 'How come everyone knows Poppa?'

"Now that she's in high school, she understands it. She's in a class with a lot of high school hockey players, and they were all talking hockey one day and she spoke up: 'My grandfather knows a lot about hockey.' The boys said to her, 'Who's your grandfather?' She said, 'Don Cherry.' So needless to say, we had to get a bunch of autographed pictures for the kids at school."

"I have three goldfish, they eat their food right out of my hand . . . see, now that's a penalty, the ref has to call that one . . . the goldfish have no names. I just call them goldfish. They're koi. They're hearty."

After all these years of going to minor hockey games together, Tim and Don have their routines down pat.

It's hit and miss as to whether Don actually gets to see the game on any given night. As one might imagine, Grapes showing up in a rink full of minor hockey players and parents is bound to create a stir. Cherry has actually given up on going to tournament games— the crowds around him tend to be overwhelming, "Which is too bad," he says, "because I really enjoy the tournaments"—but at a lot of games he'll just tell kids and/or fans looking for autographs and/or pictures to wait for a whistle or the end of the period. Sometimes, though, there's no stemming the tide and he ends up not actually seeing much of the game.

On this night, nary a soul approached him during the game. But that's highly unusual, Tim says: "Sometimes it's just one long autograph session for him."

Most times, Tim and Don will slip into the rink just as the teams are taking to the ice for the warmup, and if it's possible, depending upon which arena they're in—and they've come to know them all (Westwood, Chesswood, Buckingham, Vaughan, Etobicoke Ice, Herb Carnegie)—they'll take up their favoured spot in the corner at the glass.

Don will immediately identify a player or two that he likes the look of in warmup. He'll ask Tim what round the player is projected to be taken in.

"I'll say, 'Fourth round,'" Tim says.

"And I'll say, 'F---,'" Don adds with a laugh. "Then that kid will score a goal in the game or play really well. I won't say a word to Tim. Drives him crazy. He gets mad."

Tim laughs. "It true," he adds. "Does it to all me the time. Picks a guy in warmup and the kid usually scores. It's maddening."

There are also unwritten rules. Such as, once Don starts watching a game, he can't leave it until it's over. It's non-negotiable.

"Even if it's 9–0, I can't leave," Don says. "I can't do that to the kids. I can't have them looking at me and seeing me walk out on them and their game. It's not right."

Even on the long-ago night when Tim and Don went all the way to Welland, Ontario, to see Jamie Tardif, who got kicked out of the Junior B game on his first shift. Most of the scouts there to see Tardif left the rink immediately. Don and Tim stayed to the bitter end.

"Tim said, 'We can go now if you like,' and I said, 'I can't leave . . . what will these kids think if we walk out of here right now?'"

Of course, there was one night when they did leave early. It was a Junior C playoff game in Uxbridge against archrival Little Britain.

"It was into triple overtime on a Friday night," Tim recalls. "Unbelievable game. They're ringing shots off the post at one end and then at the other. Nothing was going in. It was 1 or 2 in the morning. It was really late—"

"So we had to leave," Don picks up the story. "Everyone's yelling at me, 'Hey Grapes, we can't believe you're leaving.' I'm apologizing to everyone. But I gotta work Saturday night. I gotta get home."

The hockey gods, though, often smile on him. Tim says no one is as lucky as his dad when it comes to winning 50-50 draws. Don buys the tickets, Tim checks the numbers, Don wins time after time and, of course, donates all the money back. On the night they stayed in Welland after Tardif was booted out of the game, Don won a free pizza in a draw.

The two of them have stories. Oh, so many stories from over the years.

"Tell him the Tipoff story," the father implores the son.

"Well," Tim says, recounting a tale that has no doubt been told many times over, "[Matthew] Tipoff was a real good player on the same Markham Waxer team Steve Stamkos was on. Tipoff and a player from another team were battling in the corner in a tournament semifinal game. They were really getting after it, and just when it looked like it was over, they both looked over at Dad, who was right there at the glass, watching. They looked at him, they looked at each other, they looked back at Dad again, and then they really started whaling on each other."

It was never deemed an actual fight, as the gloves never came off— much to the relief of Markham head coach Paul Titanic, who didn't want to lose Tipoff for the tournament final. Titanic supposedly asked Tipoff what he was thinking and Tipoff replied something along the lines of "Hey, what did you expect me to do? It was Don Cherry." The story speaks to the reaction of 15-year-olds when they happen to be in the corner during warmups or the games and come face to face with Canada's most recognizable face.

Now, Cherry's critics, and he has more than a few of those, would cite the Tipoff story as Exhibit A on why Cherry's pro-fighting, old-school mentality is precisely what kids shouldn't be aspiring to. Trouble is, the first guy who would agree that kids shouldn't be fighting is Grapes himself.

"First thing, [Tipoff's] wasn't really a fight," Cherry says. "Second, I was watching [kids'] hockey when it was worth your life to go on the ice in the old days, with the Streetsville Derbys, when everyone used to think it was good to intimidate. There was hitting from behind all over the ice. Well, you know what, the last fight I saw in this league was four years ago, and you won't see one here tonight, and that's fine with me. There's far less hitting from behind and fewer cheap shots than there was before. It's good, fast hockey. Best hockey in the world if it's reffed right. I love it."

"It's all about speed now," Tim adds. "If you're a step slow in this hockey, it's really noticeable now."

The other surprising thing about Cherry and his love for minor midget hockey is that he's got a huge soft spot for the smaller players.

"Dad really likes all the little guys," Tim says. "The smaller and more skilled they are, the more he likes them. He likes the underdog."

"It's funny the way Mother Nature works," Don adds. "The smaller the kids are, the smarter they seem to be. They have to be [smarter] if they're going to survive. Tim, who's that kid on Markham . . . Cocker? Crocker? Anyway, really small kid, really smart and skilled. I love that guy."

"Who's that white-haired guy over there [referring to Young Nats organizational manager Garry Punchard]? I see him at all the games. No one will
ever give that guy credit, but you know what, if it wasn't for him and guys
like him, sitting here in a cold arena, there'd be no hockey for these kids."

Minor hockey arenas are bubbling cauldrons of emotion.
The vast majority of the time Donald S. Cherry is in the house, he
views proceedings with a cool detachment, quietly sharing an observa-
tion with Tim, or maybe asking a question about this kid or that kid.
But there are times . . .

There are three things that occur in minor hockey arenas that drive
Grapes crazy and potentially could set him off. Tim knows them well,
knows his dad well, and knows how to navigate around them.

One is the incessant blabbermouth, who positions himself within
earshot of Don in the rink and talks loudly enough for Cherry to hear,
in hopes of impressing him with his superior knowledge of the game
of hockey.

"I'm watching and some guy will be talk, talk, talking the whole
time," Don says. "I get very upset. I hate guys yapping like that."

"They're just trying to impress you," Tim says.

So Tim is asked if sometimes he has to keep one eye on the game
and one eye on his dad, to head off any potential trouble and take care
of dear old Dad when he suspects there may be imminent danger of
Don blowing his stack. Before Tim can answer, though, Don jumps
right in: "No, he doesn't need to take care of me, but he might need to
take care of the guy who's been yapping."

Tim smiles, and adds, "I don't want to see Dad end up on the front
page of the [*Toronto*] *Sun,* so, yeah, I'm always aware . . ."

The second transgression that could solicit a . . . uh . . . response
is players hot-dogging or showboating on the ice. This was actually

included as a scene in one of the Cherry biographical movies. It involved future Carolina Hurricane Ryan Murphy, a Cherry favourite, and his team, the York-Simcoe Express. Murphy's team was down 4–0 and the team in the lead was hot-dogging and showboating all over the ice. Cherry fumed, and at the end of two periods, Don told Tim that Murphy's team would come back to win. And they did.

"So we're walking out of the arena after the game, and the coach of the losing team sees Dad and says, 'Hey, Grapes, we just had a tough loss. Would you come into the room and speak to the boys?'"

Don picks up the story.

"Tim says to me, 'No, Dad, don't do it.' So I did it. I went in and gave it to them all: 'You little [expletive deleted]. You had 10 times the talent, you were f---ing around, you turned everyone against you, looked like a bunch of soccer players.' We walked out of there, and it was dead quiet. The captain of the team was sitting by the door, and I whacked him on the shoulder and said, 'You're supposed to be leading them. Smarten up.' The coaches just looked at me."

Cherry's aggravation hat trick is completed by the thing that bothers him the most: mistreatment of the poor goalies. This one's personal. Cherry's grandson Del, Cindy's son, was a goalie in minor hockey. The experience left Cherry scarred.

"I feel sorry for all the people who have kids or grandkids that play net," Don says. "You can never really enjoy the game. It could be going great, and in the last 10 seconds, the goalie lets in a bad one and everyone's mad at you."

There was one game in particular when Don was going to see Del play. He arrived a minute after the game had started, only to find out from Cindy that Del had let in the first shot and the coach had pulled him.

"I told Cindy, 'I have to leave now, because if I stay here, it's going to be murder.' And I left."

Tim says many minor hockey coaches are too quick to pull the goalie, and if he sees it happening at a game with his dad there, Tim knows to tighten the reins.

"Remember the game at the Hershey Centre?" Don says, shaking his head. "Poor kid in net, gave up two in the first minute. Never had a chance on either of them. Tip-ins. From the point. Gets pulled. I felt so bad for that kid—a minute in—so I was going to go over there talk to the [coach]. I wasn't going to hit him or anything, but I thought, 'You [expletive deleted].' Tim talked me out of it."

You don't grow up as Don Cherry's kid without realizing controversy is a constant bedfellow. But that doesn't mean you surrender to it, either. Each Saturday morning, around 9 a.m., Tim phones his dad to get a preview of what Grapes is thinking of saying that night on "Coach's Corner." If Tim thinks it's inappropriate or sounds too harsh, he'll tell his dad so. He knows once Don makes up his mind, though, it's tough to get the train off the tracks. On Sunday, Tim will tell his dad what he thought of the segment. Even Don's son occasionally finds some of what his dad says on the air cringeworthy, because he has a pretty good idea of what might do some damage beyond any given Saturday night.

"My mom was always Dad's sounding board about what to say on 'Coach's Corner' and how to handle issues," Tim says. "When we're at the rink together, when it's quiet, we talk a lot about what he's going to say on 'Coach's Corner.' Mom might chastise Dad when she thought he stepped over the line. I don't do that so much. We'll also talk about things going on in my life. My dad is very good at helping to put things into perspective for me. He's the same with me as he is on 'Coach's Corner.' He won't sugarcoat things. It's nice for us to be able to talk to each other about things. We are both lucky, at our ages, that we can share time with each other."

Tim may be Don's biggest fan, but there was only one time, and it wasn't even on "Coach's Corner," when Tim couldn't bear to watch his dad and had to turn off the TV.

It was in October 1992. Cherry was appearing on the CBC's *Friday Night with Ralph Benmergui,* a talk show. When Cherry's interview with Benmergui was over, the next guest was Scott Thompson, a gay member of the Kids in the Hall comedy troupe. Thompson came out and camped it up pretty good, telling Don he was a big fan because the European homosexuals cower in the corner when there's a fight in a gay bar. At one point, Thompson sat on Cherry's lap and they were holding hands.

Tim was at home watching it all on TV.

"I had to turn off the TV because I thought, 'This is it, this is going to be the end of Dad's career and I'm not going to watch it.' It was live. I was afraid that Dad might have thought this whole thing was a setup to make him look bad, and who knows how he would react, what he might say or do. I couldn't even watch it. I had to turn it off."

Cherry was quick on his feet that night. He camped it up himself with Thompson, made fun of the both of them, and disaster was averted.

"If I hadn't been sharp that night, I was in deep shit," Don says. "Turns out it was the best show [Benmergui] ever had. It was all downhill [for Benmergui] after that."

Don Cherry smiles as he says that. Then he laughs.

"The best hot dogs of all are at Herb Carnegie Arena. The same lady serves them all the time. She's always been there, she's been there forever and she stays right to the very end every night."

"You're the first person who has ever stood with us for a game," Don tells his visitor to Victoria Village Arena on the cold December night. "No scouts, nobody ever stands with us."

"I'm honoured," the visitor tells Don and Tim Cherry.

"Well, [Ron] MacLean stood with us for one period once," Don says. Which leads to one more story.

"Ron came down to watch the second period with us at a game in Etobicoke," Tim says. "Right at the end of the period, right in front of us at the glass, a kid got hit and the hit knocked the kid's tooth out. The tooth fell out over by the players' bench. The Zamboni is getting set to come on the ice, but the players and coaches are down on the ice, looking for the kid's tooth. So Ron and Dad decide they're going over to help look for the kid's tooth."

Picture it: Ron MacLean and Don Cherry, on their hands and knees on the ice, looking for a kid's tooth. It gets better.

"The kid's mom was just livid her son lost a tooth," Tim says, "and she comes steaming out of the stands and onto the ice—"

"I see the mother," Don says, "and I get up [from looking for the tooth] and intercept her. Her kid is so embarrassed. His mother's on the ice and she's hot. I say to the Mom, 'Ma'am, do you love your son?' She says, 'Yes, but—' I cut her off, I tell her: 'You're embarrassing him. Just get off the ice quietly. We'll find his tooth, but for your son's sake, please, just get off the ice right now.'"

Tim says the woman did leave the ice, but wasn't happy about it. Well, at least they found her son's tooth, didn't they?

"Nope, they never did find it," Tim says. "I guess it got sucked up into the Zamboni."

"Here we go again . . . another night in the books."

Game over.

The Flyers beat the Young Nats, beat them handily. No contest.

The father and son make their way through the arena. As they say goodbye and head into the cold, dark night for the drive home, their guest thinks of a story the father told an hour earlier.

"It was after he had the kidney transplant," the father says of his son. "I bought a boat to take him fishing. We'd go fishing a lot on Lake Cochichewick [near North Andover, Massachusetts]. He always liked fishing. Except, it turns out he didn't like going fishing at all. He only went fishing with me because he thought I wanted to go fishing. I didn't like fishing that much. I was only taking him fishing because I thought he liked it. Twenty years later, I find out neither one of us really wanted to be there."

That's not something they'll ever have to worry about with their trips to the rink.

CHAPTER 6

Growing Up Exceptional

Connor McDavid and the Chosen Few Navigate
the Great Canadian Torture Test

———

The cub reporter for the *Toronto Star* was sent to cover a peewee hockey tournament in 1978. The headline on the story read: SUDBURY PEEWEE ONE-MAN BAND: PIERRE DUPUIS BAFFLES WEXFORD TO LEAD TEAM TO CHAMPIONSHIP.

The first paragraph of the story was as follows: "Hockey coaches will tell you that there is no such thing as a one-man team, but 12-year-old Pierre Dupuis comes close to refuting that theory."

It went on to chronicle the exploits of the five-foot-four, 140-pound Dupuis, who scored five of his team's six goals en route to a prestigious minor hockey tournament victory, and how no one could quite believe how exceptional the Sudbury player was compared to the other elite-level kids his own age.

> *"He's a coach's dream," Sudbury coach Dan Heaphy said. "He's a born leader, an unbelievable hockey player, an A student at school and a wonderful kid."*

"We don't have anybody on our team who can even keep up with that kid, so what use was there in shadowing him," Wexford coach Gerald Payne said. *"If it wasn't for him, I think we would have won 3–1. Our club is as good as theirs, but they've got Dupuis."*

Another minor hockey coach and hockey school operator of some note, Frank Miller, called Dupuis the best 12-year-old hockey player he'd ever seen: "I've never seen a kid skate so well and he showed me he is the complete hockey player. He passes the puck, backchecks, he does it all and very well."

The cub reporter, who was still in his final year of journalism school, was pleased with the story. He got paid for it, which was nice; a byline in the *Star* would look good in his story file and on his resumé; all that for watching a phenomenal 12-year-old kid put on a hockey clinic at St. Michael's College School Arena.

Not a bad day's work, he mused; it doesn't get any better than that.

Note to self, he thought after writing the story: remember the name Pierre Dupuis. That kid is going places.

. . .

If there's a rule, there's always an exception.

It's a universal truth, isn't it?

So when Hockey Canada, in 2005, was instituting and approving what it called the Canadian Development Model (CDM), the systematic blueprint of rules and regulations governing how young players would proceed on a year-by-year basis through the Canadian minor hockey system to the junior level, there was indeed a clause dealing with "exceptional" 15-year-olds.

What's amusing about this, truth be told, is that the exception to the rule actually preceded the rule itself.

The CDM became reality on May 23, 2005, when it was approved by Hockey Canada's board of directors in Saint John, New Brunswick.

Eighteen days earlier, though, the Ontario Hockey League declared soon-to-be 15-year-old John Tavares an "exceptional" player.

"The CDM was being put in place because there were large numbers of 15-year-olds playing Junior A, B and C hockey," Ontario Hockey League commissioner David Branch said. "It made sense to slow down that progression and keep kids in minor hockey longer and the [CDM] was Hockey Canada's way to do that."

The OHL hadn't had a 15-year-old in the league since 1998, when Jason Spezza played one season for his hometown Brampton Battalion, thanks to an old rule permitting 15-year-olds to play in the league only if it was in their hometown, with the player remaining eligible for the OHL draft in the off-season after his first year in the league.

During the 2004–05 season, Hockey Canada was formulating the CDM with an eye towards not allowing any 15-year-olds to play any brand of junior hockey. But Branch was made aware that season of the existence of Tavares. As he recalled it, Branch was talking to his son Barclay, the assistant general manager of the Belleville Bulls.

"The very clear reason for [having an 'exceptional' clause] was John Tavares," Branch said. "I was talking to Barclay and he told me, 'Not only is John Tavares good enough to play [in the OHL] as a 15-year-old, if he were eligible in our draft, he would be the No. 1 selection.'"

That got Branch to thinking on two levels. First, he called Hockey Canada president Bob Nicholson, advised him of the potential Tavares scenario and asked whether the still-in-the-works CDM might allow for an "exceptional" provision for the Canadian Hockey League. (Ultimately, it did.) Next, Branch went about the business of defining "exceptional" and determining what process and criteria the OHL could use to ensure the integrity of the "exception." He had no appetite for an exception becoming the rule if the player in question wasn't truly "exceptional."

Branch put together what he described as an arm's-length committee comprising four expert individuals: Frank Bonello, the head of the NHL's Central Scouting Bureau, who could speak to Tavares's on-ice ability as a hockey player; Paul Dennis, a noted Toronto-based sports psychologist with an NHL and OHL coaching background, who could, after meeting extensively with Tavares and his family, work up a full psychological and sociological profile to determine the player's maturity to deal with both on- and off-ice challenges while playing and interacting with 16-to-20-year-olds; Kevin Burkett, a lawyer and renowned arbitrator with both a strong legal, educational and hockey background (Burkett was a longtime Junior A hockey coach and his son, Kelly, played college hockey at Michigan State); Doug Gilmour, the retired NHL star who played for the Cornwall Royals in the OHL and knew firsthand the physical, mental and emotional skill sets required to play at that level.

"The mandate was very clear," Branch said. "We had to develop a process that was beyond reproach, something with a real focus on whether the player was mature enough to handle the on-ice challenges, any off-ice issues pertaining to school, social settings and whether this individual had the support system in terms of family and friends, to say nothing of whether the individual had the skills and ability to play against players who were four or five years older than him. It had to be done right, because there was lots of speculation we were doing something that was going to open the floodgates."

And all this at a time when the Canadian Development Model was being put in place to keep 15-year-olds playing minor hockey.

· · ·

Brian and Kelly McDavid knew their son Connor was any-thing but "normal" when it came to hockey—his interest in it, his passion for it, how he watched it, how he played it, how he basically lived it.

It didn't take them long to know it, either.

"Almost from the word go," Brian McDavid said. "He was maybe two and a half years old, he definitely wasn't three, and I got him Rollerblades, the little plastic ones. He put them on and he just took off, he started skating around the basement."

By age three, he had graduated to taking shots on his Nana (Kelly's mom), who was a fine play-against-a-toddler-in-the-basement goaltender.

"Connor would be downstairs for hours on his Rollerblades," Kelly said. "He would take all his stuffed animals from his bedroom down to the basement. They were the fans watching him play. He'd be yelling play-by-play up the stairs, he would so get into those games. 'So-and-so just scored the winning goal in Stanley Cup.' He'd do that for hours at a time."

Kelly also remembered having to play him in air hockey games, and having to let him win because she simply wasn't prepared for the consequences.

"If he lost, it was horrible," she said. "I'd let him win, I knew I was just enabling him, that he needed to learn to lose, but . . ."

When Connor was all of four years old, he tormented his parents to sign him up to play hockey in his hometown of Newmarket, Ontario. Brian fudged Connor's age when he was four, allowing him to play against the five-year-olds. And when he was five, he played against the six-year-olds. Playing against older kids would become a recurring theme for him.

Connor McDavid couldn't get enough hockey. His brother Cameron, four years older, was playing atom AA for Newmarket. Five-year-old Connor wanted to be just like Cam. When Cam would get dressed up in the minor hockey uniform of shirt and tie to go to the games, Connor also wanted to wear a shirt and tie. So off he would go, wearing an oversized team jacket, team hat, shirt and tie, dressing the part of a rep hockey player. Brian McDavid, along with Hockey Hall of Famer Steve Shutt's brother Dana, were assistant coaches on the team. Connor would help the trainer fill the water bottles before the game. He would get to sit in on the pre-game chalk talks, and when the coaches would ask the players on Cameron's team where they should be on the ice in a certain situation, Connor would put up his hand and answer.

When Cameron's game would begin, Connor sat in the stands with Kelly and the other mothers.

"We had no idea what was going on a lot of the time," Kelly said. "A play would happen and we would be saying, 'What happened there?' and Connor would, in great detail, explain exactly what had happened. All the other little brothers and sisters were running around the rink, but not Connor. He would just sit there and watch."

When Brian took little Connor to a St. Michael's Majors OHL game at St. Mike's Arena, it was the same thing. He would never take his eyes off the play, focused intently on the puck and every move being made.

"It was like he was studying it," Brian said. "He was processing it on some other level you wouldn't expect from a five-year-old. . . . It was the same thing when he played. Every kid on the ice would be in a scrum to get the puck, and Connor would stand back a few feet from the pile, on the defensive side of it, just waiting for the puck to squirt out. He would take it and go. How did he know to do that?"

By the time he was six, it was obvious he was too good to play house league against kids his own age, so the McDavids tried to move him up a year, to play against seven-year-olds in more competitive select hockey.

But the minor hockey association in Newmarket put up a roadblock. Rules were rules, they said, and six-year-olds weren't allowed to play seven-year-old select. Brian McDavid protested, appealed the decision, but was denied. So the McDavids signed Connor up to play house league hockey in neighbouring Aurora. Against kids as old as nine.

"If a student in school is advanced, they'll promote them, move them up," Brian said, "but they didn't want to hear it."

Even then, playing against older kids, Connor was frustrated playing house league. He craved higher competition, desperately wanting to play AAA rep hockey, so much so that his mother devised a visual way to track that goal, drawing a set of stairs on a piece of paper, each one representing a single house league game to the end of his six-year-old season. Each week, after he played a game, Connor would cross off one of the stairs and see clearly that he was one step closer to his goal of playing at the most competitive level of minor hockey.

At the end of that season, Connor tried out for the York-Simcoe Express AAA novice (eight-year-old) team and was the last player chosen, because the team wasn't sure until the last minute whether they wanted to carry an underage player.

After that first year of novice AAA, Brian became York-Simcoe's head coach. Connor's game flourished and so, too, did the team. The Express won four consecutive Ontario Minor Hockey Association (OMHA) titles, an Ontario Hockey Federation (OHF) provincial championship in peewee, and were finalists in the prestigious Quebec International Peewee tournament.

Connor enjoyed great success playing for his dad and alongside another incredibly gifted player, Sam Bennett, who went on to star for the OHL Kingston Frontenacs and was selected fourth overall by the Calgary Flames in the 2014 NHL Entry Draft.

Through it all, Connor continued to demonstrate an insatiable desire to win, to be successful. He was absolutely driven.

In minor atom, during a game on the bench, he heard two teammates talking about playing a video game. He told his dad afterwards, "If other kids aren't on board, we have to do something about it."

In London, at the atom OHF tourney, a season in which the team went 33–0, York-Simcoe lost 6–5 in a shootout in the semifinal. When the team came back into the dressing room, Connor, in tears, ripped the participant medal from his neck and threw it in the garbage. It was retrieved by Brian, who gave it back to Connor on the long ride home.

"We were driving home from London and I'd given the speech that we had a good year and you can't win every time," Brian said, "and Connor is in tears in the car and he says to me, 'Promise me, you have to promise me that you will do everything you can to make this team better next year.' That's Connor. . . . I've known for a long time he has that 'something.' It's his passion. I've always felt that he's had that, that it's hard to find someone who feels about the game the way Connor feels about it."

Coaching his son, and his son being such a phenomenal player, was at times a double-edged sword for Brian. The McDavids spent a tremendous amount of quality time together, sharing their perfectionist's mentality and a lot of really good family times.

"When I coached, there was a lot of routine for the team," Brian said. "We'd have a warmup stretch, a whole team meeting, separate meetings for the defence and forwards, but Connor and I would have our own routine, too, where we would do this little stickhandling ritual. Connor is superstitious. We'd have to pass the ball the same number of times. He'd flip it up and bounce it, but if we dropped it, we had to start over again."

But there also were the usual minor hockey politics, talk of alleged favouritism from a father coaching his son, and both conceded it was, at times, uncomfortable and difficult.

"Every year, the kids on the team would vote Connor as the captain, and every year I would give it to someone else," Brian McDavid said. "People would say Connor was only good because his dad was the coach. I was so offended by that, because he deserved better. Another coach would have played him more; another coach would have made him the captain. Whatever Connor got, he earned it."

"I liked [having his dad as coach] but it was hard sometimes," Connor said. "A lot of stuff would be said, but in peewee, for example, I wasn't even an assistant captain, so I'm not sure how anyone could talk about favouritism. All I know is that my dad taught me everything I know about hockey. Every kid wants to play in the NHL, and that's something I became focused on. The best advice I ever got was from my dad. He told me, 'If you want to do something in life, you have to do something every day to help make it happen.'"

Connor took that advice to heart with passion and zeal. Every day. Literally.

"Every day, he would come home from school, and his routine would be the same," Brian McDavid said. "He would do his homework, and then he would get on his Rollerblades in the driveway, shoot his pucks, set up obstacle courses, skate around paint cans, time himself. He did that every day for years."

Connor created a virtual hockey Camp McDavid in the driveway of the family home. Both garage doors would be opened up. Whatever he could find in the garage was likely to find its way onto the obstacle course. The routine was more or less the same each day, though he would refine his drills by adding an extra twist or deleting a turn.

"I would always shoot pucks, at least 100 pucks, that was always part of it," Connor said. "Then I would set up the pucks all over the driveway and stickhandle through them, like Patrick Kane did in that video. I would do some footwork. I took old paint cans out of the garage and set them up, one here [pointing], one here [pointing to a different spot] and one here [pointing to a third spot]. Then I would skate through them, weave around them, stickhandle through them. I had one stupid drill where I would have two paint cans set up beside each other and I would lay a stick across the top of them. After I would weave through the first cans, I would then flick the ball over the stick or under the stick and jump over it."

Sometimes he would work his skateboard into the routine, making it the final obstacle, passing the puck or ball to himself under the skateboard before shooting it into the net.

McDavid didn't just do this every day. He timed himself doing it. Or sometimes he would call for his mom to do the timing for him. In the summer, when he had more free time, he would do this routine two hours a day.

"Two hours would be the minimum," he said. "On a school day, I'd only be able to get an hour in."

Brian and Kelly would marvel at Connor's dedication, but they became a little self-conscious about it, too.

"People would see him out there every day," Kelly said, "and they would think or say we forced Connor to do it."

"And by 'we,' they meant 'me,'" Brian said, shaking his head.

"I used to want him to come in," Kelly said. "Sometimes he was too tired, but he would say to me, 'I won't be happy with myself if I don't do it.' Some days he would come home from school and say he was tired, and I would say, 'You don't have to go out there. We don't care. You don't have to do this. Listen to your body.' But he would always say, 'I'm going to be mad at myself if I don't do it.' So he would go out and do it. After the fact, we found out people thought Brian was making him do it."

The look on Connor's face as he heard that said it all. He took it as a personal affront, an insult, for anyone to even consider he was being pushed by someone other than himself or something other than his natural passion for the game.

Mind you, he comes by his competitive streak honestly. All the McDavid men, when it comes to hockey, have demonstrated a desire to play for keeps.

"Me and my brother would play in the driveway, one on one, and there's not a lot of space in our driveway, and it would get intense," Connor said. "I was four years younger than him, and if I beat him, he would get so mad. He high-sticked me a couple of times, and I had to get stitches. He'd go after my eyes."

But nothing rivals the intensity of three McDavids—Brian, Cameron and Connor—putting on the Rollerblades in the summer and a playing a cutthroat game of one-against-two hockey in the library parking lot near their cottage in Thornbury, Ontario.

"One ball, whoever has it is against the other two," Brian said. "Connor would almost always win, but it's really intense. There are usually some pretty serious injuries."

"One time I was sure I broke my wrist," Connor said, "but the worst was my dad."

"Oh, man, I got some gravel under my wheels and I went down hard," Brian said. "The gravel was embedded in my leg. We had to go home, and Kelly said, 'Why are you guys home?' Then she saw my leg. It was a mess. It was for weeks, with road rash."

Connor laughed at the memory.

"It was," he said, "the worst road rash I've ever seen. When we play hockey, it gets pretty heated."

· · ·

That cub reporter from 1978 went on to become editor-in-chief of *The Hockey News* in 1982. In all the comings and goings of the hockey world, from the NHL on down to the low minors and junior hockey—What was that old hockey saying? "We'll send you so far away, not even *The Hockey News* will be able to find you."—the editor-in-chief did make good on his vow to remember Pierre Dupuis's name.

But a funny thing happened on the way to future stardom, on that road to "going places." Pierre Dupuis never got there. Not really.

His entire hockey resumé on the HockeyDB website shows four games in 1981–82 as a 15-year-old with his hometown Sudbury Wolves, followed by 64 games the next season with the Windsor Spitfires (13 goals and 26 points), plus only eight more OHL games (one more goal and three more points) over the next two seasons, split between Windsor and Belleville.

By the time he turned 19, in 1985, Pierre Dupuis had, for all intents and purposes, dropped off the face of the hockey earth.

The editor-in-chief didn't attempt to reconcile it, or investigate the specific whys and wherefores, as much as he just duly noted it, tucked it away as a future reference point and hopefully some sage hockey context: as in, "Be careful, all things are not always as they appear, especially with precocious puck talents"; as in, "Beware: if a 12-year-old kid who was that good in minor hockey couldn't even make it as an everyday junior player, never mind pro hockey . . ." Well, you get the picture.

Eventually, the editor-in-chief went on to become the *Toronto Star*'s hockey columnist and ultimately a national broadcaster, the so-called Hockey Insider on TSN, yet through all the job description and title changes, the lesson of Pierre Dupuis was never really forgotten: "When reporting on teenage puck prodigies, tread carefully. Very carefully."

So, it was with some trepidation, on November 30, 2004, that the Hockey Insider introduced 14-year-old John Tavares to a national television audience for the first time:

> In the hockey vernacular, J.T. is a late-1990 birthdate, having just turned 14 on September 20. For the purposes of the NHL draft, for example, he wouldn't be eligible until 2009. But he's already turning heads. Playing up a year for the Toronto Marlboros 1989s of

the Greater Toronto Hockey League, Tavares is, on any given night,
one of the very best players on the ice. He's not eligible for the OHL
draft until the summer of 2006, but to give you an idea of where
he fits in, he would be one of the elite picks if he were available this
year . . . It's never a great idea to put unrealistic expectations on a
kid who just turned 14, but J.T.'s exploits force you to take notice.

If you must know the truth, the Hockey Insider believed he might
have gone with a harder sell on Tavares. He'd actually seen Tavares play
both minor hockey and minor lacrosse and seemed reasonably certain
that this was no Pierre Dupuis, that Tavares was an exceptional two-
sport athlete. He knew there was already a buzz within the OHL about
Tavares and the possibility of a new rule to allow a truly exceptional
15-year-old to play in the league.

But still, Tavares had only just turned 14. Fourteen. It's so young,
isn't it? And if, for some unknown reason, this Tavares kid didn't turn
out to be as good as advertised, if he wasn't as exceptional as his billing, who would have been responsible for putting him in the glare of a
national spotlight, perhaps creating unrealistic expectations and additional pressures he never asked for?

· · ·

No sooner had the OHL officially declared John Tavares
"exceptional"—the Oshawa Generals made him the first pick in the
2005 OHL Priority Selection, ahead of the talented, one-year-older
prospect Logan Couture, who had expected to be taken first overall—
than OHL commissioner Dave Branch figured the league needed to get
out of the exceptional-player business.

Sort of.

Branch didn't have any problem with the notion of a legitimately exceptional 15-year-old playing in the league, provided he went
through a rigorous vetting process; he just envisioned some thorny
issues if it were the OHL that had to tell a talented 15-year-old, "Sorry,
we don't think you're that exceptional."

"There was lots of speculation at the time [Tavares] would open
the floodgates and would invite many more applications for exceptional status," Branch said. "As a league who wants these players, be
it at 15 or 16 or 17 or whatever, was it wise for us to be so closely
associated with the process, even though we set it up as an independent, arm's-length committee? So I phoned [Hockey Canada president]
Bob Nicholson and asked him if Hockey Canada would be interested
in taking over the administration of the exceptional player program,
and he said it would. I sent him our model, [Hockey Canada] took it,
adopted it and [Hockey Canada] uses virtually the same standards and
methodology as we did. It's now a fully independent process."

Sure enough, Hockey Canada's current mission statement on
exceptional players reads as follows:

> The purpose is to develop a map that would aid in discovering
> an exceptional player. A player that is uncommon, superior,
> distinguished, remarkable, exclusive. Such a player is deserv-
> ing of reward to participate in Major Junior Hockey and whose
> development might be significantly impaired if not permitted to
> participate in Major Junior hockey. This is a map of values or a
> map of the way things should be to ensure a deserving journey.

Any player applying for exceptional status must do so by submitting
an official application prior to February 15 in the year preceding the season for which exceptional status is being sought. It costs $1,000 to apply.

Ultimately, the decision on whether exceptional status is granted rests in the hands of a three-person Hockey Canada National Evaluation Panel comprising Hockey Canada's chief scout, a designate of Hockey Canada's board of directors, and a member at large appointed by Hockey Canada.

It's designed to be a highly confidential process, with no public acknowledgement of which players have even applied so as to protect the identity of those who are unsuccessful. If an applicant is successful, there's a straightforward and simple announcement in late March or early April saying the player has been deemed exceptional and is therefore eligible to play Major Junior Hockey as a 15-year-old.

The three members of the Hockey Canada National Evaluation Panel must be unanimous in their support for a player to be granted exceptional status. In effect, the national panel subcontracts much of the detailed due diligence to a three-man regional committee: the local branch administrator, to oversee the process; a life-skill interviewer to make subjective evaluations of the player's maturity and support system; and a regional hockey scout who can assess the player's physical attributes and on-ice skills and ability.

A plethora of questionnaires are required to be completed. The player and parents must fill out one, and the player must write an essay explaining why he should be granted exceptional status. Additional questionnaires must be filled out by a current teacher of the player, a coach of the player as well as a separate hockey evaluator, in addition to the report of the regional scout. Perhaps most important of all, the life-skill interviewer conducts at least one, and often more than one, in-depth interview with the player and his family, providing both written and verbal submissions to the national panel.

When all the forms have been filled out, all the questionnaires completed, all the interviews and research considered, only then does the National Evaluation Panel make its ruling. It's all or nothing; an exceptional player gets three of three votes, or he isn't exceptional.

Oh, yeah, one other thing: If the applicant is successful, $500 of the initial $1,000 fee is returned to the player; if unsuccessful, no money is refunded.

• • •

Kids' hockey is supposed to fun and games, and for the most part it is, but as a player climbs up the minor hockey ladder—especially if the player is a high-end performer who shows signs of elite ability—it begins to change in minor bantam. That's when the players become teenagers, 13 years old, and if life in general becomes more complicated and serious in those teen years, the same is true of life and times in minor hockey.

It's as if minor bantam signals the start of a testosterone-fuelled three-year sprint—minor bantam, major bantam and minor midget—that gets progressively more serious each year. But it's a run that can open doors to the next level of junior or college hockey—businesslike worlds that require teens to grow up even more quickly—and ultimately the pro game.

By his minor bantam year, Connor McDavid had already made enough of a name for himself that Reebok Hockey (RBK), the sports equipment manufacturer that has endorsement deals with Sidney Crosby, Pavel Datsyuk and countless other NHL superstars, came calling. Connor had been identified by RBK as a "key influencer," which is the corporate euphemism for "rising star."

The equipment companies give these "key influencers" free equipment and sticks. They want these high-profile athletes wearing and exposing their brand, as well as developing brand loyalty at an early age. The parents of "key influencers" merely breathe a sigh of relief: they no longer have to pay for sticks and equipment, which is extremely costly in hockey. For the minor hockey player, what's not to like about getting the latest and best gear, and all of it for free?

But it does come with a price. Other players and families who aren't "key influencers" take notice. It can put a spotlight on a young player sooner than perhaps it should. And while the free equipment comes with no real strings attached—it's low-risk, low-cost investment spending for the equipment company—it can skew perspectives and expectations at a time when nothing goes unnoticed in the green-eyed world of minor hockey.

If getting free equipment didn't set Connor McDavid apart from the other kids, getting attention from player agents did. Like RBK, the agents recognized that McDavid was a precocious hockey talent. At the age of 12, the McDavids were being contacted by prominent player agencies that represented superstar NHL talent.

"We had agents knocking on the door, and while we were flattered by it, we never got too wound up about it," Brian McDavid said. "We just said, 'Connor is only 12 years old. There's nothing we need to do about this right now.'"

Change was the operative word for the McDavids in the 2009–10 season. Bearing in mind he was only 12—and not 13, like those he was playing with and against—there was a lot to process, on and off the ice.

In his minor bantam year—his Grade 7 year at school—Connor not only left his hometown York-Simcoe Express of the residency-based Ontario Minor Hockey Association to play for the vaunted Toronto Marlboros of the Greater Toronto Hockey League—which required a bureaucratic battle to get through Ontario Hockey Federation transfer regulations—he also switched schools, leaving Clearmeadow Public School in Newmarket to attend PEAC School for Elite Athletes in Toronto. PEAC is a private school that combines academics and daily sport-specific training. So if, like Connor, you're a hockey player, then your curriculum includes being on the ice every day at school, and in the gym doing off-ice hockey training daily, while also attending your academic classes. All of this in addition to playing AAA hockey after school for the Marlies, who on average would have two games and three practices per week.

"I was on the ice five times a week with the Marlies, but those were games and practices," Connor said. "There's not a lot of time for skill development, so being on the ice every day at PEAC, that really helped me."

Because he was going to school and playing hockey in Toronto, not at home in Newmarket, there wasn't the same free time to set up Camp McDavid in the driveway.

"That had always been Connor's way of getting his skill development," Brian said, "so being on the ice at PEAC kind of replaced being on the driveway. He was still getting skill development, which was important to him."

There were many long days, though. Connor would leave his Newmarket home at 7:15 a.m. to go to school in Toronto. His grandparents would pick up Connor and some Marlie teammates who also attended PEAC and drop them off at the rink for their Marlie practice. Brian, who was helping out as an assistant coach on the Marlies, would meet Connor at practice and drive him home. From start to finish, it was often close to a 12-hour day for Connor. And then he would have to do his homework once he got home.

"PEAC was a really positive experience for Connor," his mother, Kelly, said.

But the same couldn't be always said for his first year playing hockey in the GTHL.

Maybe, in part, it was to be expected. The experts on physiology will tell you the physical differences between kids the same age, at 12 or 13, are greater than at any other age. It's a time when some kids have gone through puberty and others haven't. Go to a peewee or minor bantam game, and the physical maturation gap between players of the same age is greater than at any other time in the development cycle. Sizewise, it often looks like men against boys.

"In the 1996 age group, people were aware of who [1997-born] Connor was, so when he went [to the GTHL], there were a lot of expectations," Brian said. "But Connor hadn't grown like other kids, so minor bantam was a very tough year."

"It was a horrible year," Kelly added. "At the time, I thought we made a mistake."

Connor had gone to the Marlies because he wanted to play with and against better competition. Brian wanted him to play on a team where his dad wasn't the head coach, although he was still there as an assistant. But it was such a difficult year, they had to ask themselves whether Connor was in the right spot, whether it was still prudent for him to be playing against kids a year older.

"Connor and I would always talk at the end of each year to discuss whether to carry on in the 1996 group," Brian said. "We relied on those conversations more than any feedback we were hearing from other people."

Still, the McDavids knew there were skeptics, but Connor was already demonstrating a trait that so many great hockey players employ: using the negativity and/or doubts of others as fuel to drive him. So, confident he would bounce back, Connor stayed the course; the 1997-born kid continued in major bantam and minor midget to thrive and excel and dominate against the 1996-born class.

Connor's speed and skill, as well his high hockey IQ and ability to process the game, were eye-popping, off the charts. He was becoming the talk of the hockey town in Toronto minor hockey circles.

In the summer of 2010, when Connor was 13, one of his hockey instructors at PEAC, Joe Quinn, was working a summer hockey camp. Quinn told player agent Darren Ferris about Connor McDavid and Connor was invited to skate at a mini-camp for clients of the Orr Hockey Group, an agency that, of course, is headed up by Hall of Fame defenceman Bobby Orr.

"I was in the stands, watching the kids skate—they're doing drills—and I'm looking at this kid, he's not nearly as big as some of the others," Orr recollected of his first time seeing McDavid on the ice. "I said to someone, 'What is *that*?' That's exactly what I said. 'What is *that*?' His hands, the way he skated, the way he could flip and handle the puck, he was incredible. . . . They said to me, 'Do you know how old he is?' He was 13."

Bobby Orr shook his head with a degree of amazement, which is funny if you think about it. Orr was only 14 years old when he left his home in Parry Sound, Ontario, to star for the Junior A Oshawa Generals. Fourteen. Exceptional and then some. And there was no panel of evaluators to bestow any official status on him.

"They found me by mistake in a playoff game I was playing in Gananoque," Orr said. "The Generals were there watching. No one would ever come to Parry Sound to scout. It's different today."

So different.

Connor McDavid's hockey IQ extends off the ice, too. He's finely tuned to who's done what on their path to get to the NHL. For the longest time, he envisioned himself going off to Shattuck-St. Mary's prep school in Minnesota at age 14 or 15, just like Sidney Crosby did. But after he saw John Tavares blaze the exceptional-player trail from the GTHL's Toronto Marlies to the OHL in 2005, he knew he wanted to do the same.

In the summer of 2011, when Connor was 14, he was invited back to the Orr Hockey Group summer camp. Not long after that, in time for the start of his minor midget season with the Marlies, Connor McDavid had himself an agent.

The McDavids went with the Orr Hockey Group. If anyone could understand the journey Connor was embarking on, it was Bobby Orr. There was also the familiarity of having been to two Orr Hockey Group summer camps. But Connor was set on getting exceptional player status and early admission to the OHL for the 2012–13 season, the same as defenceman Aaron Ekblad had just gotten for the 2011–12 season.

Connor and Aaron had been friends dating back to their time as teammates on a spring tournament team in peewee. McDavid wanted to follow in Ekblad's footsteps.

"That was important to us," Brian McDavid said. "[Orr Hockey] had been through it with Aaron Ekblad the year before, and that's what Connor wanted, too. We didn't really go through the whole interviewing process with all the other agents. Bobby was our guy."

Connor had an outstanding minor midget year. He was the best player on the best minor midget team in the province. He went through the same evaluation process as Tavares and Ekblad; he had Paul Dennis come out to the house to compile the psychological and sociological profile of him and his family, but there was never any doubt. Hockey Canada deemed him exceptional and he became the first-overall pick in the 2012 OHL draft, going to the struggling Otters franchise in Erie, Pennsylvania.

The summer before he started in the OHL, McDavid got to do something he'd never really done: play with and against kids his own age. The top 14-year-olds in the country are assembled annually each summer in Toronto for the Allstate All-Canadian Mentorship program, an event headed up by the NHL Players' Association. NHL superstars—in 2012, it was John Tavares and Taylor Hall—act as mentors to the gifted bantam-aged players who learn, train and compete in an intense five-day camp.

In addition to measuring himself against players his own age— McDavid led Team Tavares to victory over Team Hall—he got to spend time with Tavares, pick his brain on what it's like to go through the exceptional-player process and size up the challenges that lay ahead.

"He was great," Connor said. "It was good to speak to someone who had been through it. It made me realize there's a lot of hard work to be done."

A lot of hard work; many lofty goals to be realized.

"Connor has always been different that way," Brian McDavid said. "He's driven to reach goals he sets for himself. Originally, his goal was to leave home at 14 and play at Shattuck, the same as Sidney. Then it was to get exceptional status, be drafted No. 1 into the OHL and play as a 15-year-old. He wants to win a Memorial Cup. He wants to play for Team Canada at the World Junior Championship as a 16-year-old and win a [world junior] gold medal. He wants to be the first-overall pick in the NHL [in 2015], win a Stanley Cup and have a Hall of Fame career. He's had these goals for a long time. He's always known what he wants."

And getting exceptional status was the first leap on the 15-year-old's quest to turn those dreams and goals into reality.

·   ·   ·

It was November 8, 2012, the date of a Subway Super Series game in Guelph, Ontario, between OHL stars auditioning to play for Team Canada at the World Junior Championship and a team of Russian stars.

Fifteen-year-old first-year OHLer Connor McDavid was in the lineup against the Russians, and while he showed a couple of brilliant flashes in the game and there was no denying the phenomenal skill set and long-range potential, Hockey Canada wasn't taking a still physically immature 15-year-old to its national junior team camp in December. In a postgame interview on TSN, the Hockey Insider was asked about McDavid and said pretty much all of that, noting his time would come, that he would likely play in two or three WJCs and observing that he was the early favourite to be the first player taken in the 2015 NHL draft, although a lot could happen in two or three years.

It wasn't so much a throwaway line at the end as it was a recognition that NHL scouts love to extol the virtues of 15-, 16- and 17-year-olds in their non-draft years, but the longer they watch a player play junior, the more likely they are to pick apart his game in his draft year and fall in love with new flavours of the day who haven't been in the spotlight nearly as long. The Insider was thinking in particular of Tavares. By the time he got to his draft year, after four OHL seasons, the scouts were shredding Tavares's game, questioning whether he could skate well enough to be an "elite" or "franchise" player in the NHL. He still ended up going first overall, but Tavares's draft year was rife with negativity; it was as if the scales were being balanced after years of unbridled enthusiasm and accolades for his talents.

The Insider didn't think too much of his comment about McDavid as he made it, but he woke up the next day to see it had become something of an issue on Twitter:

Connor Crisp 🐦
@Connorcrispp

@TSNBobMcKenzie say lot can happen in 2 years about @cmcdavid97 implying he may not shine in the future, best player in the #OHL at age 15 #FIO. 9:47 a.m. • 9 Nov 2012

Figure it out, indeed.

Crisp, who played with McDavid in Erie, was rallying to a teammate's defence on what he perceived as a slight. That prompted the following exchange between the Insider and Crisp:

Bob McKenzie 🐦
@TSNBobMcKenzie

@connorcrisp23 That wasn't implication at all. Connor is a special player but I'm not into burdening 15 year olds with absurd expectations. 10:39 a.m.• 9 Nov 2012

Connor Crisp 🐦
@Connorcrispp
@TSNBobMcKenzie I see his skills at practice, and the humility he
has on and off the ice, I'm implying that he is only getting better.
12:45 p.m • 9 Nov 2012

Fair enough, not much doubt about that. But it's also a given that
others will burst onto the scene to mount challenges and make their
cases. It was only 14 months after that Twitter exchange, at the 2014
WJC, that the performance of American-born centre Jack Eichel was
so impressive that NHL scouts suggested *he* should be in the conversation as a potential No. 1 in the 2015 draft, that he could be a legitimate
challenger to McDavid.

That didn't take long.

• • •

Two questions have arisen regarding Hockey Canada's
exceptional-player process.

One, if players are granted exceptional status year after year after
year, can it still be considered a truly exceptional process?

Two, is Ontario the only place to find an exceptional player?

If the "exceptional player" floodgates were supposed to open up
after Tavares in 2005, they must have been on a time-release formula,
because it wasn't until 2011 that Hockey Canada next granted exceptional status. And again in 2012. And then in 2013, too.

Defenceman Aaron Ekblad of Belle River, Ontario, was the first of
the three, and by any objective measure, he met or exceeded expectations. He was the first player taken, by Barrie, in the OHL draft, and
he excelled as an under-ager with the under-17, under-18 and World

Junior Championship programs. Ekblad was chosen first overall by the Florida Panthers in the 2014 NHL draft.

McDavid was the second of the three in 2012. He, too, quickly demonstrated "exceptional ability," following the same path as Ekblad—going first overall (to Erie) in the OHL draft, playing and excelling as an under-ager with the under-17, under-18 and World Junior Championship teams and being forecast as the No. 1 prospect in his NHL draft year (2015).

Defenceman Sean Day, a dual Canadian-American citizen who was living and playing minor hockey in Detroit, was the third exceptional player in three years. Unlike Ekblad and McDavid, Day did not go first overall in the OHL draft. He went fourth, to Mississauga, and while he was only just beginning his "exceptional" journey, some were questioning whether he was as blatantly exceptional as Tavares, Ekblad or McDavid.

Time will tell, but Day was subjected to the same rigorous screening process as Ekblad and McDavid and was unanimously approved by Hockey Canada's National Evaluation Panel.

The entire process is supposed to be conducted with the utmost secrecy and confidentiality, especially as it pertains to identifying or naming which players have applied for exceptional status.

Sheldon Lanchbery, a longtime member of the Hockey Canada board who was appointed a judge of Her Majesty's Court of Queen's Bench for Manitoba in the summer of 2007, was, as of 2014, the chairman of Hockey Canada's National Evaluation Panel, though it's all kept under such tight wraps that Lanchbery not only wouldn't talk about the process, but wouldn't even acknowledge he chaired the panel.

Kevin Prendergast, who was Hockey Canada's chief scout until 2013, was also on the panel that granted exceptional-player status to Ekblad, McDavid and Day. Ryan Jankowski was named Hockey Canada's chief scout in 2013, so for any future exceptional player applications, he would be on the panel with Lanchbery and one more

Hockey Canada member-at-large appointee. And Paul Dennis, the sports psychologist who worked up the profile on Tavares for the OHL in 2005, is the regional life skills interviewer for Hockey Canada's Ontario branch who vetted Ekblad, McDavid and Day, too.

It's often said there are no secrets in hockey, and if that's true, it's even more pronounced in minor hockey in Canada, where everyone, it seems, knows everyone else's business.

For example, as confidential as the exceptional-player process tries to be, it's a well-known fact within the Canadian minor/junior hockey community that, as of 2014, only Tavares, Ekblad, McDavid, Day and one other player even applied for exceptional status, with the unnamed player being the sole applicant who didn't get the panel's approval. That happened in the time period after Tavares in 2005, but before Ekblad in 2011.

It's no secret, not really, who the sole unsuccessful applicant was. Anyone with a computer can figure it in two minutes, but the process is not supposed to be about highlighting failure, so that player's name and identity won't appear here. Suffice it to say the Hockey Canada evaluation panel got it right. While the player appeared to be at the elite level in minor hockey, he did not go on to dominate junior hockey. He was not a first-round pick in the NHL, he did not represent Canada at the World Junior Championship, and while he's playing professionally in what is a still relatively young career and still working towards being an NHL player, there were by no means any guarantees that would happen for him. In fact, he's already perceived as a long shot to be an NHL regular.

What's curious is that every applicant for exceptional status, from Tavares to Day, has been in the OHL. It's almost as if the exceptional-player process doesn't exist in the rest of Canada. Some, especially in western Canada, mock it as just another bit of evidence that people in Ontario or Toronto believe they're in the centre of the universe, in a rush to

Colin Campbell looks at the frozen pond that almost claimed his life when his tractor fell through the ice. Bob McKenzie

A proud father: Campbell celebrates son Gregory's Stanley Cup victory with the Boston Bruins. Bruce Bennett/Getty Images

A 17-year-old John Tavares celebrates Buffalo's 2008 NLL championship with his namesake uncle, lacrosse player John Tavares, and cousin Justin (*centre*).
COURTESY OF BARB TAVARES

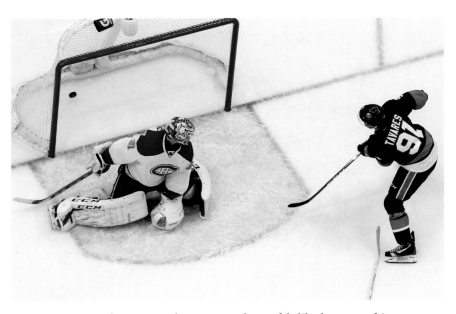

Born to score goals: Young John Tavares always felt like he wanted it more than anyone else. BRUCE BENNETT/GETTY IMAGES

Although Don Cherry and his son, Tim, will sit in the seats to watch minor midget hockey, they prefer to stand at the glass in the corner.

It's not a Fifty-Mission Cap, but Gord Downie of the Tragically Hip understands what it's like to be at the Lonely End of the Rink.

Even as a little guy playing for the York-Simcoe Express, Connor McDavid was exceptional.
COURTESY OF THE McDAVID FAMILY

No one has had a bigger impact on McDavid's hockey life than his dad, Brian, who coached his son throughout much of his minor hockey career.
COURTESY OF THE McDAVID FAMILY

McDavid got a surprise during a February 2013 visit to a Penguins game in Pittsburgh: a photo with heroes Mario Lemieux and Sidney Crosby. © PITTSBURGH PENGUINS

ROOKIE AND COACH OF THE YEAR 1988-89

Whether he was playing street hockey as a little kid or playing junior in London, Brandon Prust always had his Granda Jimmy McQuillan in his corner. COURTESY OF THE PRUST FAMILY

Getting a broken jaw, courtesy of Cam Janssen in December of 2008, was one of the worst events of Prust's life, but not so bad he couldn't take a selfie. COURTESY OF THE PRUST FAMILY

Prust doesn't possess the physical dimensions of an NHL heavyweight, but that doesn't mean he won't drop the gloves with one, even Boston behemoth Milan Lucic. CHRISTOPHER PASATIERI/ GETTY IMAGES

AUG 71

A 12-year-old Karl Subban, his mom, Fay, and younger brothers Markel (*far left*) and Patrick (*far right*) marvel at snow in the family's first Canadian winter in Sudbury. COURTESY OF KARL SUBBAN

The Subban brothers—Jordan, Malcolm and P.K. (*left to right*)— join TSN's James Duthie not long after the Vancouver Canucks drafted Jordan. Just prior to going on air, Jordan burst into tears. BOB MCKENZIE

SHELDON
KEEFE
2006-2012
HEAD COACH
GENERAL MANAGER

LEAGUE RECORD FOR
FASTEST COACH TO 200 WINS
SIX YEAR W-265 L-76 T-20
FIVE CONSECUTIVE CCHL
CHAMPIONSHIPS 2007-2011
2 FRED PAGE CUP
CHAMPIONSHIPS 2007 & 2011
2011 NATIONAL CHAMPIONSHIP

In 2006, Sheldon Keefe thought he might be run out of Pembroke. Seven years later, Keefe returned with his family to see his banner raised to the roof and receive a key to the city.

Tina Peplinskie, *The Daily Observer* (Pembroke)

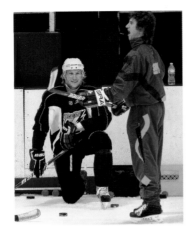

A singing Jari Byrski gets a laugh out of Tampa superstar Steven Stamkos before proceeding with an off-season skating and skills session in Toronto. COURTESY OF JARI BYRSKI

After the death of Byrski's fiancée, eight NHL stars—Steve Staios, Steven Stamkos, Manny Malhotra, Alexei Ponikarovsky, Wojtek Wolski, Jason Spezza, Mike Cammalleri and Andrew Cogliano—rallied around Byrski at a special skills session on August 8, 2008 (Byrski and his fiancée's planned wedding date). COURTESY OF JARI BYRSKI

Byrski's painting of Steve Stamkos, a piece of art that went a long way towards saving Byrski's life. COURTESY OF JARI BYRSKI

display a superiority complex. Is it actually possible that the only exceptional players in Canada in a nine-year stretch are from Ontario? That there are no exceptional players in western Canada, Quebec or the Maritimes?

"Sidney Crosby applied for exceptional status with us," Gilles Courteau, commissioner of the Quebec Major Junior Hockey League said, "but that was before 2005, when there was no program in place. We turned him down. Since 2005, we haven't had a player who has applied. I have no problem with the exceptional-player program. It's a good one, but we just have not had that player yet. One day we will, and if he's ruled as exceptional by Hockey Canada, we'll welcome him to our league. We would definitely embrace that."

Western Hockey League commissioner Ron Robison espouses the same view as Courteau: "We are fully in support of it, we just haven't had that player come along yet." Despite Robison's words, many are skeptical the WHL truly wants any part of it.

"Don't kid yourself," one player agent said, "the WHL owners and GMs don't want anything to do with the exceptional-player status. They discourage kids from going that route."

Robison did concede that two factors—the WHL bantam draft and the expansive geography of a league that stretches from Manitoba in the east to the U.S. Pacific Northwest in the west—may play a part in the practicality of not having had an exceptional player and why some players and/or parents maybe aren't as eager to apply as in Ontario.

In the WHL, players are drafted, or have their rights assigned, at age 15, after their major bantam year. In the OHL and QMJHL, players aren't drafted until they're 16, after their minor midget season. A 15-year-old drafted into the WHL is entitled to play only five games as a 15-year-old, but he knows where in the WHL he will play when he eventually gets there as a 16-year-old.

"There could be an issue related to schooling, where a 15-year-old would have to travel great distances to play, which is different than Ontario," Robison said. "And for many 15-year-olds in our league, they're satisfied to play the five games for the team that has drafted them—that's enough for them."

Even the skeptics who believe the WHL has anti-exceptional sentiment concede there hasn't been an obvious slam dunk exceptional superstar like Tavares, Ekblad or McDavid in the west.

Some believe Ryan Nugent-Hopkins and Mathew Barzal, two British Columbia kids, were the best bet for exceptional status, but as highly skilled and talented both were as 15-year-olds, they were also quite physically immature at that age. There have been highly touted prospects since then—Tyler Benson of Edmonton (first overall to Vancouver Giants in the 2013 bantam draft) is one who comes to mind, but he opted to go to the Pursuit of Excellence Hockey Academy in Kelowna, British Columbia, for his 15-year-old season rather than push the exceptional envelope.

"We've had some special kids, especially those taken in the 2013 draft, but I'm not sure you could say we have one who is as clearly exceptional as McDavid," Kelowna Rockets owner and general manager Bruce Hamilton said.

On the flip side, the exceptional player concept didn't exist in 2002, when Crosby was attending Shattuck-St. Mary's prep school in Minnesota, awaiting his chance to play in the QMJHL. As Courteau said, Crosby inquired and was denied by the Quebec league. Not getting exceptional status certainly didn't hurt his development.

"I think our results thus far speak for themselves," Branch said, citing the accomplishments of Tavares, Ekblad and McDavid. "I believe it's been a good process for the players involved and our league. It's working as it was intended to work when we introduced it. There hasn't been a rash of them. There haven't been abuses of it. It's a good process."

• • •

The old African proverb says "It takes a village to raise a child," and that most definitely rings true when the goal is to shepherd an exceptional and gifted young Canadian through the meat grinder that is elite-level hockey.

Connor McDavid's first line of defence will always be his dad, Brian, mom, Kelly, and older brother Cameron. There's no substitute for family. But if a phenom like McDavid is going to fulfil his potential and get to where he wants to be—the summit, if you will—he's going to need an extended family of sorts to help him climb that mountain. And like any talented young player in today's game—even those not deemed "exceptional" per se—McDavid's support team is in place.

There's Bobby Orr, of course, and the advisors and consultants who work with Orr. It was Darren Ferris who originally recruited McDavid to Orr Hockey, but Ferris left the company to start his own business. Former NHLer Jeff Jackson, a lawyer now, replaced Ferris and works closely with Connor and the McDavid clan to ensure the sailing is as smooth as it can be. Jackson's good friend, former NHLer Dave Gagner (father of Arizona Coyotes centre Sam Gagner) is the agency's director of player development. Gary Roberts, the former NHL player turned strength, conditioning and nutrition guru, oversees McDavid's training and conditioning program.

Collectively, between Connor's actual family and his extended family/support group, the mandate is twofold: one, give him the tools necessary to be successful; two, put up walls around him to protect him from any pitfalls or distractions that may prevent him from being successful.

"Kelly and I, we both spend a lot of time making sure he's good," Brian said. "We can't imagine the pressure he feels sometimes. Those pressures come from the outside and we try to insulate him. We just want him to be a kid and play. Connor has very high standards—no one is going to be harder on Connor than Connor. He sometimes gets down on himself; it's how he motivates himself. It's a fine line."

In a sense, the process is almost counterintuitive. Connor has an insatiable desire to be special, to be noticed, to do things most kids his age couldn't even dream about. To be exceptional on the biggest stage possible. But doing so creates attention and a wave of pressure on so many levels, with all those around him doing everything they can to diffuse that pressure. If there's anyone who can identify with that, it's Orr. He knows what it is to be phenomenal, though phenomenal today is a far cry from what it was in the 1960s.

"All I was told when I was a young guy was, 'Be home by dark,'" Orr said. "We'd go out on the pond all day. That was it. Times change. The world is more organized now. There are more distractions. The Internet, Twitter, rankings and ratings, haters, coaches, friends . . . what kids go through today is incredible. I never had to worry about any of that in Parry Sound. TSN wasn't coming to Parry Sound. [He laughs.] Our job [as McDavid's representatives] is to just make sure he's able to play to his level, play at the level he's capable of playing consistently, play to his strengths. That's it."

It's easier said than done. Sometimes, the enemy lies within. Which is to suggest that a teenager's desire, even that of an exceptional one, to just be a teenager can be problematic. And that's something Orr can mostly certainly identify with.

"That part hasn't changed," Orr said. "I tell him, 'Connor, you have to get your sleep because the level you are expected to play at it is a great responsibility. If you're tired, you can't do that. I was in the same position as you. I know you want to be with the guys, have fun, go here or there, but between the bus trips, all the games and practices . . .' These kids, they want to be on the ice all the time. In the summer, they want to go to this camp or that camp or this event. . . . I never went to a summer hockey school until I turned pro, and I went as an instructor, not a student. There are just so many things that can make them phys-ically or mentally tired, and if he's tired, he can't play to his level, and his level is high and so are the expectations."

It's a message that has been received loud and clear by Connor.

"If I'm talking to Bobby for five minutes, he will mention five times I have to get my rest," Connor said, laughing. "We talk a *lot* about sleep."

That's because talking about sleep habits is more productive than talking about, say, pressure that is ubiquitous and always will be. McDavid and Orr know it's always there; they don't dwell on it. But Orr knows if McDavid takes care of himself, his ability and passion will make the pressure manageable.

"He'll have a chance to be a very good player," Orr said. "He's not Sidney Crosby. Sidney Crosby is Sidney Crosby. Connor McDavid is Connor McDavid. He's 16 years old; give him time to put his own stamp on the game, whatever it is. Lots can happen. He's got a lot to learn, but that will come. He's so smart. Watch how he gets up on his skates. How he sees the ice, how he passes the puck, how he shoots it. He just loves to play. As long as he keeps that passion and never loses it, as long as he is able to play at his level, that's all he needs. Our job is to talk to him, keep his feet on the ground. I'm certainly not going to tell him how to play. The pressure is always going to be there—it's everywhere he goes. I never had to deal with that. No one in my time did. So we'll all work together to protect him as best we can from that."

Of course, there's only so much anyone can do. He can't be put in the mental equivalent of bubble wrap. If a pressure-free existence were the goal, McDavid wouldn't have played hockey. Pressure has been a constant companion since he started playing. At times, he even welcomes it, uses it as fuel. Other times, though, he knows it can gnaw at him.

"Honestly, I felt pressure more when I was a lot younger," McDavid said. "I never played against my own age, and I was one of the best players. That's when I would get really nervous, maybe not sleep the night before a game. I still feel pressure—I'm sure everyone who plays feels pressure—but I don't feel as it as much now as when I was younger."

Still, he welcomes those rare moments, the so-called "quiet times," when he's hanging with teammates, grabbing a bite to eat, horsing around and thinking or talking about anything other than hockey.

Most of the time, though, Connor McDavid is constantly being figuratively weighed and measured. If you get exceptional status, if you get called a generational talent the likes of which hasn't been seen since Crosby burst onto the scene, every time you step on the ice is a test. Someone is seeing you for the first time; someone is making a judgment: What's all the fuss about?

Growing up exceptional is like a Canadian torture test. The bar is set high, perhaps unattainably so, on an endless series of challenges. Crosby never escapes the scrutiny. Regardless of what level McDavid finds for himself, that, too, will be his lot in life. Some days, he'll come out on the right side of the ledger; sometimes the wrong side.

He passed his first major test after getting exceptional status by playing well in his OHL rookie season. He scored 25 goals and 66 points in 63 games as a 15-year-old with the last-place Otters. Phenomenal numbers. He might have made it look a lot easier than it was.

"It was hard," McDavid said. "I was putting up numbers. I started a 15-game point streak in my second game of the [rookie] season. It was amazing, I loved it, but it wasn't easy at all. It was hard. The league was so fast. The physical demands were really tough. I wasn't that strong, and I was going up against Dougie Hamilton, Cody Ceci, Scott Harrington and Olli Maatta. I didn't do a very good job of taking care of my body. I let little injuries slip by."

And while his season totals were terrific, the 15-year-old suffered more than enough angst over the course of a tumultuous rookie season in Erie, as the Otters finished with only 47 points, second-fewest in the entire league.

His dad can laugh now about Connor's first few days in Erie, coming out of the dressing room after three consecutive lopsided preseason losses.

"He comes out looking pale and distraught," Brian said. "He's saying, 'I can't take this, I can't take all this losing.' It was the preseason. I told him, 'It's early. It's going to get better.' He told me, 'It's gonna be a long year.'"

And it was. In late November, head coach Robbie Ftorek was fired by the Otters. Kris Knoblauch was hired as his replacement. There was more losing; it seemed like the team was spiralling downwards. Connor called home late one night. He was homesick, sick of losing, feeling like he was on a sinking ship where some of the players had checked out. In that regard, there was nothing exceptional about a homesick 15-year-old. His was a call that lots of parents get from their kids playing junior hockey. Brian McDavid drove to Erie that next day to make sure his son was okay, settle him down and help him work through his upset feelings.

At Christmas in that rookie OHL season, he played as an underager for Team Ontario at the World Under-17 Challenge. It was a disaster of sorts for what many thought was a stacked Ontario team that should compete for gold. They finished a disappointing sixth. McDavid led his team in scoring with six goals and nine points in five games, but he took it as a failed test.

"He was crushed," Brian McDavid said. "He took that all very personally."

By all accounts, the team was plagued by jealousy and infighting. McDavid was often the target. A couple of teammates reportedly rode him hard on the exceptional angle, and as the tourney wore on, Team Ontario more or less unravelled.

But there were many good times for a 15-year-old kid, occasions when the perks of being Connor McDavid paid big dividends. Like in February, when McDavid and a couple of Erie teammates got to go to a Pittsburgh Penguin game. And watch the game with Pens owner Mario Lemieux in a private suite. And meet Crosby after the game. And get a picture taken between Mario and Sid, a photo that was widely circulated in the media and on the Internet, dubbed by many as "The Past, Present and Future of Hockey."

"It was weird, it was wild," Connor said. "It was pretty cool."

It was, however, also an illustration of how a simple "cool thing"— getting a picture taken with a couple of your hockey superheroes— can amplify the pressure and expectations. As in the "Past, Present and Future" angle. Mario did his thing; Crosby's doing his; where's the new kid going to fit into that pantheon of greats? Is he worthy of being in their universe?

The truth is, there's no escaping it. The photo was, on one level, just McDavid being the same as any teenage kid getting to meet his hockey heroes. But McDavid isn't just any teenage kid, so there's always another layer to it.

The Crosby comparisons are inevitable. McDavid grew up idolizing Crosby; Crosby saw McDavid play once and immediately pronounced that he reminded Sid of himself. They have different body types—McDavid is going to be taller and rangier than Crosby—but their dynamic first-step acceleration, otherworldly hockey IQ and insane ability to score or make plays can't be ignored.

Oh, there's one other thing they share. Crosby is one of the most superstitious players in the NHL. McDavid will challenge him for that title.

"He's got his lucky underwear, and they could walk out of the arena,"

Brian said. "If we drove to the rink, we had to listen to the same songs and drive the same way because we won or he had a good game when he did it that way last time. We would have to park in the same spot. He packs the bag exactly the same way every time: left shin pad, right shin pad, he zips it, he unzips it—he has his routines. When he gets dressed, it's always in the same order—one side, and then the other."

"If Brian and Connor drove to the game together last time and they won," Kelly added, "Connor would tell me I'd have to sit in the backseat because he didn't want to change things up. Good luck with that. It's not happening."

The best part of that OHL rookie season, as fate would have it, was that the Otters were a non-playoff team. So Hockey Canada added McDavid to its roster for the 2013 World Under-18 Championships that April in Sochi, Russia.

McDavid turned the hockey world on its ear. A double under-ager, two years younger than everyone else in the tourney, he shredded the competition, leading Canada to a gold medal and being named tourney MVP, scoring eight goals and 14 points in his first five games before being shut out in his final two contests. A number of the games were televised nationally in Canada on TSN.

As well known as he already was, it was a huge coming-out party for him. NHL scouts returned from Sochi raving about his dynamic play, mentioning him as a challenger to inherit Crosby's "best player in the world" mantle one day. They declared him the prohibitive favourite to be the No. 1 pick in the 2015 NHL draft. It was all quite heady stuff, even by exceptional-player standards.

"It was such a good end to a season that was a lot more difficult for him than people realized," his father said. "When he came home, he was so tired. The first thing he said to me when he got back was, 'My legs are done.' He was gone for a month. He said it was the biggest grind he'd ever been through. It was so intense. But he loved it."

McDavid spent the summer of 2013 working hard with fitness guru Roberts. He took to heart Orr's pleas to take care of his body, to get rest, to eat properly, to train hard and get a lot stronger.

Again, a positive performance by McDavid presented new challenges. He was so dominant, so off-the-charts good at the Under-18 World Championship, it set the bar that much higher again.

The following October, early in McDavid's second OHL season, a Canadian sports magazine came out with a front cover sell line boldly stating: BETTER THAN CROSBY. It wasn't a question; it was a declaration. The story inside the magazine was a fine and reasonable account of McDavid's exploits at the U-18 tournament and how not even Crosby at the same age had done what McDavid did in Sochi, how McDavid was, in the eyes of some NHL scouts, perhaps tracking ahead of No. 87, who had been playing prep school hockey when he was 15.

Still, Brian and Kelly McDavid cringed when they saw the magazine cover.

The New York Times, USA Today and *Sports Illustrated* had all published McDavid stories and features in the spring of 2013. But that one magazine headline—BETTER THAN CROSBY—left a mark.

"We were really upset by it, Connor was upset by it," Brian said. "The story was fine, but it was referencing just one tournament where Connor did something Crosby didn't. That's all it was."

The McDavids went into protective mode. A scheduled interview for a feature story on CBC's *The National* was cancelled by the McDavids after that. So were a number of other interviews that had been arranged.

"We just felt we all needed to take a step back and give Connor some space," Brian added. "Connor's focus was trying to make Canada's team at the World Juniors, and we didn't need to be adding to the pressure. Connor can be a sensitive and introspective kid. He's very guarded about attention being on him. He doesn't crave to be the exceptional guy all the time."

There's no avoiding it, though.

It was demonstrably clear early in the 2013–14 OHL season that McDavid was so much bigger, faster and stronger than he had been in his rookie season. He struggled to score goals in the first half of his OHL sophomore season, but his improvements in speed and power were noticeable.

"It's weird looking back on that first year," McDavid said. "I felt like a little rat on the ice. I felt that way all season. It bothered me. This year, I can challenge people physically. I can hold off a defenceman and drive the net. Last year, I would have just got pushed outside. Last year, when we played three games in three nights, it was embarrassing. I might as well have not even played that third game. I had no legs."

Erie went from being one of the worst teams in the Canadian Hockey League in McDavid's rookie season to being ranked No. 1 in the CHL on and off in 2013–14. It wasn't all because of McDavid— the Otters assembled a deep, talented lineup from top to bottom—but McDavid was clearly the catalyst.

In his second OHL season, McDavid achieved one of his goals by becoming only the sixth 16-year-old to play for Team Canada at the World Junior Championship, joining the exclusive company of Crosby, Eric Lindros, Jason Spezza, Jay Bouwmeester and Wayne Gretzky. But it was a difficult tournament for Team Canada, who finished fourth and out of the medals for the second consecutive year. And it produced, at best, mixed results for McDavid.

The mere fact that he made it as a 16-year-old probably should have been enough to declare it a modest success. In the days leading up to the final selection camp, he was perhaps 50/50 in the eyes of the coaching staff to make the team. But when he was the best player on the ice in an evaluation camp game against university competition, it was clear he would make it. Still, only Gretzky dominated the tourney as a 16-year-old. Lindros played very well at it when he was 16; Crosby was more of a depth player (two goals and five points in six games); and Spezza and Bouwmeester played only sparingly.

McDavid played out of position, at left wing instead of centre, but started the tourney in a relatively prominent role on one of the top offensive lines. He had three assists in the first two games, showing flashes of brilliance, but took a pair of minor penalties in that second game, against the Czech Republic. Head coach Brent Sutter benched him for most of the third period and all of overtime, but took him off the bench for the game-deciding shootout. McDavid missed on his attempt, and the Czechs won the game. Canada lost a game it was supposed to have won, and the McDavid angle was front and centre. It was a tough night for the 16-year-old, and even though he bounced back to score a key goal in a 3–2 win over the Americans, as the tourney wore on, his role on the team steadily diminished. When it was over, Team Canada was branded a loser; McDavid was judged by many to be a non-factor, betrayed by his youth.

The first judgment was accurate. Canada hadn't gone without a medal at the WJC for 14 straight years, but now had done it in back-to-back tournaments. The second was perhaps somewhat true, though maybe unreasonable when weighed against expectations, given that Gretzky and Lindros were the only 16-year-olds to have ever made really strong contributions at the WJC.

It's all just part of the torture test the truly exceptional players go through. McDavid was hailed as a hero at the Under-18 World Championship, and then dismissed as a zero at the 2014 WJC. Build them up; tear them down. There hasn't been a young Canadian hockey superstar who hasn't experienced it. It's like a rite of passage.

The relentless judgments passed on a talented teen who is just trying to find his way in the world unquestionably builds up a tough outer layer of skin—"if it doesn't kill you, it makes you stronger" seems to be the applicable catchphrase here—but for both the player and his family, it's also about trying to maintain degrees of normalcy, to keep from becoming too cynical or bitter in the process.

The McDavids are really quite nice people. Brian is a hockey dad, no question about that. Kelly is the furthest thing you'll get from a hockey mom; if she had her druthers, when the kids were young, they would have skied instead of playing hockey. As competitive as they were when they were younger, older brother Cameron is supportive of his little brother. Connor is a warm, friendly kid, obviously intense and driven to be successful, but the whole family recognizes they're all being constantly measured and judged to ensure they don't violate the Canadian hockey culture's cardinal sin: displaying cockiness. Confidence is okay; cockiness, no way.

The McDavids are constantly striving to be normal in what is so clearly not a normal situation.

How many 16-year-olds, for example, have yet to get their driver's licence, but do have a family trust bank account with tens of thousands of dollars in it—the by-product of a five-year endorsement deal with RBK Hockey signed when Connor was just 15—to say nothing of a deal with a trading card company and other paid business opportunities? Still two or three years away from actually playing professional hockey, Connor McDavid didn't have a six-figure annual income as a teen in junior hockey, but it was quite likely in the range of $50,000 to $100,000.

"My dad has the bank card and I don't have the password," Connor said with a smile. "But, yeah, I know there's money there if I need it."

"It's in a family trust," Brian added. "There's a separate business company for Connor's endorsements. We pay taxes on it. It's his money. He has access to the money, more access to much more money than kids his age."

Within the McDavid family, there is certainly an awareness of how Connor is perceived from the outside looking in. That, because he has more fame and talent and money than not only average teenagers, but many of those he plays with and against, there's an effort made to demonstrate he's a good guy, a good teammate, a good person. But he doesn't have to try too hard.

"Kind of, yeah, that's a really big fear of mine," Connor said of sometimes feeling like he should go the extra mile not to be perceived negatively. "One of my own biggest pet peeves is cocky people, people who think they're so much better than everyone else. I cannot stand that, I really can't. I certainly don't look at myself any differently than anyone else. It's not too hard at all for me [to project a positive image]. I don't feel like I have to go out of my way to do that, because it's who I am, it's what I believe in and it's what is right."

. . .

You may be wondering what ever became of Pierre Dupuis.
His story was told as part of a book, *Selling the Dream: How Hockey Parents and Their Kids Are Paying the Price for Our National Obsession*, by Ken Campbell, with Jim Parcells, which was published in 2013.

Campbell wrote that, after Dupuis quit junior hockey, he took a job as a hydro lineman in northern Ontario, getting married and raising a family, but also struggling for a time with what might have been—what never was—for him in hockey.

But he was able to let go of his resentment. One night, he packed his hockey bag, and off he went to the local arena.

Campbell wrote:

It wasn't long before Dupuis was once again leaving people amazed with his skills—on a much smaller stage. Playing against huffing and puffing recreational players whose best days had passed them by, Dupuis was once again filling the net and gaining legions of fans. People from town—and even from other small towns nearby—flocked to the arena to watch him play. Kids asked for autographs.

"Pierre became the little superstar all over again," [wife] Nicole Dupuis said. "He was doing what he loved to do and I saw that twinkle in his eye like it was when he was younger. Then Pierre was happy. He realized, 'You know what? I've got my kids coming to see me and the kids at school were talking about Pierre Dupuis.' It was fun because people would come from all over to watch him play. It came back to what it was."

• • •

The year 2014 was noteworthy on the exceptional-player calendar.

That's because there wasn't one. After Ekblad (2011), McDavid (2012) and Day (2013), no one applied to Hockey Canada for exceptional status in 2014. Therefore, no one crowned; no one rejected.

It's difficult, if not impossible, to predict when the next kid will willingly vault himself into the glare of the hockey world. Or from where in Canada he'll emerge. There was talk of a young Quebecois star who dazzled the prestigious 2014 Quebec International Peewee Tourney. Might it be him, three years later, in 2017?

The cub reporter turned Hockey Insider does the math. Pierre Dupuis was 12, the same age as the young star from Quebec who turned so many heads at the Peewee Tourney.

All in good time . . .

. . .

There are two questions often asked about an exceptional
player. One doesn't have an answer, at least not a very good one. The
other is a question you hope never comes into play.

WHY ARE THESE EXCEPTIONAL PLAYERS SO, UM, EXCEPTIONAL?
It's not hereditary. Not really. Brian McDavid played Junior A hockey
with St. Mike's back in the day, and still loves to play whenever he can.
He has a real passion for the game. He may have passed *that* along to
Connor, but Brian was not a great player, never mind a star or super-
star. Bobby Orr's dad, Doug, played some hockey, but he was, uh, no
Bobby Orr.

"I'm not sure you can ever explain it," Orr said of why Wayne
Gretzky is Wayne Gretzky or what makes Mario Lemieux Mario
Lemieux. "There's something there. There has to be. I have no facts to
back it up, but when you watch Gretzky or Lemieux or Sidney Crosby,
go look at the video of them, and I think they just 'see' the game differently, they think so far ahead, they process things completely differently
than everyone else. I don't know how you quantify that. Everything in
our game happens so fast, but the special few can process it faster and
better than everyone else. That, to me, is what separates them. They
can take a really fast game and slow it down in their mind so they know
where every player is on the ice."

WHAT IF?
What if these extraordinary teens don't turn out to be as great as their
billing? Or, more important, what is it that could prevent them from
getting to where they're expected or ordained to go?

"I can tell when a kid is having a great time, and my biggest fear is we take that love and passion out of the game," Orr said. "We have to be so careful with our kids who play now. My biggest fear is always that they'll stop enjoying it. When Connor plays, you can see he is having fun. We have to be really careful to protect that for all the kids who play. We screw up a lot of players with the pressures. Connor is going to feel pressure, it's everywhere he goes, and I never had that—no one who played in my time did. I can't imagine what it's like now. If pressure is worry, I didn't feel any pressure until I couldn't skate anymore [because of knee injuries at the end of his career]. . . . My greatest fear with Connor is he's a young boy who won't get a break, and everyone is on him all the time. That's why we all have to work together to protect him and just let him play."

It's something Brian and Kelly McDavid have thought about, too. What is the job description of parent, after all, if not to be concerned or worried for their child's future well-being? We all want our kids' dreams to be realized, not crushed. Yet we also know there are so many variables, so many hurdles to overcome, so many holes they can fall into. There's nothing exceptional about that. That's life, as they say.

"I worry about injury sometimes. I do," Brian said. "But there's no control over that. I've known for a long time Connor has a shot to play [in the NHL]. His demeanour, his passion, I've always felt it he would have that chance. . . . The other thing that worries me a bit is that Connor can be really hard on himself. I worry that he sometimes doesn't give himself the luxury of making a mistake. I'm sure he feels the pressure—that's his 'normal'—but we talk to him a lot about that to make sure we don't let the negative things affect him. He's got lots of good support from a lot of people, and he's matured so much in the last couple of years. It's really heartwarming to us as parents to hear him say, 'I don't like cocky people,' because we've always tried to raise both our boys to be humble and sincere."

"I always worry," Kelly McDavid said. "I'm his mother. That's what mothers do. I just want him to be a normal kid. If he's going to shoot pucks for two hours, I want him to not feel like he has to do it. He's so focused on hockey all the time, I didn't want him feeling like he missed out on being a kid. That was always my big worry with Connor. But I've learned over time this is what he wants, this is what makes him happy. If he's happy, I'm happy."

The formative years—from Connor McDavid's emergence into the hockey world's consciousness at age 14 to when he'll turn 18, eligible to be taken six months later in the 2015 NHL draft—are quite likely the most difficult and challenging he'll ever face. The mercurial world of being a teenage prodigy will steel him and test him. If he's able to successfully navigate the choppy waters as a boy, like John Tavares, you would have to think he'll be ready for whatever awaits him as a young man. That isn't to say there aren't a plethora of pressures in store for a potential first-overall pick in the NHL, but just getting there without cracking under the enormous weight of expectation is a tremendous accomplishment in its own right.

Then again, maybe it's not so different for Connor McDavid than when he was six years old, crossing stairs off the diagram his mom had made for him as he eagerly anticipated ascending from house league to AAA rep hockey. Single-minded, focused and driven; intent on getting to that next level, but one step at a time.

"It all seems so far away," Connor McDavid said in November 2013 of his NHL draft in June 2015, "but at the same time, it's hard to believe I'm already in my second year in the OHL. It's weird. The years seem to be flying by, but the NHL draft, that still seems so far away. And it *is* far away. There's still a lot of hard work to be done."

CHAPTER 7

Warrior Elite

Brandon Prust Fights the Good Fight, and All Comers,
to Fulfill His NHL Destiny

————

The NHL's self-made man always knew, even as a young boy, that he was going play professional hockey. He told his parents exactly that one night while watching an NHL game on TV. He wasn't sure how it would all come to pass, but he never doubted it would.

You could even say Brandon Raymond James Prust was destined to be an NHLer, but for a young player whose skill set and physical tools were decidedly average, and as someone who believed far more in self-determination than fate, he still isn't entirely sure where he comes down on the destiny thing.

There's no debating this: the extraordinarily ordinary young man from London, Ontario, has gone on to do ordinarily extraordinary things as a highly valued, uniquely talented member of the Montreal Canadiens, one of the toughest players in the entire NHL, in spite of not quite being six feet tall and weighing less than 200 pounds.

"I always believed I would find a way to do it," Prust said on the eve of the 2014 Stanley Cup playoffs, his ninth year as a professional hockey player. "So I guess that means I was destined for it, but when I was growing up, I never really believed in fate, to be honest."

Looking back on it now, though, he's not so certain what he does or doesn't believe, though he most certainly will acknowledge he needed a little help along the way.

And he got it from the most unlikely sources: a broken-down Zamboni, a bad golf shot and a sound beating.

Brandon Prust's career in minor hockey was somewhat undistinguished.

Oh, he was a good player in the Forest City Hockey League, always playing up a year against older players, but he was never one of the really high-end players for his age who played on the prestigious London Junior Knights AAA team.

In his major bantam year, when he was 15 years old, he decided if he was going to get noticed for the Ontario Hockey League draft and truly begin the quest to be a hockey player, he needed to play AAA. So he tried out for the Junior Knights.

He got cut.

Rejection would become a recurring theme.

Disappointed, he planned to return to his Forest City team, but the coach of the London AA team asked him to play. He had a good year playing AA, but still not good enough to get drafted into the OHL. The following year, his 16-year-old season, he tried out and made the Junior Knights AAA midget team. He had an excellent season in his first year of AAA, but London was no match for its rival from Kitchener. London lost the first two games of its playoff series against Kitchener by lopsided scores, and what would almost assuredly be the last game of the season was scheduled for Kitchener.

Minutes before game time, though, the Zamboni in Kitchener broke down and effectively ruined the ice. "Burned a hole in it," Prust said. The game had to be postponed, rescheduled for the next night, but back in London. The inevitable occurred—Kitchener wrapped up the series with its third straight decisive win—but Prust had a strong game. Staff from the London Nationals Junior B team happened to be in the arena that night. After the game, Prust was invited to finish the season as a practice player with the Nationals, a team for which he would play full time the following season.

"I wonder sometimes, if the Zamboni hadn't burned a hole in the ice in Kitchener, what would have happened," Prust said.

At the very least, it was a break. Practising with the Nationals at the end of his midget year got him a spot on the team for the next season as well as an invite to the London Knights' Ontario Hockey League training camp in the fall of 2001. Of course, the Knights cut him. That was okay; Prust was thinking he might like to try to get a scholarship to a U.S. college, so a full season with the Junior B Nationals was the perfect situation. He had a solid year as a 17-year-old in Junior B—17 goals and 52 points with 38 penalty minutes in 52 games—and played well enough in his own mind, by season's end, to consider playing in the OHL the next season instead of going the college route.

It was the week before the OHL Knights' 2002 training camp, and Prust was still waiting for his invitation to try out. He was getting a little anxious. Prust's father and mother—Kevin and Theresa— were out golfing that summer week in August when they had a close encounter of best kind.

"[Knights' co-owner and head coach Dale Hunter] was golfing at the same course as my parents," Prust recalled. "He and my dad will argue about who hit the ball into the other guy's fairway—it was Dale's into my dad's—and they crossed paths. My dad introduced himself to Dale and said, 'Why haven't you called my son?' Dale told him they thought I was going the school route, and my dad told him, no, that I wanted to go to [the Knights'] camp. A couple of hours later, I got the phone call inviting me to the Knights' camp. That was a weird one, for sure."

Another break.

So Prust attended his second OHL training camp.

He was cut. Again.

This time, though, before being sent back to Junior B, Prust made a plea to Knights co-owner and GM Mark Hunter and his brother, head coach Dale: "I told them, 'Just put me in, you'll never take me out. Just give me a chance.'"

Prust went back to the Nationals, though not for long. A few games into the OHL season, the Knights ran into injury problems. They recalled Prust. He went into the lineup.

"And he never came out," Mark Hunter said.

Finally, at age 18, two years after the really good 1984-born hockey players made it to the OHL, Prust had arrived. He wasn't a big kid, not highly skilled by OHL standards. He had a lot of heart and a work ethic, not to mention a special quality that set him apart from pretty much every other player.

"He's got charisma," Mark Hunter said. "When Brandon walks into a room, he lights it up. He doesn't have any bad days. He's a very special person, he cares about everyone he comes into contact with, he's always smiling, laughing, having fun. You could see that right away."

What no one could have seen, though, was the average-sized late bloomer with modest skills would become a way-above-average NHL tough guy who would fight more than 260 times over 12 junior and professional seasons, an average of more than 20 fights per year.

"Outside of a couple of scraps when I was really young, in elementary school, I'd never been in a fight in my life," Prust said. "It wasn't my nature to fight [off the ice]. I never had a hockey fight [before playing in the OHL]. I always played the game hard. I loved to hit people, I could really hit. My favourite player growing up was Wendel Clark."

If a broken-down Zamboni and a chance meeting on a golf course helped to steer Prust on his chosen path, so, too, did getting beaten up in a fight.

The hockey fight website *HockeyFights.com* identifies Prust's first OHL fight as taking place on November 2, 2002, against Plymouth's Nate Kiser. Though that isn't exactly how Prust remembered it.

"It wasn't much of a fight," Prust said. "Kiser jumped me. He beat the crap out of me. That was the fight that scared me. I said after that one, 'I gotta learn to fight.'"

Prust had already become good friends with the Knights' designated tough guy, Chris Bain. After every practice, Bain and Prust would stay on the ice and fight—or at least, Bain would teach Prust how to fight, show him the tricks of the trade. Prust was like a sponge, soaking up all that fistic knowledge.

"I felt I needed to protect myself," Prust said. "I was hitting [bodychecking] people hard, I crushed some guys, and I realized if you hit people hard, they're going to want to fight you."

Under Bain's tutelage, Prust started feeling more comfortable, much more confident. He wasn't just ready to protect himself; he was prepared to initiate, to do battle, to protect teammates and fire up his team.

"My first real fight was against Guelph," Prust said of his bout in a game on December 20, 2002. "We were at home. The guy had a really long last name [Steve Zmudczynksi]. I started that one. Guelph had just scored. He lined up beside me. He was a pretty big guy. I knew he wasn't their toughest guy. That was my first 'Let's go' moment, and we squared up."

Prust won the fight. He fought some more that season (13 fights in total), even more the season after that (35 fighting majors), moving up in weight class to take on legitimate OHL heavyweights. He won a lot more than he lost.

"I had a knack for it," he said. "It seemed to come naturally to me, even though I'd never done it before."

The truth is, he liked it.

"Off the ice, I would always do anything to avoid [fighting], and still do," Prust said. "But in hockey? The switch goes off."

In the span of about a year, the charismatic kid who was so caring and congenial off the ice, this late bloomer of average size and skill, had charted his course. He knew where he wanted to go and how he was going to get there, and no one was going to get in his way.

Destiny? Whatever.

Brandon Prust was on his way to establishing himself as a member of hockey's warrior elite.

A four-year, $10 million contract with hockey's most storied franchise, the famed *bleu, blanc et rouge* of the Montreal Canadiens?

Check.

A home in the hip Plateau neighbourhood that he shares with his stunningly beautiful girlfriend Maripier Morin, a Montreal television personality and model?

Check.

A hometown charitable foundation, Prusty4Kids, which finances the Kids Kicking Cancer program at the Children's Hospital in London?

Check.

A respected leader on his hockey team, a model citizen in the community and a close-knit family that taught him to love life and laugh, that it's as important to care for others as yourself?

Check, check and check.

Life's good for Brandon Prust; he's living the dream, and then some.

"How can I not be happy?" Prust said. "I'm so fortunate. I've been blessed with good people in my life and a life that is so unbelievably fantastic, I'm not sure I could even dream about having it."

Well, there are the nights when his heart pounds so hard with anxiety before he drops the gloves to fight a foe who may be as much as six inches taller and 40 pounds heavier. And there are those mornings when Prust hauls himself out of bed and feels like he's 100 years old, when he tries to block the pain of myriad injuries suffered in what is, without any doubt, hockey's most physically and emotionally taxing job, that of an NHL tough guy. It can be a good pain, though. Reminds him how lucky he is to be in the NHL, though there have been too many occasions to count over the years when Vicodin or a shot of Toradol was required to numb the physical misery, just to allow him to stay in the game and do his job.

Fighting, hockey's dark science, can be scary and gut-wrenching. It can eat away at the soul of those who embrace it. For however much it may wear on Prust—and at times it does (see the interview that follows this story)—the smile on his face, his eternally sunny disposition, a legitimate *joie de vivre*, suggest he's found a way to stay on the right side of that fight.

Prust is good at it, too. Fighting, that is. He's not just a face-puncher, though that is the platform on which he's built his career.

One-dimensional palookas don't make $2.5 million a year. Disposable 13th forwards with no discernible hockey-playing skills don't get courted by the head coach of the Montreal Canadiens, who on the first day of unrestricted free agency in the NHL showed up at the Prust family home on Fanshawe Lake in Thorndale, Ontario, carrying a Habs jersey with PRUST and the number eight on the back.

"It was actually [Habs coach] Michel Therrien and [director of player personnel] Scott Mellanby who came to the house," Prust said. "They had a bag with them; they pulled out this Canadiens jersey with my name and number on it, gave it to my dad [Kevin]. It was funny. We grew up in our house as [Toronto] Maple Leaf fans. My dad was the biggest Leaf fan ever. He held it up, he looked at it . . . they were looking at him and he was looking at them, like 'What am I supposed to do with this?' I hadn't signed anything yet, hadn't made a decision. So my dad just hung it over the chair. I knew I wanted to go to Montreal, but I still asked my dad, 'Would you be okay with this?' And he just told me, 'I'm behind you 100 per cent whatever you decide. Whatever is best for you.' Once I signed, he put on the jersey."

Montreal, known as a skilled but undersized finesse team, had targeted Prust as their primary free-agent consideration on July 1, 2012. They wanted to get bigger, stronger and tougher. They wanted a robust winger who could get in on the forecheck and bang bodies, someone to block shots and sacrifice his body for the team. They wanted someone who would fight for the right reasons, to stand up for teammates. They wanted a character leader, on and off the ice, a presence in the dressing room, a player who would relish fourth-line duty and minutes but have the skills and wherewithal to play on any line at any time, as required, with a chance to play as much as 14 or 15 minutes a night. They wanted intangibles; they wanted a role model for their younger players; they wanted someone tough as nails.

They wanted Brandon Prust.

"He was the guy," said Montreal general manager Marc Bergevin. "He was the guy we really wanted. We were looking to establish a new identity and new culture in our dressing room and on the ice. Brandon is a glue guy. He changes the dynamic of a room when he walks into it. Players look up to him."

Bergevin had just one fear. "After [Brandon] signed, I had a conversation with him and told him, 'Don't change who you are because of the contract, the money. We're paying you to just be yourself, to be the same guy you were in New York.' Some players get a big contract and they try to change to live up to it. All we wanted from Brandon was the same thing he's done for any team he's played on. That's what we needed, and that's what we got."

The Canadiens paid handsomely for it, too, giving Prust more than three times the $800,000 annual salary he was earning with the New York Rangers.

There were those who suggested Prust was simply chasing the dollars, looking to cash in. If that were the case, who could blame him? Fighting in the NHL is oftentimes a high-risk, low-reward proposition, with a short shelf life. There was much more to it for Prust. It was gut-wrenching to leave New York and his posse of close friends that included Brad Richards, Brian Boyle, Michael Del Zotto and Henrik Lundqvist.

"The contract . . . for sure, if you asked me when I was 18 years old, could I ever envision making $2.5 million a year . . . a guy like me, not the most skilful. . . . No way. I couldn't imagine it," he said. "But it wasn't just about the money."

Ironically, Prust had met the lovely Maripier in New York while he was with the Rangers. The Canadiens knew he might look favourably on moving to his girlfriend's hometown. He was also hopeful of an expanded role, maybe more minutes of ice time, a chance to get in on the ground floor of a new culture in Montreal being established by a new general manager (Bergevin) and new head coach (Therrien).

"I loved New York City, the organization, the players. I knew I was leaving a very good situation," Prust said. "It was the weirdest time for me. For two days after I signed, I was the happiest and saddest, all at the same time, I've ever been in my life. So happy to be part of something new in Montreal, so sad to be leaving New York."

The Prusts didn't just talk about family values; they lived them.

When Kevin Prust's father, Raymond, died—Brandon was 11 years old at the time—Kevin moved the whole family from their home in London to nearby Thorndale, where Kevin's mother, Georgina, was still in the family cottage overlooking Lake Fanshawe. They built an addition to the cottage—one big, happy, mixed-bag family.

Raymond Prust, Brandon's Papa (grandfather), was of Welsh-English origin. During World War II, he met Georgina Miliardi in Italy. Their relationship was frowned upon in Naples, so Raymond and Georgina left for Canada and got married. Brandon's Nonna (grandmother)—or as he called her, his Nonni—was as Italian as Italian could be. Brandon's mom, Theresa, was born and raised in Glasgow until age seven, when the family moved to Canada. She was a McQuillan, the daughter of a colourful Scotsman, Glaswegian Jimmy McQuillan.

"Italian and Scottish," mused Prust. "I grew up with Italian home cooking and kilts. I lived with my Nonni. My *Granda* was a real Scot, one of the funniest men you would ever meet. My family, all we ever did—and all we ever do when we're together—is laugh and have fun. That was instilled in me from a very young age."

Brandon and his sister, Carla, three years his senior, came by their love of hockey honestly. Their home on the lake provided some of the best outdoor skating imaginable, no doubt part of the reason why Carla, who grew up to become a schoolteacher, not to mention a mother of three, played varsity hockey for the University of Western Ontario.

Brandon's dad worked as a salesman for a safety company, travelling throughout southwestern Ontario; his mom spent more than 35 years with the Canadian Imperial Bank of Commerce.

When Brandon, at age 18, finally made the hometown OHL Knights, it was a cause for celebration for the whole family. Well, almost the whole family.

"My Nonni, she would come to the games or watch them on TV, and as much as she liked me playing [for the Knights], she didn't like me fighting," Prust said. "She would say, 'You don't have to fight. Why do you fight?' She tried to offer me money [$20] for any game I didn't fight. I never took it, but it was always offered."

Meanwhile, there wasn't a game Prust played as a Knight that he didn't give or get a high five from his "Granda," Jimmy McQuillan, whose Knights season tickets were right on the glass, alongside where the players would walk out onto the ice.

"He loved it, and so did all the guys [on the team]," Prust said. "He had front-row seats and I'd say, 'Hi Granda,' every night on my way to the ice, and we would all give him high fives."

Jimmy McQuillan wasn't offering Brandon money not to fight. Neither was Kevin Prust, who Brandon said was a "little more naturally aggressive off the ice, with more of a temper, than me."

The Hunter brothers, meanwhile, were instilling in Prust, and all the Knights, their own set of hockey family values.

"[The Hunters] taught me what it is to be a professional," Prust said. "That's what they do there—teach all the kids who go through there how to be pros. I was like a sponge, soaking it all up."

It was in Prust's second season in London, when he had 35 fights, that his game blossomed, and not just the face-punching part. He showed more dimension than many imagined he possessed. He scored 19 goals and 52 points, with 269 minutes in penalties, in 64 games. In the playoffs, he scored seven goals and 20 points in 15 games and was named the Knights' playoff MVP.

"He showed he could play," Mark Hunter said. "He wasn't real big, he wasn't real fast. He killed penalties, he made plays. Tough? Oh, yeah. He could fight. Totally fearless. He was a leader. He cared so much for the team."

The combination of pugilism and production didn't go unnoticed. The Calgary Flames drafted Prust in the third round, 70th overall, in the 2004 NHL draft. It was an amazing step forward for a kid who had played Forest City hockey before one year each of AA and AAA without being drafted into the OHL.

"That's when I knew [he was going to fulfil his destiny to be an NHLer]," Prust said. "I needed some luck, some breaks—the broken Zamboni, my dad golfing—to get to that point, but once I'd been noticed, once I was drafted, I knew it was in my hands now. I could take it from there."

The real dream season was Prust's overage year, 2004–05. The lockout wiped out that entire NHL season, so all eyes were on junior hockey's most dominant team. London was a star-studded group—future NHLers Corey Perry, Rob Schremp, David Bolland, Marc Methot and Dan Girardi, amongst others. The Knights started the season with an OHL-record 31-game undefeated streak, went on to win the OHL championship on home ice, and hosted—and won—the Memorial Cup, beating Sidney Crosby's Rimouski Oceanic in the championship game before a rabid hometown crowd.

"The guys on that team are best friends to this day and always will be," Prust said. "There's such a tight bond. It was a fairy-tale season. We made a statement. No chance anyone was beating us. We were dominant. I got to hold up the OHL championship trophy and the Memorial Cup on home ice, right there in front of my family and friends, my Granda in his seats at the glass. It doesn't get any better than that."

Nine years into his professional career, Prust was still looking for that elusive Stanley Cup championship, but simply forging that length of career was quite an accomplishment for someone who easily could've been a dead-end kid.

In his first three years as a pro, in the Calgary system, he fought all comers, had decent offensive output for a fighter—12, 17 and 10 goals— in the AHL. He showed he could play some to go with the fighting.

"I was trying to make an impression, trying to make a name for myself," Prust said. "I was playing a lot, putting up some goals and points, and I wasn't backing down from anybody. If I didn't lead the league in fights, I was close to it. I fought anyone . . . John Scott, Rocky

Thompson. I fought some scary dudes, but I was confident. I'd become a good fighter. I knew if I played well, did my job, any team [in the NHL] would need a guy like me."

By 2008–09, his fourth year as a pro, Prust was an NHLer, never to play another game in the minors. He was traded that season, from Calgary to Phoenix, but was immediately dealt back to Calgary in the summer of 2009.

Prust liked playing for Flames coach Darryl Sutter in his first go-round in Cowtown; not so much in his second tour of duty, playing for Darryl's brother Brent. So when Prust was traded from Calgary to the Rangers in the 2009–10 season, he welcomed the fresh start under hard-rock Blueshirt coach John Tortorella. Prust flourished there, providing abundant grit and even scored 13 goals—his NHL career high—in 2010–11 while becoming a fan and media favourite who hit, fought and cemented his reputation as the consummate tough-guy teammate, all heart and soul and nails.

"I've yet to hit 20 goals," Prust said, with a grin and a puncher's lament. "I had 19 in my second year in the O, 17 [in his second year] in the AHL and 13 [in his second year] with the Rangers. Lot of good years, but I couldn't quite get to 20."

Brandon Prust smiles easily and often, but his chipper demeanour can sometimes belie the brutal physical punishment that's been inflicted on his body over a dozen seasons of high-level hockey. It's not unique to him; every hockey player goes through to it to varying degrees, but the United Brotherhood of NHL Fighters and Tough Guys must withstand a level of searing pain that is almost obscene, difficult for an average man to even comprehend.

It's often said that professional athletes must understand the difference between being "hurt" and "injured." You can play hurt, but not injured. For tough guys, though, in a world where a spot in the lineup isn't as certain as it is for the goal-scoring winger or playmaking centre, the line between hurt and injured is more easily blurred, to the point where it's often indistinguishable. It's unimaginable pain, not to mention unspoken painkilling remedies, often game after game for the better part of a season.

"It is a worry," Prust conceded. "Some days, you feel like you're 100 years old. You think about 20 years from now and how you're going to feel. You want to be able to live, to play golf when you retire. I'm trying to take care of my body differently now. I train and stretch differently. I'd like to play 15 years in the NHL."

But fighters, and hitters, have no choice but to sacrifice themselves. It's in their job description; it's in their DNA.

Prust underwent hip surgery after his second year of junior hockey. He had a hairline fracture of his jaw in his third year with the Knights. In his first real NHL season, in December 2008, the Flames winger paid the price for renewing acquaintances with old Windsor Spitfire OHL rival Cam Janssen of the St. Louis Blues. The two fought early in the game in St. Louis—that was the norm—but Janssen later lowered the boom with a violent hit to the head that smashed Prust's jaw, badly fracturing it. His recounting of the incident is not for the faint of heart.

"We were in St. Louis. The doctor gave me three Vicodin to get me through the night," Prust said. "The team was going on to another game somewhere else, but I had to get back to Calgary the next day, on a commercial flight with a connection—I think it was from St. Louis to Denver to Calgary. I can honestly say it was one of the worst days of my life."

Prust said he couldn't swallow, could barely breathe. The pain was excruciating, and he had no painkillers. He needed to have his jaw wired shut, but that wouldn't happen until he got back home to the doctors in Calgary.

"I literally had to hold my face together, like this," Prust said, clamping one hand on one side on the top of his head and the other hand on the opposite side, along his jawline. "My face was so swollen, it was out to here . . . people in the airport were staring at me. I had to change planes. It was a long day. I was in so much pain."

Welcome to the NHL, kid.

He missed three months because of that injury, and was back in the lineup for about three weeks when Minnesota's six-foot-seven, 258-pound Derek Boogaard hit him with a forearm to the head. Prust was concussed, badly. Boogaard got a five-game suspension.

"I didn't get knocked [unconscious] but I didn't know where I was for an hour," Prust said. "I didn't know where my stall was. I went into the change room; they asked me, 'What day is it? Don't know. Who did we play? Don't know. What was the score? No clue.' It all came back to me about an hour later."

Before he was healthy enough to return to the Flames' lineup, Prust was traded to the Phoenix Coyotes.

Good luck, kid.

In his first full year with the Rangers, in November 2010, Prust tore up his shoulder in a fight with Pittsburgh's Mike Rupp. Prust never missed a game that season—it was the year he had his NHL career-best 13 goals and 29 points—but he lost count of how many pain-numbing shots he took to make it through all 82 games.

"I'd wake up in the morning and not be able to move my arm or shoulders and think there was no way I could play that night," Prust said. "But by game time, I'd be lining up against [Montreal's] Travis Moen on the opening faceoff and saying, 'Hey Mo, you wanna go?' You find a way, you have to find a way."

When the season ended, he had shoulder surgery.

The next season, his last in New York, Prust fought Ottawa's Zenon Konopka in mid-January. He snapped a tendon in his left ring finger.

The doctor told him he could have it surgically repaired immediately, regaining full use of the finger, but would miss three months—the rest of the regular season—or he could wait until the off-season to have the tendon surgically removed.

"They told me if I waited, and did it in the summer, I would never be able to bend [the top half of his ring finger] again," Prust said. "I think it was [Ranger captain] Ryan Callahan who said to me, 'Hey Prusty, it's just a finger. You don't need to ever bend it again.' The guys were chirping me because they thought I should get it fixed [in-season], but it was a contract year. I wasn't missing three months in a contract year."

Prust played with the pain, and the painkillers. Again. His whole left hand was a mess by the playoffs.

"There was so much swelling and scar tissue," he said. "I fought [Ottawa's] Chris Neil in our playoff series and I was in agony. I couldn't even grab onto his jersey; I just tried to hang on for dear life. He won that fight; I did all right. I had to do it. It helped change the series around for us."

Prust got the off-season surgery to remove the tendon. He can no longer bend his ring finger on his left hand, but he was able to sign his four-year, $10 million contract with Montreal that summer just fine.

In his first two seasons with the Habs, he had a pair of shoulder separations—one left, one right, one each season. He had an oblique strain, which he came back from, only to aggravate it and miss the last month of the 2013–14 season. He was out of the lineup for a total of 40 of his first 130 regular-season games in Montreal.

"The last couple of years in Montreal have been great years," Prust said on the eve of the 2014 playoffs. "I've had great fun, the most fun I've had in [pro] hockey. I can't imagine how much more fun it would be if I didn't have the injuries."

Brandon Prust would never ask anyone to feel sorry for him.
Quite the opposite, in fact. He chose the life he leads, and he embraces all the consequences and rewards that go with it. He couldn't be happier. He's living the dream. His Nonni Georgina passed away when Brandon was 22, in his second year as a pro. His Granda, Jimmy McQuillan, died in 2013, and lived to see Brandon establish himself as a full-fledged NHL player. Brandon knows if they're looking down on him now, his Nonni would still be offering to pay him to not fight and his Granda would be sitting at the glass, exchanging high fives on Brandon's way out to do battle as an NHL warrior. He still has his grandmother Lillian, his mom's mom, who has made a point of trying to watch, on the internet or on TV, most every game Brandon has played since he was 18 years old

His perspective on life has been shaped by a loving, close-knit family that instilled in him a sense of community and deep level of caring, evident by his charity work with cancer-stricken kids in London. The Kids Kicking Cancer program allows youngsters battling the disease to get instruction in the martial arts while they're in the hospital, which in turn helps them to learn to breathe, manage pain, feel good about themselves, live for the moment and continue to fight the good fight.

Which, in a manner of speaking, goes to the very core of who Brandon Prust is and the life he's always felt he was meant to have, the one he's living to the fullest.

"All I know is when I'm 50 years old, no matter what," Prust said, "I'm not going to say I would have done anything differently. You'll never hear me say that."

· · ·

NHL forward Brooks Laich, in one of the great hockey quotes of all time, once said: "If you want money, go to the bank. If you want bread, go to the bakery. If you want goals, go to the net." Well, borrowing a page from Brooks, if you want to talk fighting in the NHL, go to Brandon Prust. The Montreal Canadien forward is something of an expert, and over lunch on the final Tuesday of the 2013–14 NHL regular season, Prust talked candidly about all things fighting. Here's the transcript of that interview.

BM: This is probably a stupid question, but I'll ask it anyway: What's it like to get punched in the face?

BP: It doesn't feel good. [*He laughs.*] But you know, when we play with pain, it's kind of a rush for us. If, after a game, I've got a sore leg from blocking a shot or a sore face from eating a punch, it's actually a feeling of being proud of yourself, it's the proof you battled that day. I don't fight where I eat a lot of punches. I'm a smart fighter; I try to limit the number of punches I take. But, yeah, getting punched in the face is not something I look forward to.

BM: I'm guessing it's a better feeling to punch someone in the face than to get punched?

BP: It feels a lot better. [*He laughs.*] I always try to punch someone in the face more than they punch me. [*He laughs again.*] When I fight, it's not like I hate the guy or I'm mad. When I fight, I'm totally calm. It's business. I'm trying to out-strategize the guy, wait for my openings. When you hit someone and connect, it's like, "He felt that one." That's what you're thinking.

BM: Is being in a fight more exhilarating or scary?

BP: It's both. I'm nervous going into every fight, but it's that fear that makes me a good fighter. I can admit it's nerve-racking, especially some of the guys I fight. But once the gloves drop, my nerves go away. It's just me and him; nothing else really matters except how I'm going to win that fight and not get beat up. My heart is beating like crazy when I ask someone to go, but once the gloves drop, I'm calm.

BM: What's the key to winning a fight?

BP: I think you have to be in control of your aggression. I know that when I do badly in my fights, it's when I really hate the guy—it's when I really want to hurt him. That's when I don't fight so well. I fight better when I'm calm and in control. Fighting is about using your brain. You have to know what punches are coming, what hand he punches with, what hand he grabs on with.

BM: Is it important to win a fight or more important to just show up?

BP: Both. It's important for me to win a fight. I hate losing fights. But it's definitely more important to show up, to stand in there and stick up for teammates or your team. Show that courage, get your team-mates going.

BM: Do you study your own fights? Watch video?

BP: Definitely. If I get in a fight, I'll usually watch it right after the game, on the bus on the way to the airport. I watch it on YouTube or on *HockeyFights.com*.

BM: What about before a game, preparing for a fight? Do you watch video of potential opponents?

BP: Yes, I'll watch, especially a young guy coming into the league, I may not know him. A lot of the older guys, I obviously know all about them. I don't need to see video of them. But new guys, young guys, I need to know how they fight. I'll strategize, go through in my head how I'm going to fight them. I'll do that more than I will think about the game, because you just play the game. The fighting, though, is on your mind the most. I like to fight right away if I can, try to get it out of the way and focus on playing hockey. If you know a fight is coming, it's harder to focus on playing. If the fight doesn't come until the third period, I'm an awful hockey player for the first two periods, because it's in the back of my mind. I'm thinking, "When's he coming for me?" or "When am I going to go after him?"

BM: So before a game, will you look at their lineup and say, "Okay, I am going to fight this guy or that guy?"

BP: Yeah, a lot of times what I do is look at their lineup and say, "This guy might come after me, that guy might come after me." Or I'll say to myself, "I'm going after this guy tonight." I may decide ahead of time I'm going after this guy on the first shift. I'll do that more if we've lost a couple of games in a row, if I feel like I need to get the team going right away.

BM: Have you ever arranged a fight ahead of time with the guy you're going to fight?

BP: No, but there are guys you've fought your whole career, you just know you're going to fight them. You don't have to arrange it. You both just know. Like if I'm playing Cam Janssen, we know we're fighting. Now, I also know I can sometimes say no to him. Or he can say no to me. One of us is going to be looking for the other guy. That's just the [unspoken] agreement we have. Nothing's actually arranged, but it's understood. We both have a lot of respect for each other and what we do. If he says, "No, I'm not fighting you now," I'm fine with that. But there are games when I just know if I ask him, he's going to say yes. Those are the games [when] I'm most nervous, because I know I'm going to ask him and I know he's not going to say no.

BM: There's always been a lot of talk about "the Code" and what it is. Do you know what the Code is?

BP: Yeah, for sure. I could write the Code. It's all about respect and honour. I'm not sure in the old days, there was that amount of respect. They hated each other when they fought. I'm sure there was a Code back then, but it's changed. It's about respect now. If a guy falls down, you don't hit him when he's down. There are not that many rules to the Code, really. It's just about not taking advantage of a guy when he's down and out. You want to fight people, but you don't want to seriously injury them.

BM: A lot of people would say that doesn't make sense. I mean, what's the purpose of a fight besides punching them in the face and possibly hurting them?

BP: For sure, you are trying to punch a guy in the face, and yeah, it's a war, but if the guy is laying there, you have to let up and not take advantage.

BM: I think the confusion on the Code is that some will say if you're asked to fight, you have to be honourable and accept, yet some guys refuse to accept the fight and they'll have their reasons for doing that. It strikes me that there are a lot of provisions in the Code—when you have to fight, when you should fight, when you can turn down a fight—but it seems like a moving target sometimes.

BP: I definitely agree that part of the Code is you should have to answer the bell sometimes. Not all the time, but sometimes you have to. If you're a player who makes big hits—guys like [Dion] Phaneuf, even P.K. [Subban] on our team, there are guys who make big hits in hockey, and that's great, that's the way to play the game—I don't think those guys have to answer the bell *every* time they make a hit, but they should answer once in a while. I mean, a guy like Brooks Orpik, he runs around out there, makes all these big hits, but doesn't drop the gloves. I don't respect that. If you're going to try to injure our players [with big hits], you've got to be prepared sometime to face the music. That's everybody's call they have to make. You can't do what [Boston's] Shawn Thornton did [knock out a defenceless Orpik with a punch, for which Thornton was suspended 15 games], and I know Shawn feels bad about that, but you can't really do anything about it if they don't [want to fight] except maybe try to hit them even harder.

BM: In your mind, what are the best and worst reasons for having a fight?

BP: The best reason is sticking up for a teammate if it's a vicious hit on your guy. The other best reason is to help your team if it's down and needs a spark or you need to get the crowd going. Protecting a team-mate or getting your team going, those are the best reasons. The worst reasons to fight . . . hmmm, I don't think there is a worst reason to fight. [*He laughs.*] Obviously, if you're down 5–1 and it's the last five minutes of the game and you start a fight, it's like, "Why are you acting like a hero now when you could have asked me to fight in the first period?"

BM: You're a big fan of mixed martial arts fighting. Do you use any of that training to help you with fighting in hockey?

BP: When I met my buddy [UFC fighter] Sam Stout five years ago—we're both from London, we didn't grow up in the same area, but we knew of each other—we became good friends right away. I started training with him. I do my regular [off-season hockey-related strength] training, but also I train in the ring with Sammy to work on punching. It's been tough the last couple of years with my injuries. I've been lim-ited, by the time my injuries heal up.

BM: Do you know how many fights you have had in your career?

BP: Total?

BM: Yes—OHL, AHL, NHL, pre-season, regular season and playoffs.

BP: I think it's close to 250.

BM: As of today [April 8, 2014], it's 264, according to *HockeyFights.com.* That's a lot of fights.

BP: It is a lot, isn't it?

BM: Do you know who you've fought the most?

BP: It's gotta be Cam Janssen . . . or Adam Keefe.

BM: You're good. It's Keefe. Kitchener vs. London. Minor pro. I count nine fights with Adam Keefe and seven with Janssen. Imagine how much higher the Keefe number would be if he played against you in the NHL. The fights with him were in junior or the AHL—the last one was in 2008.

BP: [Keefe] is one of those guys I talked about [who, if] we were play-ing against each other, we knew we were fighting. I thought Janssen would have been the most.

BM: You've had a lot of multiple fights with the same guy—Paul Bissonnette, Mike Brown, Brad Staubitz, Kelsey Wilson, Nathan McIver, Rick Rypien, Milan Lucic, Chris Neil, Zac Rinaldo . . . By the way, is there not a rule against fighting former London Knights [like Rinaldo]?

BP: Nope. [*He grins.*] I was never teammates [with Rinaldo]. If I'm playing for the New York Rangers and he's playing for Philadelphia, it's going to happen.

BM: Do you remember who your first NHL fight was against?

BP: Rick Rypien?

BM: No, it was Jody Shelley.

BP: You're right. I was just called up. It was my second NHL game. In Columbus. I went after him.

BM: What was more exciting: your first NHL game or your first NHL fight, which came in your second NHL game?

BP: My first NHL game, in Detroit. My whole family was there. I think I played pretty good. I think I played maybe eight minutes. Felt like it, anyway. It felt like 20 minutes to me. Hasek was the goalie. I was playing against [Pavel] Datsyuk, [Henrik] Zetterberg and [Nicklas] Lidstrom. That was pretty cool playing against those guys.

BM: We went over that list of guys you've fought multiple times. Is there anybody in that group who falls into that category of someone you hated, where the fight was personal?

BP: Nobody. I've seen most of those guys outside of the rink and had conversations with them. It's just business.

BM: Is there anyone it is really personal with?

BP: Hmmm . . . you know, coming up, I really hated David Clarkson. Our fights were personal. I think we've both matured now; we maybe don't have the same hatred. There's more respect now. But as teenagers in London and Kitchener, and when I fought him when I was in Phoenix and he was in New Jersey, it was personal.

BM: You would never consider yourself a heavyweight, would you? How much do you weigh?

BP: One hundred and ninety-five pounds.

BM: How tall are you? Are you really six feet?

BP: With sandals on, yes. Six feet with sandals on. [*He laughs.*]

BM: Yet you've fought heavyweights, guys like Janssen, and even super heavyweights, you fought (six-foot-eight, 260-pound) John Scott in the minors.

BP: I don't know what I was thinking there. I also fought Steve MacIntyre. Again, what was I thinking? I did pretty well against him, too. That was my first year up in Calgary, and after I did that, I remember [Flames coach] Mike Keenan came up to me after the period and hugged me. He gave me a big hug.

BM: Has the fighting landscape changed much since you broke in? The size of the guys or the science of it?

BP: I don't know . . . it's tough to say. I've fought the same way and for the same reasons: to make a stand for our team, to stand up for teammates, to continue to make a name for myself that I'm not going to back down. I think it's an important piece of the team. I know a lot of people are trying to get fighting out of hockey, but I think it's an important part of the game. I do believe if you take fighting out, there are going to be more injuries, more guys will take liberties if there are no consequences for your actions.

BM: Do you really believe that? You've said yourself that some guys, no matter what, won't answer the bell, so how does fighting now prevent what you call the rats from being rats?

BP: Well, there aren't many rats. I think a lot of guys still play with pride and honour. It's what makes our game unique in that sense. The fact that we can police our own game a bit, make people think twice about trying to take a run at and potentially hurt a top player. And if [the rat] doesn't answer the bell, eventually, if he continues, I'm just gonna start throwing punches and give him what he deserves.

BM: Do you think the anti-fighting forces in hockey will eventually get their way?

BP: I can see it eventually happening. The game has changed so much since the [2004] lockout. It's not the same game I grew up watching, that's for sure. And I think a lot of the changes were for the good. But you see some of the penalties that are being called nowadays. It's getting softer and softer every year, it seems. A little whack, a little tug, a little hold-up. Penalty. I laugh at calls that are called on the other team sometimes. It's a different game from that "tough, battle through everything, only the men survive" style. So I imagine they will eventually take out fighting. Hopefully, not in my day. And whenever they do it, it will be the biggest mistake hockey ever made.

BM: When I hear you talking about fighting, it's as if I'm listening to Don Cherry. You're definitely his kind of player, but he went after you on "Coach's Corner" because you got into a little skirmish with a goalie [Tampa's Ben Bishop in 2013–14]. How did it feel to get called out by Grapes on *Hockey Night in Canada?*

BP: My dad and I actually happened to be watching it together when Don chirped me. My dad was more upset than I was. I didn't really care. We all know you have to discard about 50 per cent of what comes out of Mr. Cherry's mouth.

BM: Your dad had always been a big fan of Don Cherry. I was looking, and your dad has a Twitter account (@kevinprust). He's only ever tweeted a few times, but two of them were directed at Cherry (@CoachsCornerCBC): "He plays exactly how ur rock em sock em's taught him . . . my son is 1 of the most honest players in the league . . . loved by every teammate he's ever had."

BP: My dad doesn't watch ["Coach's Corner"] anymore. [*He laughs.*] Seriously, Don will come on the TV now, and I guess my dad turns the channel. That's a direct quote from my mom. [*He laughs.*]

BM: I think the fear some people have now with fighting is that, with the size of the guys fighting and how they train to punch, someone could die in a fight one day. Does that ever cross your mind?

BP: [*Pauses.*] No, not really. I think the league does a good job of controlling things—the linesmen jump in if someone gets jerseyed; if a guy is down or hurt, the other guy backs off and is more respectful. You do see guys get knocked out sometimes. Kevin Westgarth [of the Calgary Flames] last month, unfortunately, he got it bad, and you don't like to see that. That's a scary situation. But [getting knocked unconscious] could happen anywhere, not just in a fight. It could happen in any [contact] sport.

BM: Is fighting more difficult now because visors are mandatory?

BP: Yeah, but when I fought in junior, I would punch to the bottom of the visor, and that would pop the helmet off. It would kind of blind them for a second. You can cut your hand, but my hands are taking a beating anyway—what's another cut? I don't mind [fighting a player wearing a visor]. I don't want a guy to take his helmet off. I'll try to punch their helmet off or just pull it off. I can use that visor to my advantage in a fight.

BM: In the OHL now, if the helmet comes off, the fight is basically over. The linesmen jump in to break it up. Do you think that's a good thing?

BP: At that age, in junior, yeah, but if you're fighting someone, you're trying to get their helmet off. Wait—you're saying in junior now, they stop the fight if the helmet comes off?

BM: Yes, that's the rule in the OHL. After Don Sanderson died [in January 2008] during a fight where his helmet came off and he hit his head on the ice during a senior game, the OHL put in new rules about fighting without a helmet.

BP: That's a good rule for kids at that age. They're not as experienced; they're more reckless in how they fight. It's not a bad thing. But not in the NHL, no. I don't agree with that. I mean, not if you're going to have visors on, too. If you don't have visors on, there's no need to take a helmet off. I don't think you can do that in the NHL, they should just let [fights] go in the NHL.

BM: You've had 264 fights and, all things being equal, by the time you retire you're going to be well over 300 career fights. Knowing what we know now about head trauma and concussions, are you worried about what effect that could have on you for the rest of your life?

BP: Knock on wood, I haven't had a lot of concussions or head trauma from fighting. That's why I fight the way I fight. I'm not a guy who stands in there and eats a lot of punches. I want to have a long career. It's not a punching-bag match. I try to use my brain. I want to play 15 years in the NHL. Guys are protecting themselves a lot more now. You see [in] the old days, guys would just stand in there and whale away on each other.

BM: Yet you've seen a teammate go down. George Parros was knocked out a couple of times this season. How does that affect you?

BP: That first game of the season, when he went down in the fight with Colton Orr, I was right beside him. I was trying to help him. It was definitely hard, it's something you definitely don't want to see happen to anyone. But when it hits so close to home, it's even worse. That's the fear we go into every game with. I could get hit into the boards and get my head smoked every time I go on the ice. A helmet only helps so much. That's the same fear [all hockey players] live with every day. Any of us could get [knocked unconscious or injured] in any game we play. It's a dangerous game.

BM: How do you think the people close to you—your girlfriend, Maripier, and your parents—cope with the dangers of your job as a fighter?

BP: They worry, for sure. But they don't make it visible to me, because they know I don't want to see or hear that. I think they trust the way I play and the way I fight.

BM: [London Knights GM] Mark Hunter says that when you walk into a dressing room, you light it up, that you don't have any bad days and you're a really well-adjusted, happy guy who lives life to the fullest.

Many would say being an NHL fighter has a really dark side to it, that doing this job creates demons. Can you separate those two worlds? Or do you feel like there's part of this job that could eat you up?

BP: I'd be lying if I told you fighting doesn't worry me at times. But it's a healthy fear for me that helps to make me a good fighter. It's a job I've chosen. I don't let it mix me up. It's my job. It can be stressful at times. For sure. But it's something I don't ever regret. I don't plan to change my game. I'm the player I've always wanted to be ever since I was a kid and I watched Wendel Clark play. I wanted to be a leader, on and off the ice, and fighting is part of my game. That is stress I've chosen to accept. I'm good with it, I'm happy.

BM: In the summer of 2011, there were three deaths in hockey, and one of those tragedies hit really close to home for you. Derek Boogaard was a friend, a roommate, a teammate. That must have been really difficult for you.

BP: It was a really tough time. He was my roommate on the road for a month [before he got injured and subsequently died]. We were close. That was tough for our whole team. When we found out he had died, a lot of us were together, and that was really difficult. That whole summer was terrible, just awful, with the death of three fighters [Boogaard, Rick Rypien and Wade Belak]. I was so sad for all of them. I know it made people worry [that the deaths were fight-related]. I am sure fighting could have been a demon for them, but whether you're a fighter or not a fighter, everyone in this world has issues they have to deal with, and everyone deals with them differently. This is something I know for a fact. I know Boogaard could be a happy guy and loved coming to the rink. I didn't know Rypien or Belak. I had some wars with Rypien [four fights]. What a great competitor he was. What a sad story. Whether fighting was the reason or not for their deaths, exactly what part it played, I'm not sure we'll ever really know.

BM: Well, there's no doubt being a fighter is hockey's most difficult job. It certainly seems as if there's a real bond or brotherhood amongst those who do it.

BP: There is mutual respect. If you're fighting another guy who fights, you can't hate him. You're doing the same role. It's a tough job. We know what we go through to do it. We know it's business.

BM: Would you rather be known as a good player or a good fighter?

BP: Can you do both? That's the goal. I want to be both. I want to be looked at as a great fighter. I want to be remembered as a great player, a leader, a guy who helped lead his team to a championship, to a Stanley Cup.

BM: Would you rather score a goal or win a fight?

BP: Score a goal. [*He breaks out in a big smile.*] I love scoring goals. There are different days, though. Today, it's a goal. Tomorrow, it might be a fight. I love scoring, but there's something about being at the Bell Centre in front of 20,000 people, or at Madison Square Garden, squaring off at centre ice, people cheering you on. There's something about that experience that you can't touch.

BM: Would you change anything about your life in hockey?

BP: No, I'm not a guy who looks back and dwells on decisions. You can't change what has happened. I have no regrets. I'd do it all over again exactly the same if given the chance.

BM: If you were to have a son and he grows up and says, "Dad, I want to do exactly what you did, I want to fight in the NHL," what would you say to him?

BP: Get training. Get working. If he wants to be a warrior, all the power to him. I like that mindset.

CHAPTER 8

Recalculating

*Karl Subban Sets the GPS for a Legacy Beyond
Three Sons Being Drafted into the NHL*

———

The photograph, taken in the winter of 1970, was meant to be a family postcard of sorts. Just a little something to mail back home to the relatives in Jamaica, to show them the marvel of this thing called snow, this entirely new and oh-so-foreign experience of a first Canadian winter at the family's rented duplex on Peter Street in the hard-rock northern Ontario city of Sudbury.

There was the matriarch of the family, Fay, stepping outside for a quick snapshot, in her pretty pink dress and matching hairband and, funnily enough, wearing furry blue slippers, smiling, with her arms around three of her sons in the picture: nine-year-old Markel, on the left; 10-year-old Patrick, on the far right; and 12-year-old Karl, between his mother and Patrick. The snow was piled up high—mid-winter high—against the house behind them. Each of the boys was grinning, holding snowballs in their bare hands, Markel and Karl pretending to be eating them like snow cones. All three were decked out in matching dark green winter coats and boots.

No one, certainly not any of those actually in the photo, or anyone back home in Jamaica who would have seen the picture—or
another similar snapshot in which young Karl was in front of the
house, proudly clutching his first hockey stick, given to him by their
landlord's hockey-playing son—could have possibly dreamed what
it would foreshadow: that the unusually tall 12-year-old Jamaican
immigrant boy was about to embark on a Canadian hockey odyssey
that, one day, could be talked about in the same tones of wonderment
usually reserved for a Viking, Alberta, rancher who fathered six sons
who would play in the NHL or a Thunder Bay, Ontario, sod farmer
with four boys playing professionally, three of them in the NHL.

Karl Subban's school community retirement celebration was
June 25, 2013, at Claireville Junior School, where he had most recently
been the principal. It's just a four-mile hop, skip and jump from
the Subban family's six-bedroom home (two in the basement, four
upstairs) in the Humberwood neighbourhood of Rexdale, in northwest Toronto, where the family resided for 20-plus years.

The celebration of his 30 years as an educator—teacher, administrator and principal—came 10 days after his eldest son, Montreal
Canadien star P.K., was in Chicago during the Stanley Cup final to
win the Norris Trophy as the NHL's best defenceman. It was just five
days before the NHL draft in Newark, New Jersey, where the baby
of the family, Jordan, another defenceman, would be chosen in the
fourth round by the Vancouver Canucks. And about two weeks before
goalie Malcolm (in the middle, naturally), a 2011 first-round pick of
the Boston Bruins and a blue-chip netminding prospect, would head
off to the NHL team's summer development camp, in preparation for
what would be his first professional season.

On the occasion of Karl's retirement, the whole family was there to celebrate it. Karl's wife and partner of more than 30 years, Maria, herself already retired from the Canadian Imperial Bank of Commerce; eldest daughter and schoolteacher Nastasia, with her three little boys, two-year-old Legacy and his four-month-old twin brothers, Epic and Honor; second-oldest daughter Natasha, an artist turned teacher; and, of course, the three hockey-playing Subban brothers, who gave the event an air of celebrity as students and parents scrambled to get autographs and pictures with the bona fide NHL star and two more bound and determined to follow in P.K.'s footsteps.

Education and hockey; hockey and education. Teachers and hockey players; hockey players and teachers. Really, that's the interwoven story of Karl Subban's life since coming to Canada from Jamaica in July 1970, but if you don't make some distinction between the two, he'll be sure to let you know you should.

"People always believe it's my sons playing hockey, them playing or getting drafted into the NHL, that is my passion in life, but they don't understand that teaching is *my* real passion," Karl Subban said. "I'm not going to kid you. Am I proud and thrilled to have one son in the NHL and two more drafted to play there? Of course I am. My boys love what they are doing, and I'm thankful for that and the journeys they're on. And, like any parents and family, we all do whatever we can to support and help them reach their goals. But their hockey, that defines them. It doesn't define me."

Or as his son P.K. put it: "My dad will often say, 'I'm not living their [hockey] dream; that's their dream, not mine.' My dad has his own dreams he still wants to fulfill."

Karl Subban is a big man, six foot three and 260 pounds, if you're measuring, but there's a presence about him that makes him seem even bigger. He has a strong, deep voice that fairly resonates; an easy, big smile; a loud, hearty laugh; a twinkle in his eye; and a natural curiosity that has him asking as many questions as he's being asked.

In mid-August 2013, a couple of months after his retirement party, he was in a Tim Hortons coffee shop not too far from the family home, talking about life. His life, his kids' lives, where they've been and where they're going. It's obvious from the get-go that this "retirement" status is a misnomer, because Karl Subban has just reached one destination on his long and winding road; now he's moving on to other places. As the voice on the GPS says: "Recalculating." And that's not the last time you'll hear the GPS analogy.

"I see my life story as a challenge," Subban said. "I love that feeling of taking on something. As life goes on, you constantly learn about yourself, and what I've learned—and it's true for everyone—*my potential lies inside me*. We all have the ability to reach and become something. I feel like all my life I've been reaching. I'm 55 now and I'm still finding my passion, and for me, that's helping people to be better, helping children to be better. I want to write a book. I already have a title: *Saving Lives in Inner City Schools.*"

Much of what Subban plans to do in his so-called retirement years has been shaped by his career in education, specifically an eight-year stint as principal of Brookview Middle School on Jane Street in the Jane-Finch Corridor, a job he took on late in his educational career because he felt he needed some grand, new challenge. He was comfortable in his job at other schools—maybe too comfortable.

From the outside looking in, Jane-Finch is stereotyped as a notorious high-crime/low-income development in northwest Toronto. For example, a story in the *Toronto Star* on August 31, 2013, called it Toronto's "most dangerous place to be a kid" after four friends, aged 15 and 16, were gunned down within blocks of each other. While Jane-Finch residents often bristle at the stereotype and maintain there is a real community beyond the crime statistics and racial profiling, it is clearly one of Toronto's most ethnically and racially diverse neighbourhoods (a story in the *National Post* in 2011, for example, said half the student population at Brookview was black, with the majority of the rest either Asian or South Asian). By any standards, though, it's a tough part of the city. A poor part, too. The socioeconomic issues facing Jane-Finch residents, especially the children, are much more plentiful and significant than in any of the many other school districts where Subban has taught or administered in his 30 years in education.

"Jane-Finch, what it's really like?" Subban said, pausing to consider the question. "Well, I saw children who needed a lot more support, a lot more kindness and caring from adults around them, children who needed guidance and love. The staff would go home to our nice, comfortable homes at night and you didn't want to know what some of those kids were going home to . . ."

For eight years, Subban said he "gave it my heart, my soul, my money, my life." So much so, his son P.K. said, that P.K. thought it was taking too much of a physical, emotional and mental toll on his father.

"I knew as he got closer to retirement, he wanted that last big challenge in his profession," P.K. said. "I told him, 'I don't think you should go to Brookview . . . at this stage of your life you don't need to come home with grey hair every night.' You know, I talk to my mom and dad every day—not a day goes by that I don't speak to them—and back then, when my dad was at Brookview, he would be falling asleep on the phone while I was talking to him, he was that tired and drained. But that's my dad. He's so committed to teaching, and for his personal fulfillment, that's what he needed to do, that's where he needed to be."

So for eight years, Karl Subban was fully immersed in trying to make a difference for the kids at Brookview, and he did it with the zeal of a missionary, recognizing the stakes couldn't have been any higher.

"I called it saving lives more than teaching," Subban said. "That's how you have to look at it. It wasn't teaching reading and writing so much as saving lives. I told the staff, it's like being in an emergency room: kids are wheeled in and lives are hanging by a thread, and you have to do what you can to save that life . . . you can't convince me it's not emergency room work. I've been at other schools and observed the kids as they walk in each morning, and they enter that school ready to learn, work and cooperate. Those [teaching] jobs, they're a lot easier. Many of the kids [at Brookview], you have to get them ready to learn before they can learn. We're dealing with 11-to-13-year-olds—those are the critical years, the troublesome years. We have kids who come in and they don't know why they are there at school. It's a simple thing, but they just don't know why.

"If you don't get them going down the right path, they're taking the wrong road, and there's a consequence, a cost to society, for failure. And it's a major, major cost when a child doesn't do well or does nothing at school. If they're failing middle school, they're going to fail high school. If they fail high school, they're going to be on the street. This is very costly to society . . . children headed for the unemployment line, children being incarcerated, children being dead."

Subban experienced some moments of incredible angst and heartbreak at Brookview, like the time the school had to call 911 for an out-of-control boy who ultimately had to be sedated against his will by EMS personnel while he screamed, "Please, Mr. Subban, don't let them do this to me." Subban was so distraught by it all, he punched a wall and cried.

But many days, as challenging as it was, the immediate goals were relatively simple.

"At this school, students smoking or drinking or taking drugs were not a big problem," he said. "Coming late was the big problem. Getting them to focus and pay attention once they were there, that was the big problem. You can't learn to read or write if you're not there on time, if you're not focused when you're there."

Like all good teaching situations, the teacher often ends up learning as much as, or more than, the students. From the students. And so it was for Subban at Brookview. And the revelation for him, what those kids taught him, was that when children come to school and they're tired or hungry or scared or even scarred by their lives outside of school, a much broader reprogramming is required before there's any chance to begin the teaching process.

"Every child, regardless of their situation in life, comes with a built-in GPS," Subban said. "P.K., for example, told me when he was very young, 'Daddy, I want to be like those guys on TV playing hockey.' His GPS was programmed to be a hockey player. That just happened naturally for him. So it was our job, as parents, to do the things to allow him to try to be like those guys on TV. That's how it's supposed to work. Every kid has that GPS in him or her, but these kids in the priority neighbourhoods like Brookview, their GPS is there, but it isn't always loaded. They've had to deal with so many other things in their lives, they can't see any destination. Our job, as educators, is to load their GPS. And until we can come up with something better, their GPS has to be loaded to simply be a better student and a better person every day. Every child must have a pledge. That's what I learned at Brookview. As teachers, we can make a case to them why it's important to be a better person, a better student. Most parents do this naturally for their children. But if there's no role model of a mom or dad going to work, if parents are not able to do that for their children because of whatever circumstances at home, well, the school needs to step up."

So Principal Subban instituted the Brookview Pledge, a daily reminder for students, said aloud, of why they're in school and how they're going about it.

"I come to school to save my life," the pledge reads, "by working hard to be a better person and a better student."

In addition to the pledge, there were also the 4 Ts, the tools necessary to fulfil the pledge: *time*—be on time for school and make time to do your schoolwork; *task*—complete the assigned work; *training*—practice makes us better; *team*—cooperate with peers and adults.

Subban remembers one little boy in particular. The principal would see him every morning and ask him, "Why are you coming to school?"

"And this little boy, he would say to me, 'I'm coming to school to be a better person and a better student.' Then I would ask him how he's going to do that. And he would tell me. And by the end of the year, that little boy had really turned it around. His GPS was loaded. I'm very big on telling kids, 'You have greatness inside of you, and you can develop it.' There's no timetable here; it takes time and we have to work at it."

Subban also utilized his own love of hockey, even traded on some of P.K.'s burgeoning celebrity status, to implement the Vancouver-based HEROS (Hockey Education Reaching Out Society) hockey program at Brookview. HEROS is a charitable foundation, founded in 2000 by former Western Hockey League player Norm Flynn, that solicits corporate support and charitable donations to "use the game of hockey as a catalyst to attract youth to a program offering support for education, self-esteem building and life-skills training . . . focusing on boys and girls of diverse ethnicity from economically challenged neighbourhoods."

"Hockey is a big part of my life, and I wanted to bring it to the kids there," Subban said. "P.K.'s status in hockey gave me a lot of credibility with the kids. A lot of them wanted to be P.K. So I announced, 'If you want to play hockey, come see Mr. Subban in the office.' Seventy kids showed up."

And the Brookview HEROS program was off and running. Willie O'Ree, the first black player in the NHL, dropped by to support the cause. It became a thriving community project, with volunteer help from the Toronto Police, Big Brothers and Big Sisters, and countless other organizations. Every Tuesday was Hockey Day at Brookview, and the kids would go to the nearby multi-pad facility at York University, where the donated new equipment was stored. Subban fondly remembered a huge hockey jamboree, not just for the Brookview students on the ice, but the entire school and surrounding community, where more than 700 people showed up in the stands to cheer the kids on. It was an excellent tool to keep the kids' GPS loaded.

"The hockey was fun, it was great, but it was all about imparting the values, about using hockey to reinforce expectations," Subban said. "If you come to school on time, if you do your work, you could leave school early on Tuesday to go to the rink. But if you don't show up to school on time, if you don't do your work, you can't leave early. Hockey—sports, for that matter—are such a wonderful tool to reinforce listening and cooperation and helping another person. We had more kids who wanted to play than we had equipment. It was wonderful to see how all these children of diverse backgrounds wanted to play Canada's game, just like I wanted to play when I came to Canada."

While Karl Subban's time at Brookview came and went, and official retirement from the educational system ultimately beckoned, it's clear to anyone who knows him that this work to "save lives" and "loading the GPS" didn't end with his retirement party in June 2013.

"There's something about poverty and achievement," Subban said. "If you look at income level, the higher the income, the higher the achievement. The lower the income, the lower the achievement. It doesn't mean those lower-income children can't learn. It just means the schools need to do things differently, and that's what my book is going to be about. I love my children, I share in their passion for what they do, but *this*, that's *my* passion."

From the moment Sylvester Subban's family arrived in Sudbury from Jamaica in that summer of 1970, it was almost as if they were destined to connect with the game of hockey—and the Montreal Canadiens. Sylvester, a diesel mechanic, had a good job in Jamaica but wanted to give his family more opportunities, and a job with mining company Falconbridge in Sudbury in faraway Canada seemed a good start. It was almost impossible to not come into contact with hockey once the Subbans arrived in the Big Nickel.

Sylvester's wife, Fay, got a job doing laundry at Memorial Hospital and worked alongside former NHL player Eddie Shack's mother. Living on Peter Street (now known as Mountain Street), the Subban boys met the anglophone and francophone kids who also lived on the street, where they were introduced to Canada's game. They'd play road hockey there. Karl got his first hockey stick from their landlord's son, he got his first pair of skates from the Salvation Army, and he'd try skating and playing hockey at the outdoor neighbourhood rinks, though he knew, at age 12, he wasn't going to be able to catch up to the Canadian boys who had been skating almost as long as they were walking.

The Subbans had their choice of only two TV stations—one English, one French. Karl immediately became infatuated with the Montreal Canadiens. He'd watch their games in English on *Hockey Night in Canada* every Saturday night, and on weeknights, *les Canadiens* were *en français* on the French channel.

"We would have big fights in our home," Subban said, laughing heartily at the memory. "I was the only one in the family who wanted to watch games in French. My poor parents; here they move to a new country, the snow, the cold, all of that, and now they're watching a foreign game they don't understand in another language."

Karl loved the Canadiens, especially netminder Ken Dryden, and Dryden's number, 29, became his favourite number, especially after his daughter Natasha was born on October 29. Karl loved hockey, and it was seemingly all around him. He attended the same high school as members of the Sudbury Wolves of the Ontario Hockey League—guys like Dave Hunter, Alex McKendry, Hector Marini and Ron Duguay. When Karl wasn't watching his beloved Canadiens, he would go to the Sudbury Arena to watch the Wolves.

But he was a good athlete himself. He played basketball and lacrosse in the summer, and though he remembers being cut from his school's Grade 7 basketball team—"a setback is a set up for a comeback," he said, one of many motivational slogans he's liable to throw at you—he went on to be a very good player in high school, moving on to play varsity basketball at Lakehead University in Thunder Bay.

"Not bragging," he said, "but I was pretty good."

Indeed he was. He played for the Lakehead Thunderwolves, often a top-10 team in Canada, from 1979–84, amassing enough points (2,019) to be No. 5 on the school's all-time scoring list, twice leading the team in scoring. He was team MVP in 1981 and co-MVP in 1983. He played varsity hoops, but also intramural hockey at Lakehead. And he still loved his Canadiens, watching their games religiously on Saturday night before he would go out to parties.

But it was while working as an instructor at a Lakehead basketball camp for kids that he heard his calling to be a teacher. He got his Bachelor of Arts degree in 1983 and a Bachelor of Education degree in 1984.

"I was in the business program and I switched to education after working that basketball camp," he said. "I loved working with kids. I just knew teaching is what I would do, it would be my life's work."

Once he had his degrees and was ready to embark on a career in teaching, he moved to the big city, Toronto. He coached the men's basketball team at George Brown College. He eventually was hired to teach at a Toronto elementary school. He also met the love of his life when they were introduced at a New Year's Eve party.

Like Karl, teenaged Maria St. Ellia Brand immigrated to Canada from the Caribbean, the island of Montserrat. Like Karl, Maria was a fine athlete, a track star at Bathurst Heights Secondary School in Toronto, a sprinter who ran against future Olympian Angella Issajenko (then Angella Taylor), amongst others. But unlike Karl, Maria was an unabashed supporter of the Toronto Maple Leafs. Oh, the horror. Could a diehard supporter of the *bleu, blanc et rouge* find love and happiness with a true blue Maple Leaf fan? Apparently so, and the result was Nastasia, Natasha, P.K., Malcolm and Jordan.

And as was the case in Sudbury when Karl arrived in Canada, the Subban family fully embraced the Canadian way of life in Toronto.

"We were living in Brampton, and the girls were on skates before they ever bounced a basketball," Karl said. "We enjoyed skating as a family. We'd go to the outdoor rink at the Bramalea City Centre, it would be 30 below zero and we'd be the only ones out there, skating around the big Christmas tree. We must have been quite a sight, the only ones out there."

Karl and Maria, with their athletic backgrounds, obviously allowed their kids to swim in the deep end of the gene pool. Nastasia went on to become a top basketball player on the York University women's varsity team before she became a teacher. Natasha also played basketball growing up, but showed great flair for art and went to the Ontario College of Art and Design before deciding to switch to teaching. And, of course, quite remarkably, not one, not two, but all three Subban boys were drafted into the NHL, and one of them was named the NHL's best defenceman a month after his 24th birthday.

Good athletic genes are one thing, and the Subban kids have them. But a work ethic? Advanced coaching and training techniques? They had all those, too. Karl Subban's passion may be teaching and working to help kids less privileged than his own to learn, but don't think for one moment he wasn't involved every step of the way in the hockey development of his kids, notably P.K. A voracious reader and seeker of knowledge, Karl was gobbling up information on training, conditioning and coaching techniques even back in his Lakehead days, and he has never stopped, reading everything from Malcolm Gladwell's *Outliers* to . . . you name it.

Make no mistake, Karl and Maria Subban didn't just raise their kids; they taught, trained and coached them, too. If Karl would push a little too hard, Maria was there to pull back and maintain some balance. "They were," P.K. said of his parents, "a very good team. And when my dad thought it was time to move us on to someone who knew more than him, to go to another level with someone else, that's what he did. He knew when it was time [to let go]."

"I knew hard work, I knew a lot about training from my days at Lakehead," Karl said. "I introduced the girls to basketball and I trained them. If the boys were going to play hockey, I knew the value of practice. Of being on the ice every day. Time skating is time well spent, but I would skate, too. I didn't sit in the car and read a book. A lot of parents don't go on the ice with their children. I think that's so important. The really young kids, they want you out there with them. Looking back on it now, it was a great strategy with P.K. We would do it every day. I'd get home from work—he was still in diapers, two and a half—I'd grab the baby wipes, and off we'd go in my old Corolla. He liked it. Some kids wouldn't. He did. He always wanted more. P.K. couldn't get enough."

Karl was quite taken with the 10,000 Hour Rule Gladwell wrote about in *Outliers*—that it takes that much practice to become phenomenal at anything—and decided to try it with P.K. So the plan was to skate every day from the end of October to the end of the season. Keep in mind that P.K. was all of five years old at the time. That is, of course, what led to the well-documented story of P.K. skating at Nathan Phillips Square at Toronto City Hall late every weeknight with Karl. P.K. was in kindergarten at the time. Karl was working as a vice-principal of a night school to earn extra money, and when he finished work at 9 p.m., he'd go home and pick up five-year-old P.K. to take him downtown to City Hall. They'd skate for hours, into the wee hours, and once P.K. realized the older guys and rink attendants would play hockey with sticks and pucks after pleasure skating was over, Karl had no choice but to stay later. When they were done, Karl would grab P.K. a slice of pizza, take him home to Rexdale and put him to bed at 2 or 3 a.m. Karl would have to get up only hours later for his long two-job workday. But P.K. could sleep until it was time to catch the noon-hour school bus to afternoon kindergarten class. The next night, they would do it all over again.

"If I told P.K. I was too tired to go any night," Karl said, "he'd say, 'But I really want to go.' And we'd go."

"I'll never forget Nathan Phillips Square," P.K. said. "It always had that same smell, the smell of the air in downtown Toronto—you know, the hot dog vendors. I can still smell it now. We'd get a pizza slice every night. I loved that. I love the memory of it. That's what I'm going to do with my kids. I'm so lucky to have those experiences."

Karl noted that what worked for P.K. might not have worked for Malcolm or Jordan, and that what he learned from seeing P.K. embrace the nightly skates at Nathan Phillips Square is that "once kids become good at something, the younger they are, the more it fuels them.... P.K. had the advantage of me knowing the importance of practice. When he was a little older in minor hockey, P.K. would have power skating classes on the same day as his games. He'd skate with [power skating instructor] Cam Brothers at 10:45 at Westwood Arena and we'd have to be at St. Mike's for a game at 1:15 p.m. It would bother me to think he was missing practice for a game, so he would do both. Games don't make you better; practices do. It was a lot, but P.K. ate it up."

Karl would also flood the backyard rink each winter, and P.K. would spend hours on it. So, too, would Karl, who would ask Cam Brothers for some drills and come up with his own unique take on repetition, and building more skills and moves into each, increasing the speed and degree of difficulty.

"Oh yeah, the figure-8 drill," P.K. said, breaking into a wide grin. "Do you know how many variations of a figure-8 skating drill my dad came up with? Do you know how many times I did that? Two cones, so many variations—forwards, backwards, pivot one way, pivot another way, pass him the puck, take a pass, skate with a puck, jump over sticks on the ice, pass the puck over sticks on the ice. Over and over and over again, increasing the speed, always adding a new wrinkle. I loved it."

And it no doubt explains, in part, P.K.'s masterful ability to skate, wheel and pivot and do things with the puck at top speed that so many NHL defencemen can only dream about.

"What I've learned about training and athletic performance is, yes, biology obviously plays a big part," Karl Subban said. "But a lot of it is circumstance and environment. I mean, they went looking for the running gene in Jamaica and they didn't find it. There is no running gene in Jamaica, just like there's no hockey gene in Canada. But there's a hard-working gene, and that's what I've tried to teach to all my children."

The book on the three hockey-playing Subbans has yet to be written, really. It's still very much a rough draft. There's no telling what they'll be when each is fully formed. But the amazing thing is that, as similar as they are in so many respects—as you would expect with three brothers born within six years of each other, they share many of the same physical features and personality traits—the Subban boys are unique individuals who have travelled on their very own personal, and divergent, roads to be drafted into the NHL.

P.K. is a force of nature who just can't help being P.K. He's precocious, on and off the ice. Karl said P.K.'s power skating coach, Cam Brothers, once said of him, "P.K. is a lightning rod of controversy."

"I think P.K. was eight years old when Cam said that," cracked Karl. "Eight."

Karl laughed some more at that. "P.K. is P.K."

When P.K. was young, between five and seven years old, he was something of a minor hockey phenom. He could skate like an eight-year-old. Other players and parents would marvel at how a kid that age could shoot a puck into the top of the net from so far out. He played with the elite kids all the way up—Steven Stamkos, amongst others—but by the time it was his OHL draft year, he was no better than a sixth-round pick by the Belleville Bulls. Yet he surprisingly made the Bulls as a 16-year-old, playing on their power play and on the top shutdown pairing—as a rookie. Still, as talented as he was as he entered the OHL, two years later, he was not a first-round NHL draft pick, going 43rd overall to Montreal in the second round in 2007. Six years later, he collected the Norris Trophy as the NHL's top defenceman.

"I remember P.K. sitting in front of the computer [for the OHL draft] and all those kids being taken ahead of him, not going until [the sixth round]," Karl said. "That's an emotionally charged situation. P.K. used it the right way. He's still using it."

By comparison, though, P.K.'s route to the NHL was paved with gold compared to what the more introverted middle brother, Malcolm, experienced on his path to pro hockey. Miraculously, Malcolm didn't start playing goal until he was 12, in major peewee. "Malcolm was the best skater of any of us," P.K. said. "But he wasn't a real hard-nosed physical guy. But as a skater and athlete, he's incredible. He's competitive in a different way. He just hates to be scored on."

By the time Malcolm was 15 and in his OHL draft year, with only four years' experience as a goalie, he had to wait until the 11th round to hear his name called—as fate would have it, by the same Belleville Bulls. Malcolm played midget hockey as a 16-year-old—not unusual for a goalie prospect—but even when he was 17, Belleville Bulls general manager and head coach George Burnett said, the plan was to put him in Junior A for another year because Belleville had a few other goalies ahead of him on their depth chart.

"But he came in as a 17-year-old and he outplayed the others and we made trades to make room for him," Burnett said. "He wouldn't give up the net. He made us play him—he was that good."

So good, in fact, that the Boston Bruins took him 24th overall in the 2012 draft, 19 picks higher than P.K. went to Montreal.

Jordan, meanwhile, was another story entirely. Throughout his minor hockey career, the smallish defenceman, who may actually be able to outskate P.K.—and that's saying something—was always one of the best kids, playing on the best teams. In Jordan's draft year, 2011, Burnett completed the Subban trifecta in Belleville by drafting him fifth overall.

"If his name was Smith, not Subban, we would have taken him there," Burnett said. "We didn't take him because he was P.K.'s and Malcolm's little brother. We took him because he's a dynamic, skilled player. In his first two years in our league, Jordan outscored P.K. in P.K.'s first two years here. He's an outstanding player and athlete. He just hasn't grown to be the size of P.K."

And yet, largely because Jordan was five foot nine and 175 pounds, he wasn't taken by the Vancouver Canucks until the fourth round of the 2013 NHL draft. The scouts would tell you Jordan is the longest shot of the three Subban boys to be an NHLer, fighting a decidedly uphill battle to make it because of his size.

"Let me tell you, Jordan's GPS is loaded," P.K. said of his little brother, stealing his dad's analogy. "The best thing that could've happened to him is people telling him he's not going to make it, that he's too small. That's all he needed to hear."

There was a telling, and poignant, moment at the 2013 draft when the three Subban boys were all together, preparing to go on TSN's live broadcast of the draft, not long after the Canucks had ended Jordan's agonizing wait by drafting him. During a commercial break, the Subban boys were just getting into place alongside host James Duthie when Jordan, in his Canuck jersey and hat, suddenly burst into tears. He buried his face into his hands. He was immediately comforted by his two brothers. He wiped away the tears just before the interview began. An observer watching this all unfold wondered to himself whether Jordan was crying tears of joy, relieved at being drafted, or showing a raw, emotional reaction—upset at not being taken until the fourth round.

"People don't understand how emotionally charged the draft is," Karl said. "Yes, Jordan cried. Malcolm cried, too, after he was drafted and he went in the first round. P.K. didn't cry, but . . . [he wasn't happy going in the second round]. Honestly, if you're a kid sitting there, whether it's the first round or the last round, you just want to hear your name called. That's it. It's a difficult time as a parent when you're waiting. You want to say the right things to them; it's difficult because there's nothing you can say. They only want to hear their name."

As important as his kids' hockey is, Karl Subban, ever the teacher, is always looking for that moment where there's a life lesson to be learned. And as Jordan waited to be drafted, along came a moment—for Karl, anyway—that transcended the entire draft and hockey.

Max Domi, the son of former NHLer Tie and a longtime friend of

Jordan's—as well as a teammate and opponent in minor hockey—had already been selected much earlier, in the first round, by the Phoenix Coyotes. But immediately after Max had finished with his media obligations and met the Phoenix management, Max came up into the seats and sat alongside his pal Jordan for moral support. Finally, the Canucks took Jordan in the fourth round, and relief washed all over the Subbans.

"That was such a grown-up thing for a kid like Max to do," Karl said. "Imagine that. It was Max's day. He went in the first round. But he thought of Jordan and came to be with him. Parents are always trying to teach their kids the right values, you want them to be humble and thankful and considerate and to give back to others who need help and support. What Max did there . . . what a great example for Jordan and my boys to see it. So, yes, Jordan cried . . . there was a lot of emotion there."

While there were no words Karl or Maria could say to Jordan as he waited to hear his name called, the father/teacher/trainer most certainly had some perspective for Jordan after the fact.

"I've been around hockey a long time, and one of the things that is hard to see is someone's potential, even for the best scouts in the world," Karl Subban said. "You can't tell Jordan he's not going to make the NHL. Just don't even bother, because he's not having it. We don't get too caught up in what other people see in our children. Jordan believes in himself. There's lot there for him to improve upon. Size is his prize, but he has a desire to achieve and be successful. He has lots of fire in him.

"It's not really any different for P.K. or Malcolm. You have to listen to what people say, you have to be open to ideas and opinions. I try to be objective about my children. But if people say P.K. can't play defence, if P.K. believes that, those people will be right. Your kids are always going to get criticized by someone. That's part of the game. People say all sorts of things about P.K.—who he is, making judgments on what kind of person he is, making a diagnosis from afar when they don't even really know him. If they were all doctors, they'd be charged with malpractice." He laughs.

"I've always believed that before you become a master mechanic, you have to be an apprentice, so you can't get too hung up on labels. Experts are wrong a lot of the time. Scouts are wrong a lot of the time. Scouting is a fascinating thing. It's a very difficult job. I have nothing but respect for the scouts who work so hard at it. But Malcolm was an 11th-round pick into the OHL, a first-rounder in the NHL. P.K. was a sixth-round pick in the OHL, a second-rounder in the NHL. P.K. won a Norris Trophy. So, good or bad, don't get too hung up on labels or what other people say about you. Yesterday's achievement is yesterday's glory. You can't tell Jordan he won't make it to the NHL. Who knows, maybe he only gets as far as the AHL, but he's on his path and journey and what he does will determine how far he goes, not what round he was drafted in or whether someone thinks he's too small."

No one in the Subban family worries too much about Jordan. His brothers and parents know him better than those who size him up, and what they know is that he's the most competitive member of the entire family, that it's a mistake to underestimate the youngest Subban boy, the smallest Subban boy.

"Put it this way," P.K. said. "If there are six slices of pizza and our family of seven is sitting around the table, Jordan can't tell you the one person who won't get a slice, but he can tell you the one who *will* get one. It's Jordan. Every time . . . people look at Jordan's size and they don't get him. Honestly, he can squat more [weight] than me, he lifts more than me—not in the bench press, but in everything else. He sprints better than me, he has a fire in him like you can't believe. He wants [to make it to the NHL] more than me and Malcolm, and believe me, me and Malcolm really want it. But Jordan is on another level."

As similar as his boys are, Karl knows there is much that is different about them. Not that there are many days when all three are in the house at the same time anymore, but if they are, Dad can pretty much predict what they'll be doing.

P.K., Karl said, will be watching video of his games. In the summer, he reviews every game from the previous NHL season—the good, the bad, the ugly—and breaks it all down. If not a game tape, then Don Cherry's *Rock'em Sock'em* videos. P.K. can never get enough hockey.

Malcolm, the most introspective of the three, might be likely to go off on his own, teaching himself how to play guitar or chilling and playing a video game—maybe Call of Duty. P.K. said he didn't even know Malcolm could play the guitar until, to P.K.'s surprise, he heard him playing and singing a song.

Jordan is the outgoing imp of the bunch, the one who'll grab his mom's laundry basket, turn it on its end to make it into a goal in the hallway, use a rolled-up sock as a puck and anything he can get his hands on as a stick and play his own version of floor hockey, all the while calling play-by-play. Karl is convinced Jordan has the best hockey hands of the bunch, in large part of because of his extensive mini-stick prowess, which he's taken to another level as a shootout specialist with the OHL Bulls. When he was very young, Jordan would have the whole family laughing hysterically at his preoccupation with mimicking an NHL referee, including blowing a shrill whistle, sliding across the kitchen floor and calling penalties on the rest of the family.

Getting three boys to the NHL would be a grand achievement for any family. Karl Subban would never minimize that; he well knows the odds of putting one son in the NHL, never mind three. But he's probably more gratified at what his kids have learned on their journey to pro hockey than the achievement of just being there. In other words, whatever niche the three Subban boys carve for themselves in the professional hockey world, having all three influenced and mentored by Bulls GM and head coach Burnett is the real payoff for Mom and Dad.

"Maria and I couldn't have scripted it any better," Karl said. "The hockey's the hockey, but when you send three boys away from home at 16 or 17, you're putting them in someone's hands. It better be the right person. We're so fortunate to have had George Burnett look after our boys. George had such a big impact on P.K. that P.K. has started to sound like George—"

(Interruption: this is very funny if you know P.K. and you know George. In terms of personality, style and approach, they are at opposite ends of the spectrum from each other. Two people simply could not be more different. Okay, back to Karl's observations).

"—now Jordan is sounding like George. George taught P.K. how to dress, how to be a professional person. He has taught all three boys so much about being professional people, not just professional hockey players. George is a teacher by trade. There should be a George in every school, because he knows how to develop people, not just hockey players."

"George is a tough-ass, no-nonsense, old-school guy," P.K. said. "I remember my first OHL game, I was taking my suit off and George saw me and said, 'What are you doing?' I told him, 'I'm hanging up my pants.' He told me, 'That's not how you hang up pants.' He showed me how to match the creases, fold them neatly over the hanger. He taught me everything about being a professional. He's a parent, he's a teacher. He still calls me, we still talk and he still intimidates me."

Burnett, meanwhile, who played for the London Knights in the OHL in the late 1970s and early 1980s and who coached professionally in the NHL and AHL with Edmonton and Anaheim, probably knows the Subban family better than most anyone in the hockey community. He is uniquely qualified to offer an assessment.

"It's an extraordinary family," Burnett said. "Everyone always talks about the three boys, but Karl and Maria have two daughters, and they are as big a part of their daughters' lives and fully committed to the girls as any of the boys. As a family, they have made enormous sacrifices for their children. They've done everything to support their children, given them everything, and I'm sure it wasn't easy.

"There haven't been many games here in Belleville or anywhere else where you don't see Karl and Maria. When you consider the time and energy both of them have spent to work their jobs, to support their family . . . for Karl to spend all those years in the challenging job he had—it's incredible, really. They've been very kind to us as an organization, trusted us to look after their children. Outside of making sure their kids were set up in school or their billet family, there's never been any interference or involvement on the hockey side of things. You couldn't get a better set of parents to deal with. And they've instilled in all their kids great family values. They're respectful, they're care about other people, and they do a tremendous amount of charity and community work. They are all high achievers."

Karl Subban loves Canada. He feels as though Canada has done so much for him and his family, from that first day he arrived on Peter Street from Jamaica. He's a celebrity of sorts now, appearing with P.K. in the Hyundai Hockey Helpers commercials on TV, part of a sponsored program that helps underprivileged kids play the same game Karl immediately fell in love with in that first Canadian winter of 1970. And he wants to pay all of it back, with interest.

This so-called retirement of his will no doubt allow him to support P.K., Malcolm and Jordan on each of his three boys' quest to live out their version of the Canadian Dream, as they strive to etch the Subban family name alongside Sutter or Staal, the gold standards for Canadian hockey siblings in the NHL.

"I wouldn't trade their situations for anyone's," Karl Subban said. "Their situation will define who they're going to be. I would ask them, 'Who are you going to be, Jordan? Who are you going to be, Malcolm? Who are you going to be, P.K.?' You know what I mean? I know how difficult it is. You know what they say, eh? The only place you get a free lunch is a mousetrap, and you know what happens to the mouse." He laughed. "You have to pay the price, you use your situation as fuel to light your fire."

Ultimately, though, for as much as the father wants his sons to fulfil their hockey dreams, he has loftier goals for them, just as he does for himself. And those goals mean more than scoring in the NHL.

"The boys may make it in hockey, but they have to make it in life, too," Karl said. "There's more to life than hockey. P.K. could win six more Norris Trophies, and that would make him a great player, but is he a great person? I think he's seeing that now. P.K. went to Haiti after the earthquake there to do work with World Vision. He doesn't miss an opportunity to visit a sick child, he's seeing that [is] as important as hockey is. You have to give back. I want to give back. If people knew how many times others reached out at various times to help us up when we needed it . . . we've tried to teach our boys the importance of giving back."

But retirement is also a time for the simple pleasures in life—driving or taking the train, here, there or anywhere with Maria, to watch one of the boys play a game. Or maybe time spent with Maria, just being grandparents to Legacy, Epic and Honor, the second generation of Canadian-born Subban boys. When Legacy was 27 months, he skated for the first time.

"He cried for 30 minutes," Karl Subban said, laughing. "I told his dad, 'You have to go out on the ice with them.' They love mom and dad being there with them for comfort, if you have the time. It's good family time. . . . Legacy, he just doesn't know what he was born into."

He will find out soon enough.

Karl Subban didn't write the book on parenting or training or coaching or teaching or putting three sons in professional hockey. But that's most certainly the plan.

CHAPTER 9

Fully Completely

At the Lonely End of the Rink or On Stage,
Gord Downie Was Born to Love the Bruins

————

Gord and his younger brother, Pat, talk on the phone.

Every day.

They talk about what is near and dear to them: the Boston Bruins. During the playoffs, contact is even more frequent and intense, upgraded to a combination of phone calls, texts and emails on pretty much a shift-by-shift, running-time basis during every Bruin game. As it should be. When the Bs up their game in the postseason, so too do Gord and Pat.

Gord and his older brother, Mike, will speak to each other about the Bruins—it isn't like they *never* break bread over the Bs; it's not as if it's *forbidden*—but it's not as frequent, not as naturally simpatico as it is with Gord and Pat. You see, Gord and Mike know that sometimes, in the interest of peace and love, it's best to steer clear of certain topics, at least since the infamous Ray Bourque blowup of 2001. That's when Gord left Mike's house in a huff because Mike was mad at Gord for not being happier for the ex-Bruin great winning his first Stanley Cup with the Colorado Avalanche. Gord and Mike are kin, flesh and blood, brothers in arms, but when it comes to the Bs, they sometimes tend not to see things the same way, so they will opt for the path of least resistance.

Now, whether it's Gord talking to Pat, or Gord talking to Mike, or Pat and Mike talking to each other—they're all Bruins at heart, dammit—it should go without saying, but needs to be said for emphasis nonetheless: the Downie brothers are not what you would call casual fans of the spoked B.

Their passion for the black and gold knows no bounds. It is deep and abiding, communal, maybe even tribal.

"It's how we connect," Gord said. "We have deep discussions every day about the Bruins or other stuff that may or may not be important in our lives. So, yeah, mostly about the Bruins."

Could you really expect anything else from Gord and Pat, two boys who, when they were christened, had Harry Sinden, the architect of the Big, Bad Bruins and the team's longtime head coach general manager, as their godfather?

Not every song the Tragically Hip sings is about hockey; it just seems that way sometimes.

The iconic Canadian rock band, which came together when five young guys from Kingston, Ontario, got together in 1983, writes a lot of music and sings a lot of songs that dissect, reflect or chronicle what it is to be Canadian, everything from Jacques Cartier to Tom Thomson to Hugh MacLennan to David Milgaard to Bobcaygeon. Hockey just happens to be one of those things, the organic by-product of, well, being Canadian.

Gord Downie, the front man and lead singer, as has been duly noted, is a diehard Bruin fan, but even before discovering the Bs, he was a goalie in Amherstview, Ontario.

Guitar players Paul Langlois and Robbie Baker are fervent fans of the Montreal Canadiens and Toronto Maple Leafs, respectively. Bass player Gord Sinclair describes himself as a "floater," a Chicago Blackhawk fan in his youth but now quite content to cheer for any team that is contending for the Cup. Drummer Johnny Fay always liked the Philadelphia Flyers.

They all like hockey; they like watching it; they like playing it— or at least, to varying degrees, they did. In the early or middle years of the band's existence, in the 1990s and early 2000s, the boys in the Hip would go to great lengths while touring to organize hockey games. Sometimes it was just ball hockey in an arena parking lot, but often-times it would entail finding ice and equipment to play a real game with the crew.

"I remember when we opened for [Jimmy] Page and [Robert] Plant, we did two legs of America as their opening act," Downie recalled, "and we had this ferocious three-on-three game on Rollerblades in the parking lot of the [Philadelphia] Spectrum right before we went on. I remember our tour manager coming out and yelling at us, 'You're on in eight minutes.' When you're opening for someone, there's no pressure. It was like, 'Okay, backstage, skates off, on stage.' We would do that a lot.

"We had a lot of band and crew games [on ice], too. We'd rent gear, find ice, play a game. Not the band, but some guys would have a few [cocktails] and play. Or some of them hadn't played in a long time. Someone would always get hurt. We haven't done that as much in the last 10 years. To be honest, it feels like the right time to do this [convergence of Hip and hockey] interview would have been 10 years ago. I used to run the band hockey pool—regular season and playoffs. I would write weekly reports, which were meant to demoralize and diffuse enjoyment for others." He laughed.

So many of the venues the Hip plays are hockey arenas. So many of those who have come backstage to meet them after shows are NHL players. The Hip has always been an in-arena music staple at hockey games and in NHL and junior team dressing rooms, too.

"There is that connection," Downie said of the link between band and hockey and vice versa. "We've met a ton of pro hockey players, got to know them, our music plays in their locker rooms. We've always taken pride in that."

Maybe it's become a bit of a cliché, too, this seemingly inexorable link between hockey and the Hip. Although maybe that's a harder case to make when one of the band's own iconic symbols is the official Tragically Hip hockey sweater, available for purchase ($150 Canadian). The Hip jersey has had multiple incarnations in colour and design, everything from traditional Canadian red-and-white with a maple leaf crest to the more recent Boston-style black and gold, emblazoned with Gus the Polar Bear (after the title of a Hip song) on the front.

"The jersey, yeah, it's become kind of the trademark of the band," Downie said. "It always changes [colours and style]. I had nothing to do with [the Boston colours] this time. If we were smart, we'd have one for every [NHL] town . . . on one hand, we're saying, 'Let's exploit this love of hockey,' but we're also saying at times, 'Hey, we're not all about hockey.' I guess we're kind of sucking and blowing on that one."

Edgar Downie, whose parents came to Canada from Belfast, Northern Ireland, was a travelling salesman based out of Oakville, Ontario. He would peddle his wares—cutlery and flatware from Wallace Silversmiths, corsets and women's underthings from Dominion Corset—all over Ontario and Quebec. He was on the road a lot, with his wife, Lorna, back home taking care of the family's three children—eldest daughter Charlyn, son Mike and youngest daughter Paula. Lorna was pregnant with their fourth child when Edgar decided to get off the road and try to settle into a sales job with less travel.

So the Downie family left Oakville, moved to the Kingston area—
Amherstview actually, on the north shore of Lake Ontario, just west
of Kingston. (Between Millhaven and Collins Bay, if you're into cor-
rectional facility geography.) Edgar got his real estate licence and a job
selling new homes in a new subdivision, so it was there in Amherstview
that the family put down roots. Soon after, on February 6, 1964, Gord
was the first of the Downies to be born in Kingston, his brother Pat
arriving four years later.

At the time, Harry Sinden was in the final stages of his playing
career, as a player-coach with Minneapolis and then Oklahoma City in
the old Central Pro Hockey League. In 1966–67, Sinden became head
coach of the NHL Bruins, but whether he was in the minors or the
NHL, he always returned home in the summer to Kingston, where he
and his wife, Eleanor, became part of a group of friends that included
Edgar and Lorna Downie.

Soon after Pat was born—Gord was four at the time—Lorna
wanted to get her two youngest boys christened. A chaplain who lived
across the street from the Downies offered to do it in the family's living
room. Lorna asked Harry and Eleanor Sinden to stand in as the boys'
godparents, an invitation they readily accepted.

"In the years since, I've sort of wondered about all of that, what is
the role of a godparent?" Downie said. "They're meant to be in charge
of the spiritual development. In the definitive and traditional sense,
that's their job, to educate you in the ways of the Bible and the ways of
the spirit. While [the Sindens] didn't do that in the traditional biblical
sense, they mentored us in a way just as meaningful to us. They have
done that in spades. Really, I've always thought that, even though we've
been in rare touch and rarer all the time. But I would see [Harry and
Eleanor] at my brother's wedding and they would ask me about my
kids, remember all their names. It's really been great. Harry has taught
me a lot."

Yes, the ways of the spirit; also, the ways of the Bruins. Sinden went on to be inducted into the Hockey Hall of Fame, an NHL coach and later a general manager, the face and vision of a franchise synonymous with Boston and the Bs.

"The Bruins have become so much more to me than some boyhood fascination," Downie said. "That's why I talk to my brother in Boston every day for more than 30 years, and I imagine we always will. Back in the day, we supported every move Harry made. It wasn't just bias; we honestly believed in what he was doing. . . . He had this sort of blue-collar budget, trying to compete with white-collar teams. He made competitive teams in his own image, that shared his work ethic, and he managed to walk that tightrope with ownership. Everyone has their stories about him, their thoughts on him, but every move he made, even trading Espo [Phil Esposito] was, in our minds, spot on. We really admire Harry in every way. He was a mentor. He taught us more than he will ever know. And I will always be grateful to him."

Downie doesn't really remember the Big, Bad Bruins' first Cup in 1970—he was six at the time—but vividly recalls the Bs beating the New York Rangers for their next Cup in 1972.

"It was May 11 when they beat the Rangers to win the Cup. It was my little brother's [Pat's fourth] birthday, and me and my older brother [Mike] were dancing in the rain, whooping and realizing how quiet it sounded—*whooooo, whooooo*," Downie said.

But Downie didn't just like watching the Bruins; he liked to play hockey, too.

His first year of organized hockey, in novice, he played defence. Wore No. 4, naturally. But when he and his brothers and friends would play road hockey, he always enjoyed playing goal. He was hooked on it and became a goalie in minor hockey, too.

"I really got into the nobility of it, what Jacques Plante would call the noblest position in all of sports," Downie said. "I felt it was the position where you could be the cause, where you could have the biggest effect on the game. I liked everything about it. You can't play goalie harder or faster. I liked that aspect of it. Rarely would a coach say anything to me. Coaches never know what to say to the goalie. 'Go stretch, we'll get to you later.' I liked that independence. It's still the case, really; it's just a very different game than what everyone else is playing."

Downie was good in net. Good enough that the Kingston AA rep team came calling, but with a schedule that included travel as far away as Oshawa, Edgar Downie said no. He hadn't moved his family to Amherstview to put down roots only to go back on the road for kids' hockey. He was too busy trying to sell homes, to make a living.

But it wasn't long before a rink was built in Amherstview, with a team that started in the small-town Ontario double-C loop but quickly moved up to the more competitive B level. Downie loved playing goal. It loved him, too. There was his dream season in major bantam, when Downie's Amherstview team won the provincial B championship.

"It's not like it happened yesterday; it's not like I dined out on it," Downie said, with a laugh. "But we played Picton, Campbellford, East Gwillimbury, Gravenhurst and Exeter to win the champion-ship." Downie seemed to recall that future NHL defenceman David Shaw, coached by his father [Bruce] at the time, was on the Exeter team Amherstview beat, mounting what Downie referred to as a "Hendersonian" comeback from a 5–1 or 7–1 deficit in the eight-point series, which was played to capacity crowds in each of their towns.

But he also learned it can be a cruel game, especially in the cruel-lest of positions.

"It was a game in that dream season, our run to the Cup year, and it was a very special weekend because everyone in my family—I mean everyone—was there to see me play," Downie said. "My grandparents, my parents, all my brothers and sisters—and my sisters didn't even care about hockey, but for some reason, everyone was there on that one weekend.

"We got up on this team 5–0 after two periods and there's a break to flood the ice. We come back out for the third period and they score early in the third. It's 5–1. Then it's 5–2, 5–3, 5–4. I'm thinking, 'This can't be f---ing happening.' Then it's 5–5, they go ahead 6–5. They have scored six goals in less than 10 minutes, and something happened in me. My whole family is there, my grandpa is a huge sports fan, a hero in my life, and I'm like, 'Wow, this isn't really happening.' So I take my stick and start whaling on the crossbar. I didn't hit it seven times, I hit it 14 times until it broke. I was taken out of the game, to the bench—thank you, Coach, do you think it's time for me to come out?—and I went to the dressing room. Our other goalie goes into the game, our team ties it up and we win it 7–6, but no thanks to me. The president of the league comes into the dressing room after and says, 'I've never been more ashamed of a player in my life.' I'm crying and my dad comes in and says, 'Get your stuff, let's go.' It had all turned to shit. I went home and I was in the laundry room, the mud room, crying. My grandfather had to come in to talk me into moving to the kitchen. I think I'm still scarred by that game."

It's funny, but when the Toronto Maple Leafs collapsed in their historic meltdown against the Bruins in Game 7 of the 2013 Stanley Cup playoffs, blowing a 4–1 lead in the final 10 minutes of regulation time and losing in overtime, Downie thought back to his own bantam-level apocalypse. Which one might think would allow him, love of the Bruins aside, to be empathetic or even a little sympathetic towards the Leafs and their plight that night.

"Feel bad for the Leafs?" he mused. "No. It happens. I know. But I really, really didn't feel sorry for them."

No one ever said a Bruin fan is necessarily benevolent.

In some ways, the Bruins have always existed on some higher plane, beyond even hockey, for Downie.

That championship bantam season was his personal zenith as a player. The next year, in minor midget, he played on what he termed a "super-struggling team." He quickly started to lose interest in the game, and when his family moved from Amherstview to Kingston after that season, he knew it was time to quit, in part because he didn't want to start all over again with new teammates and a new team, but also because he simply had so many other interests beyond hockey.

"Living in Kingston, instead of Amherstview, there was so much more to do," he said. "Hockey just fell like a coat off my shoulders. I never looked back."

Downie had always been fascinated by music. He would listen to his sister's 45-rpm records. In Kingston, he got into a band.

"It's all I wanted to do," he said.

Downie met Paul Langlois in Grade 11 and they became best friends. Downie joined a band called the Slinks. Meanwhile, that same year, Robbie Baker and Gord Sinclair were in Grade 13, in a band called the Rodents, but they didn't know Downie and Langlois at that time. Johnny Fay was still in Grade 9 then, unknown to them all.

Between high school and Queen's University, there was for Downie, briefly, a band called the Filters, but that soon gave way to the Tragically Hip forming in 1983. And they've been together ever since.

It's not lost on Downie that his desire to be a goalie, rooted in wanting to be the individual with the greatest cause and effect on the game, was likely the same motivating force for him wanting to be the lead singer and front man of a band.

Downie was thirtysomething before he started playing hockey again. He played in a regular pickup game on Friday afternoons in Toronto, returned to his roots and played goal. He and his buddies would also play shinny when they could—he'd be a skater in that— climbing the fence and sneaking into Toronto's Withrow Park in the

Riverdale area of Toronto on Sunday nights when the lights were on but no one was home.

But he soon got tired of the rigours of even once-a-week Friday afternoon goaltending. "I'd be gobbling Advil until the next Wednesday," he said. Not unlike when he was a teenager, playing hockey just more or less fell off his shoulders like a coat once again.

With 15 albums, more than 150 songs, countless tour dates all over the world, multiple No. 1 hits in Canada, all spanning parts of four decades over 30-plus years, the Hip is a national treasure. Downie and Fay reside in Toronto; Langlois, Baker and Sinclair live back home in Kingston.

The band that plays songs about hockey.

It's a funny thing to be known for, especially since there have been only four Tragically Hip songs with a hockey connection. (On the flip side, that's four more than many popular bands). Well, five if you count Downie's live freestyling lyrical treatment of their old standby "New Orleans Is Sinking," where instead of singing, "I had my hands in the river / My feet back up on the banks / Looked up to the Lord above / And said, 'Hey man, thanks,'" he would sing, "I had my hands in the river / My feet back up on the shore / Looked up to the Lord above / And said, 'Hey man, thanks, it's Bobby Orr.'"

The first Hip hockey reference, and arguably its most famous, was "Fifty-Mission Cap," a single from the 1992 album *Fully Completely*:

> *Bill Barilko disappeared that summer*
> *He was on a fishing trip.*
> *The last goal he ever scored*
> *Won the Leafs the Cup*
> *They didn't win another until 1962,*

The year he was discovered.
I stole this from a hockey card,
I keep tucked up under
My fifty-mission cap, I work it
To look like that.

Downie had been unfamiliar with the legend of Barilko—the Maple Leaf defenceman who scored the game-winning goal in over-time of the 1951 Stanley Cup final, only to disappear the following summer in a plane crash—until he read about it on a hockey card. Around the same time, the Hip were in Washington, D.C. Downie was visiting the Smithsonian National Air and Space Museum, where he saw the cap worn by World War II American pilots, who would "crush" the standard-issue air force cap to make themselves look more experi-enced than they actually were.

"Back in those days, I was into collage or cut-and-paste writ-ing," Downie recollected of his melding of the Barilko story and the fifty-mission cap. "I wrote 'Pigeon Camera' from the same visit (to the Smithsonian) because I learned pigeons with cameras attached to them were used to spy during the war. So I took the fifty-mission cap and the Barilko hockey card ideas, mashed them together.

"I was taken with the idea of a veteran pilot whose ultimate goal is to stay alive, to fly fifty missions, that in itself is its own glory and con-trast that with Barilko's flashing moment—that 'is it better to burn out than to fade away' sort of thing. I wasn't comfortable with doing just a straight narrative of what happened to a hockey player."

It's a song that packs a powerful punch, most notably for Maple Leaf fans and especially when the song was played in Maple Leaf Gardens or at the Air Canada Centre, with a single spotlight shining on Barilko's retired No. 5 banner in the rafters as the Hip launched into the hard-driving but haunting song.

"I remember performing it at Maple Leaf Gardens—it was February 10, my sister's birthday, I don't recall the year [it was 1995] and we played that song with the light on the banner at the Gardens, in the building where the goal was actually scored. I know my dad was there. I think he fell to his knees on that one and he doesn't even play hockey. That was a special moment."

The Hip's second hockey reference in a song was "Fireworks," from the 1998 release *Phantom Power*. Most Hip hockey fans can instinctively sing the words:

If there's a goal that everyone remembers, it was back in ol' 72
We all squeezed the stick and we all pulled the trigger
And all I remember is sitting beside you
You said you didn't give a fuck about hockey
And I never saw someone say that before
You held my hand and we walked home the long way
You were loosening my grip on Bobby Orr.

The curious aspect of "Fireworks" is how the song is so often interpreted as an ode to hockey, notably international hockey, when in fact the song is actually about an opposite ideal ("Isn't it amazing anything's accomplished when you don't let the nation get in your way") and represents that period of time when Downie quit hockey as a teenager.

"Yeah, there actually was a girl who said [she didn't give a f--- about hockey]," Downie said. "On that song, I was thinking about hockey falling off my shoulders like a coat to the floor. Girls do that to you. All of a sudden, you don't want your Saturdays tied up with the sweaty game. And I had never heard a girl swear and I'd never heard anyone say that before, that they don't give a f--- about hockey. It's like there's a whole other world out there, which is hard to fathom sometimes."

Six years after "Fireworks," from 2004's *In Between Evolution*, there was a third foray into hockey, with "Heaven Is a Better Place Today":

> *Here's a glue guy performance god*
> *A makeshift shrine newly lain sod*
> *Hardly even trying gives the nod*
> *I sure hope I'm not the type to dwell*
> *Hope I'm a fast healer fast as hell*
> *Heaven is a better place today because of this*
> *But the world is just not the same*
> *If and when we get into the end zone*
> *Act like you've been there a thousand times before*
> *Don't blame don't say people lose people all the time anymore . . .*
> *It's just not the same because of this*
> *It's not the same.*

This is a song that Hip fans know was written in honour of the late Dan Snyder, but it's also very much for Dany Heatley. Snyder and Heatley were teammates with the NHL's Atlanta Thrashers in the fall of 2003. On September 29 of that year, Snyder was a passenger in Heatley's Ferrari. He suffered head trauma in a high-speed car crash and died six days later. Heatley, who had some broken bones and non-life-threatening injuries, was charged with vehicular homicide in the first and second degree, reckless driving, driving too fast for conditions, failure to maintain his lane and speeding. Heatley had alcohol in his system, but it was below the legal limit in Georgia. He later pleaded guilty to four of the six charges, with vehicular homicide in the first degree and reckless driving being dropped. He was sentenced to three years' probation.

"Like everyone else, I watched all of that pretty closely," Downie said. "Dan Snyder, I didn't know at all. Dany Heatley, I didn't know him too well but knew of him. It seemed to me that Dany Heatley needed a friend after that. It was a tough time for him. We weren't in that vehicle—none of us were. They were in that car together, they were buddies, that's something [Heatley] doesn't need a reminder of how it's going to bother him for the rest of his life. He can pay whatever debt to society that society feels it needs him to pay, and that makes [society] feel better, but that doesn't help him. That's not the real punishment here."

Downie was also greatly influenced by the Snyder family—Dan's father, Graham, and his mother, LuAnn—and how, amid their grief over the tragic loss of their son, they still managed to find forgiveness in their hearts for Heatley.

"They're such a beautiful family," Downie said. "I was struck by their reaction. That's a big part of the song, too. It was like, 'We're going to handle this between us all, all that pain, but what they did outwardly and inwardly, I was so impressed."

Even years after the fact, Downie will still occasionally get text messages from Heatley.

"It may be odd hours—I envision him on a dock somewhere and maybe the Hip has come up on someone's iPod," Downie said. "He'll hit me up with a text, which I love. I love getting those texts from people, love those little friendships with people we've met along the way, who might hear [a Hip song] and decide to reach out."

Without question, though, the most meaningful Hip-to-hockey connection for Downie is "The Lonely End of the Rink," from 2006's *World Container*:

I looked up and you were there
Just sitting there all alone
Holding your fist in the air
Like, if you need me you're on your own

You drove me home through a snowy tomb
I fell asleep in my seat
I had the dream of having no room
You were there just staring at me.
At the lonely end of the rink, you and me
At the lonely end of the rink, you and me
Oh to join the rush
As the season builds
I hear your voice 'cross a frozen lake
A voice from the end of a leaf
Saying, "You won't die of a thousand fakes
Or be beaten by the sweetest of dekes."

This song is deeply personal. It's about his father, Edgar, who was far too busy selling homes to be involved in any regular way with Gord's minor hockey, yet they still managed to connect on some deep level.

"My dad wasn't a hockey dad—he was the furthest thing from it," Downie said. "My dad could never drive me, but it never bothered me. I'd walk to practice with my gear—I kind of liked the independence of that. And my friend Phil, for games, we never had to call him, but his dad would pick me up, it was automatic. They just knew I needed a ride. But I'd be playing in a game, I would look up and my dad would just appear there. He wouldn't be with the other parents, grouped under the heaters. He'd be alone, down in my end, and I would look up at him. He would just go like this [he raises a fist in the air]. I'd make a flurry of saves, I'd look up and he would be gone. He had places to be. He's a very good dad. I was always very hard on myself; he would listen. I never really was told [by him] what I could have done better, but he always listened . . . when he showed up, when he raised that fist in the air, to me, it meant, 'I'm here, I'm with you, maybe no one else in the building is, but I am.' That's what ['The Lonely End of the Rink'] is about."

What Downie will also never forget about that song is playing it for the first time for his older brother, Mike. Gord picked up Mike, and, as is their custom when Gord wants Mike to hear some of his music, they drove to Toronto's Cherry Beach and played it on the car stereo.

"Mike heard the song and he started to cry," Downie said. "We cried together, thinking of the old man. I just admire my dad so much and how he approached things. By design or neglect, he was the perfect hockey dad, and he let me do it. I could learn from him. . . . My son plays basketball, he's a good player, but I got pissed off recently after one of his games. I was a bad basketball dad that day. I should have been more like my dad and said nothing."

Downie's passion for the Boston Bruins is impenetrable. He knows this to be true because, as much as he loves the Bs, he isn't sure sometimes how much he really loves hockey. If that makes any sense.

"In ways I don't even like the game anymore," he said, "I still do like the Bruins.

"There is a normal level of violence that erupts from the game, just from two guys who want something really badly," he added. "That, I understand. But I see some things happening now [line brawls off opening faceoffs] and it strikes me that it's nothing more than organized brutality. It's organized intimidation and it comes from the highest echelon of the game. That dude in baseball [*Boston Globe* baseball writer Peter Gammons, who said the NHL remains a fringe sport in America because of a game-opening Vancouver–Calgary brawl in the 2013–14 season] was right. It is bush."

Many of Downie's fellow Bruin supporters would no doubt strenuously object to those views—"heresy" is a word that might come to mind for some—but Downie the deep thinker has reconciled his love of the Bruins, however big and bad they may be at any given time, with his own feelings.

"I don't like fighting," Downie said. "I just don't. I don't think it does what people [who support it] say it does. It's a tired conversation. I don't think I like the NHL's version of hockey as it is practised at times. Shawn Thornton . . . I know he fights, but he can also play. You should have fourth lines who can play, like the Bruins' fourth line can play. You want to be tough like the Bruins? Fine, then have a fourth line you believe in. And have them play hockey.

"Harry [Sinden] was one of the early [old-school] guys who came around and said fighting had become too much, even for him. What the NHL is facing now is, 'Can you give up two dollars to maybe make five? Would you risk alienating a core group of fans to bring in twice as many [if there was less fighting]?' I think there's a big bait-and-switch going on in the NHL right now. It's like, 'Parents, bring your kids to the game, the kids eat half-price.' It's like taking your kid to a Disney film, and halfway through it, a porn scene breaks out. Bare-knuckle fighting scares kids more than almost anything on earth, at least until they become inured to it. I'm sorry, I don't see it. To me, sports are meant to hint at man's ideal, not just mirror our reality, which is, 'This is how we solve things in life: we fight.' There's got to be a better way."

In the absence of that, Downie will always be able to take from hockey what is forever embedded in his heart and soul—the image of his dad, Edgar, fist in the air, at the lonely end of the rink, to say nothing of brotherly love and the Downie boys' spiritual connection that includes the Bruins.

"We will," Downie said, "always be carrying on Harry's work."

CHAPTER 10

The Road to Redemption

*Sheldon Keefe's Quest to Be His Own Man and
Put His Checkered Past Behind Him*

———

Regrets?

Sheldon Keefe pondered the question and paused before he answered.

Maybe he was taking stock of them, running through the inventory in his mind, with no shortage to choose from.

Or maybe he hesitated because he's not inclined to look back, determined instead to focus on the here and now, or perhaps a future that seems as bright and promising as his past was, at times, dark and disturbing.

But the head coach of the Soo Greyhounds of the Ontario Hockey League also knows that, as hard as he runs on the road to redemption, he can't pretend his past never happened, can't deny who he was or what he did. And he knows how all of it, for better or for worse, has shaped the man he's become and still hopes to be.

"I regret a lot of things," he said. "Everything, really. Just around who I was when I played junior hockey, all of that in general—a lot of incidents, how we acted, how we conducted ourselves . . . the truth is,

I lost years of my life, especially how I lived in isolation, so focused on the task. I lost years of my life, I really did."

He knows who to blame for that.

"Just myself," he said. "Just me."

This is Sheldon Keefe's story. It is not so much a story of what he was or what he did—a lot of which has already been told—as much as it is a story of who he is and what he's doing now in his quest to be a good son, brother, husband, father, friend and member of the hockey community, working hard, one person at a time, to convince the skeptics and doubters he's worthy of their respect and trust.

This is not David Frost's story.

This is not Mike Danton's—or Mike Jefferson's—story, either.

Their stories, to varying degrees, have been told. Countless times. You're likely familiar with some aspect of a sordid hockey saga that exposed not only the dark, seedy side of the game but the worst of those directly involved with all of it for the better part of a decade beginning in the late 1990s.

Frost is a pariah in the game of hockey: a disgraced minor hockey coach turned disgraced agent turned *persona non grata*, who gained the trust and confidence of a small cadre of teenage hockey players, only to control their lives like some sinister Svengali. All the while he side-stepped intense media inquisitions, police investigations and a bevy of criminal charges, leaving him with no criminal record, though he didn't fare nearly so well in the court of public opinion. Frost pleaded guilty to assault of one his players in 1997, but was granted a conditional discharge in open court. In 2001—when a photograph surfaced of a half-naked 13-year-old taped to a chair, who subsequently alleged he was abused by Frost when the photo was taken in the summer of 2000—a year-long police investigation failed to result in any criminal charges after multiple witnesses, including Keefe, alleged the boy was lying about the context of the events leading to the photo. In 2006, Frost was charged with 12 counts of sexual exploitation involving teen-age boys and girls in Deseronto, Ontario, during the 1996–97 hockey season when Frost, then a Junior A coach, lived in a motel room with a few players, one of them Keefe. Eight of the 12 charges were later dropped, and in 2009, Frost stood trial on the remaining four counts of sexual exploitation, an offence punishable by up to 10 years in prison. But he was acquitted on all charges. He was also charged with fraud in 2007 for using a credit card belonging to Mike Danton, but was found not guilty after Danton said Frost had permission to use the card. In 2012, Frost self-published his professed own story in e-book form in *Frosty: The Good, the Bad and the Ugly, Going Up the Ranks to the NHL*, in which he said: "I am not the devil. I took a handful of long-shot kids and beat the odds. In turn, a few of my players made it to the NHL." In the years since then—as of the spring of 2014, anyway—Frost had virtually disappeared from the hockey landscape.

Mike Jefferson—or Mike Sage Danton, to which he legally changed his name in 2002 after a stormy and highly publicized estrangement from his family—pleaded guilty in July 2004 to a failed murder-for-hire conspiracy a few months earlier that the FBI said was to have targeted Danton's agent and former coach, Frost. Danton was playing for the NHL's St. Louis Blues at the time of his arrest. Danton was sentenced to seven and a half years in a U.S. federal prison, but was incarcerated for slightly more than five, transferred to a Canadian prison in the Kingston, Ontario, area in March 2009, was subsequently released and granted full parole in September of the same year. At his parole hearing, Danton maintained the target of his murder conspiracy was not Frost, but his own father, Steve Jefferson, something Frost had also claimed in the wake of Danton's conviction. After being paroled in 2009, Danton attended and played hockey for two years at St. Mary's

University in Halifax. In the years following, up to and including the 2013–14 season, Danton played lower-level European pro hockey in relative obscurity in Austria, Sweden, Slovakia, Kazakhstan, Romania and Poland. In 2011, *Toronto Sun* columnist Steve Simmons wrote a book entitled *The Lost Dream: The Story of Mike Danton, David Frost and a Broken Canadian Family.*

So there you have it, the checkered pasts of David Frost and Mike Danton (né Jefferson) in all their glory, stories the hockey world would just as soon forget.

There's no denying Sheldon's Keefe's story is, in part, inextricably intertwined with Frost and Danton's. It's not possible to tell Keefe's without touching on the others. But of the three, Keefe's story has a fighting chance to become one of hope and promise, not darkness and despair.

Here it is, through his own eyes, then and now (his comments, unless otherwise indicated, are from an interview conducted in March 2014).

Sheldon Keefe was born in 1980, the middle child to father Brian and mother Roberta, hardworking people who settled in Brampton, Ontario, a bedroom community northwest of Toronto. Sheldon's sister, Lisa, was four years older than him; his brother, Adam, four years younger. Brian Keefe was a blue-collar guy who loaded and unloaded trucks at a cold-storage plant, a hard existence he continued to work at into his late 50s. As of 2014, he was still at it. As Sheldon said, "My dad hasn't had many easy days [at work]." His mother worked in child care for many years.

Their existence was unremarkable in the sense that theirs was a normal Canadian family whose lives, more or less, revolved around a love of hockey. When Brian grew up in Prince Edward Island, he never played the game, though he was a good athlete, playing basketball and wrestling. But from a very young age, Sheldon and younger brother Adam were consumed by it.

"Growing up it was hockey, hockey, hockey," Keefe said. "I remember playing on two or three teams in the same winter."

Sheldon played in the local Chinguacousy minor association, one of the better kids, always scoring a lot of goals. Adam was always the best player on his team as he started out.

Sheldon went on to play AAA rep hockey for Chinguacousy in the Ontario Minor Hockey Association, a good player on a poor team—no match, really, for their local rivals, the powerful Brampton team.

One of Keefe's teammates from a young age was Mike Jefferson. The Jeffersons didn't live too far from the Keefes. Brian Keefe and Steve Jefferson became fast friends—drinking buddies, if you will—spending a lot of time at the Jefferson home. Sheldon and Mike also became friends.

"We lived close to each other, my dad and his dad were close. We [Sheldon and Mike] were close at times and grew more [close] because of our fathers," Sheldon said, adding he probably met Jefferson for the first time at age seven or eight. "We were very different people, but we hung out a lot."

Between his major atom and minor peewee years, Sheldon wanted to play summer hockey. The core of the Brampton OMHA team was putting a summer squad together, and Keefe, the best player on the Chinguacousy team, was recruited to be on it. So was a coach by the name of Dave Frost.

As Keefe recalled it, Frost was known in Brampton hockey circles as a hotshot in the coaching ranks, a young guy who was already coaching Junior A with the Brampton Capitals. The Brampton parents who were putting together the summer team asked Frost to be the coach. He accepted.

Keefe doesn't believe Mike Jefferson was on that first summer team, but when the team was put together again the following summer, Keefe and Jefferson were teammates. The team was again coached by Frost. Keefe's recollection is that even though Frost, at first, only coached him on two summer teams and was still busy coaching the Brampton Junior A team, he started showing up at Keefe's Chinguacousy games and "being around a lot more."

In their major peewee year, the Brampton parents who put together the summer team decided they wanted to move, as a group, to the Greater Toronto Hockey League. Again, they asked Frost if he would be the coach. And again, Keefe and Jefferson were recruited to join them. They all joined the Toronto Young Nationals major peewee team in the GTHL. Frost, who was still coaching Junior A at the time, was the coach.

"We played like a bunch of nobodies," Keefe said. "The Toronto Red Wings were the hot ticket."

Joe Goodenow, the son of then NHL Players' Association executive director Bob Goodenow, was one of the big names on the Red Wings. When the major peewee season ended, the best players on the Red Wings, including Goodenow, and the best players on the Nats, including Keefe, Jefferson and another Brampton friend, defenceman Shawn Cation, joined forces on the minor bantam Nats team, which was coached by Frost.

In minor bantam and major bantam, the Nats were a powerhouse team, winning the all-Ontario bantam championship. David Frost and Bob Goodenow—who was one of the two most powerful men in professional hockey at the time—developed a relationship.

Frost's championship Nats were a much greater team than the sum of its parts. Only one player off the bantam Nats, Lance Galbraith, was taken in the first three rounds of the OHL draft—in the third round, to Ottawa. At the time, 16-year-olds could only play in the OHL if they were drafted in the first three rounds, so Galbraith was the only team member going directly to the OHL.

Keefe was a small and physically underdeveloped player in bantam—a good player, but no longer dominant, though Bob Goodenow gave him a nickname that would stick: "The Professor," reflecting his heady ways as a player and someone who always seemed to be processing things in his mind. Jefferson was small but strong and aggressive, a relentless worker. Neither, though, was good enough to be drafted into the OHL at 16.

It was after the fact, when Frost's troubles first came to light, that newspaper stories were published, reporting Frost verbally abused and physically intimidated his Young Nats players to get the most out of them. If Keefe had any issues with Frost or his abusive ways in minor hockey, he didn't let on, citing a burgeoning and largely positive relationship between Frost and the boys from Brampton . . . at that time, anyway.

"We all looked up to him," Keefe said of Frost. "He was a young guy, a passionate coach, much different than we were used to. He was a [Junior A] coach. We all started to attend or work at his hockey school in the summer. There was a lot more interaction away from hockey. The relationship became more involved to the point where I looked at him as the guy who knew what he was doing, who would point us in the right direction and tell us what we should be doing."

And Frost didn't just forge a relationship with his players. He befriended their parents, too.

"Steve Jefferson, initially, really took to Dave," Keefe said. "Dave spent a lot of time at the Jeffersons'. My dad spent a lot of time there, too. It was a hangout for them. They would drink there. We thought the relationship was good. Both my family and the Jefferson family recognized and looked at it as a positive for our hockey [at the time]. We were happy."

For all the talk of verbal and possibly physical abuse with
the Nats, it was ironic that Frost ran afoul of the GTHL for something
relatively innocuous: forging a parent's signature on a form. He was
ultimately suspended and lost his ability to coach sanctioned minor or
junior hockey. But that didn't stop him.

There was an "outlaw" Junior A league in Ontario. Frost, along with the
Abrams brothers, Marty and Kevin, got involved with a team, the infamous Quinte Hawks, based in Deseronto, Ontario, just east of Belleville.

The Abrams brothers assembled a big, strong team, not just taking
some core players from the Nats—Keefe, Jefferson and Cation—but
also recruiting talented players from all over Ontario. Ryan Barnes,
from Dunnville, Ontario, joined the group, as did big defenceman
John Erskine, the future NHLer who had been playing minor hockey
in Ajax, Ontario. In addition to Keefe, Jefferson and Cation, Frost
placed two older players he knew from junior A, Larry Barron and
Darryl Tiveron, in Quinte.

Frost didn't have any official role with Quinte to start the season,
other than to supply his five players to the Abrams brothers. Greg Royce
was the head coach. Jefferson and Keefe were actually cut in training
camp, which prompted Frost to also pull Cation, Barron and Tiveron
out of Quinte. All five, briefly, went home to Brampton and played
for Lindsay Hofford's Bramalea Blues Junior A team in the Ontario
Provincial Junior Hockey League. But it wasn't going well for them in
Bramalea, and it wasn't going well for Quinte, either. With the Hawks
off to a slow start, the five returned to Quinte along with Frost, who at
that point was named an assistant coach to Royce. But the truth was,
Frost was effectively calling all the shots.

From a purely hockey perspective, Quinte was a good move for
Keefe and Jefferson. Keefe, a skilled, cerebral player, scored 21 goals
and 44 points in 44 games. Jefferson racked up 281 penalty minutes to
go with 28 points in 35 games.

The Hawks under Frost were a huge, physically intimidating team.

"It was a monster team," said Keefe, who estimated he played that season at 145 pounds. "So many of the 16-year-olds were huge, so much bigger than me."

Barnes was over 6 feet tall and had 245 penalty minutes; Erskine was six foot four and collected 241 PIM.

The Hawks finished the season with a 34–13–3 record, and more than half the team—12 players, to be exact—got drafted into the OHL (one scout called it the most heavily scouted Junior A team ever). Erskine went No. 2 overall to the London Knights; Barnes 40th to Sudbury; Jefferson 85th to Sarnia; Keefe 101st to Plymouth; Cation 143rd to Oshawa.

But no one remembers the hockey side of things in Quinte; it was the off-ice issues that have been well documented and chronicled by major media outlets, including the CBC's *The Fifth Estate*, amongst others. The stories are now almost too well known to many Canadians.

In a Quinte playoff game in April 1997, Frost punched Tiveron in the face on the bench. It was witnessed by off-duty police officers. Frost was subsequently arrested, charged and suspended. He would later plead guilty but receive a conditional discharge.

But the biggest headlines to emerge from the Quinte year were the salacious ones, involving sex and drinking and partying. Frost lived in a motel room, the infamous two-bedroom suite, Room 22 at the Bayview Inn, with three of his players—Barron (who was then 20), 21-year-old Tiveron and 16-year-old Keefe. Jefferson and Cation, also both 16, were reported to be regular visitors, as were teenage girls from the town. What went on there later led to Frost being charged with 12 counts of sexual exploitation involving teenage boys and girls, none of which ever resulted in a conviction. Not that the lack of a guilty verdict made the conduct acceptable, because it wasn't.

How accurate, Keefe was asked, were the published reports of the goings on in Room 22?

"Pretty accurate," he said, "in the sense that it was accurate but exaggerated. The thing that was exaggerated was that it was portrayed as nonstop, Monday-to-Sunday partying. It was the opposite, actually. We had one day a week when guys would get together and party. If you think we were up to all hours of the night on a regular basis, you don't know David Frost very well. It was very regimented."

It was, Keefe added, also totally inappropriate.

"Frost was our adult supervision and also the coach of our team," Keefe said, "and he was present for some of these parties. Clearly, now that I'm a coach myself, I'm aware of how totally unacceptable that is."

Through that entire season in Deseronto, Keefe believed he maintained a solid relationship with his family, who would regularly make the drive from Brampton to see his games.

"They were there quite a bit," Keefe said. "I thought the relationship was good. But we were away from home at age 16. Like a lot of kids, you become more independent. The influence of Frost was much greater than it had been. We started to feel less and less reliant on our parents. I don't recall any friction with my parents, but looking back on it now, that was probably the beginning of something. I never really [lived at home] after that."

If anything, Frost's influence over Keefe, Jefferson and Cation only gained momentum after the 1996–97 season in Quinte, though the members of what some had taken to calling the "Quinte cult" were going their separate ways. Briefly, anyway.

Barnes, whose association with Frost at that time was limited to one season in Quinte, went off to the Sudbury Wolves. Jefferson joined the Sarnia Sting. But Keefe, drafted by Plymouth, and Cation, drafted by Oshawa, had other ideas. They were leaning towards the NCAA route.

"Plymouth pursued me, they were trying to recruit me as a 17-year-old, and the decision was made to not go," Keefe said. "Frost was calling the shots, telling us what he thought we should do. I was really small, 145 pounds. I wasn't the same type of player as Jefferson—he was rugged, totally fearless. I had a lot of apprehension I couldn't play there. I remember feeling very insecure about my ability to play in the OHL. I wasn't ready. Frost saw that and I agreed."

Frost placed Keefe and Cation with the Caledon Canadians Junior A team coached by Greg Ireland, who Keefe said was an acquaintance of Frost's—they had coached against each other in Junior A. Keefe started to become much closer friends with Cation, whom he first got to know in those summer hockey days back in Brampton. But Cation's parents and Shawn—not back then, anyway—weren't hanging with the Jeffersons, Keefes and Frost at Jefferson's house.

So Keefe and Cation moved back home, but for Keefe, it was only home in the figurative sense.

"I started to spend a lot of time with [Frost] and his wife, Bridget, at their house in Brampton," Keefe said of life during the 1997–98 season. "I was spending nights there; I was spending less and less time at home. [Frost] didn't discourage it. We'd hang out there, it was a place to go, close to my high school. I thought it was cool. He was a young, successful guy who was fun to be around and Bridget was welcoming and took care of meals and things. Having been away from home at 16, I guess I liked the independence [of hanging at Frost's house]. I thought my family life was still pretty good."

Keefe and Cation were making major strides on the ice with Caledon. Cation played well enough—15 goals, 36 points and 231 PIM in 46 games—to earn a scholarship the next season to Northern Michigan University. Keefe was planning on going the same route—until he started getting bigger and stronger in his 17-year-old season. He had a monster year, scoring 41 goals and 81 points with 117 PIM in 43 games.

"I started to feel more comfortable with the idea of playing in the OHL," Keefe said. "It was Frost's suggestion I play [major junior]. I didn't question that. I felt better about myself as a player."

That was merely the precursor to getting all the boys in the band back together again.

With a keen eye for talent and a bright hockey mind, Mike Futa is considered an NHL general manager in waiting. In 2014, he was co-director of amateur scouting with the Los Angeles Kings, but he was interviewed for GM jobs around the league during the 2013–14 season, subsequently being promoted by the Kings to be vice-president of hockey operations and director of player personnel.

In 1997–98, though, he was a 26-year-old assistant coach of the first-year St. Michael's Majors, the OHL club affiliated with the prestigious Toronto Catholic high school that was returning to this level of junior hockey for the first time since 1962. Futa therefore had a ringside view of the master manipulator Frost, who was moving his boys around hockey like pawns on a chessboard.

In his rookie OHL season, while Keefe and Cation were playing in Caledon, Jefferson had a falling out with his team in Sarnia. So Frost helped to orchestrate a midseason trade to the Majors.

"I knew Frost from when he coached the Nats," Futa said. "And that team in Quinte was maybe the most heavily scouted Tier II team ever. We'd all heard the stories about Frost and his boys, but we figured Jefferson could help us."

So the trade was made. Jefferson broke his leg after 18 games with the Majors and didn't play the rest of the season.

"He missed the last two months," Futa said, "but there were no issues. He'd sit at all the home games in the stands and watch with Frost."

When that 1997–98 season ended—the Majors finished with a terrible 15–42–9 record—Frost approached the Majors' brass (owner Reg Quinn, former NHL GM Gerry Meehan, head coach Mark Napier and assistant coach Futa) with a proposition.

"Frost said to me, 'If you're prepared to give up some assets, you can get Sheldon Keefe's rights from Plymouth,'" Futa recalled. "He told me [Keefe and Jefferson] wanted to play together."

The Majors called Plymouth GM Peter DeBoer, offered a third-round pick for Keefe's rights and made the deal.

"I told [Frost] we made the trade and asked if we needed to talk to Keefe [about reporting], and he was like, 'Oh, no, he's out in the parking lot.' He wasn't actually, but it wasn't like there was any issue there. Frost knew Sheldon was coming."

At the start of that 1998–99 season, Jefferson was the Majors' top centre, while Keefe was the team's top right winger. The Majors got off to a slow start. Head coach Napier was replaced by Futa, a now 27-year-old rookie head coach.

"Their chemistry was unbelievable," Futa said. "Jefferson was just a beast on draws. Sheldon was the best player in the league. We sucked, but they were unbelievable."

Frost the puppet master was just getting warmed up, though.

Cation was in his freshman season at Northern Michigan, but didn't like it there. He wanted to come home. Frost told the Majors to get his rights from Oshawa. They did. Cation was reunited with Keefe and Jefferson. Then Frost told Futa that Ryan Barnes in Sudbury was available. The Majors traded for him, too, having the big, tough winger ride shotgun on a line with Keefe and Jefferson. Barnes had already been drafted into the NHL after his rookie OHL season, going 55th overall in the second round to Detroit in the 1998 draft.

The four Quinte Hawks were back together on the ice, but Frost was pulling the strings off it, too.

Futa was alternately awestruck and unnerved by what he was witnessing each and every day.

"They were the hardest-working hockey players I'd ever seen, and I had no control over them," Futa said. "Sheldon's tank would never empty. He was a machine. Jefferson was relentless. All four were inseparable on and off the ice. They were driven like I've never seen anyone driven in hockey. No one on the team wanted to do practice drills against them because it was game conditions, it was stick in your face. I would look at some of the really talented players on our team and I would think, 'If only some of these guys had just a little bit [of the drive] these four guys had.' They wanted to be players so badly. Nobody wanted it as badly as they did. I feel guilty even complimenting them, because I know where it was coming from, but their drive was unbelievable."

Futa would recall that when NHL Central Scouting was coming in to take players' official height and weight measurements, Keefe and Jefferson were rigging their shoes with lifts to gain an extra half-inch and loading up on peanut butter sandwiches to pack on the pounds before a weigh-in. It was excessive, it was crazy, but this was their life.

"All of them, including me, were just chess pieces being moved around the board," Futa said. Frost controlled everything for the four players, on and off the ice.

Futa said he would put all four on the power play, and every move the players made on the ice was scripted by Frost, not the coach. The players would look up during the game to get hand signals from Frost. They had their own faceoff alignments and set plays off the draw. As a young first-time head coach, Futa was overwhelmed. He had no control.

During one game at Maple Leaf Gardens, Futa benched Jefferson because Jefferson was only interested in fighting Kingston opponent Sean Avery, a hated foe. During a stoppage in play, Jefferson left the bench without a word and skated the length of the ice to the Zamboni door at the north end of the rink and went to the dressing room to take off his equipment.

"He'd obviously gotten his signal from up top," Futa said.

If any opponent dared lay a hand on Keefe, Barnes would come flying in, gloves off, to Keefe's defence.

They were a four-man team within a team. They might occasionally interact with another teammate or two, but it was cursory and superficial.

Frost would regularly hound Futa with suggestions or orders on how he should be coaching. In those pre–cell phone days, Futa recalled he had a pager set to vibrate. It would be sitting on his desk, where it would faithfully go off between periods of games.

"The number would come up and I'd recognize it [as Frost's]," Futa said. "It would be vibrating, flying across my desk like a little Zamboni. I think that number is burned into my memory still, like that movie: [He whispers] 'Check the children.' If [Frost] didn't get his message [to the boys] through me, he'd try to get it to them some other way. They were checking phone messages between periods. It was crazy."

It only got worse, especially after a game one night at the Hershey Centre in Mississauga. The power play hadn't gone well that night. When the game was over, the four players walked down the hall past Futa in their full equipment, minus their skates, their hockey bags slung over their shoulders.

"I said, 'Where the f--- are you guys going?' and they just kept walking," Futa said. "Frost had ordered to them a nearby arena to work on the power play after the game. I can laugh about it now, because the fifth guy on the power play—it was either Gerald Moriarity or Mark Popovic—said to me, 'Coach, do I have to go with [the four of] them?' That was one of the final straws for me."

Futa said none of Frost's boys was causing any problems away from the rink—they were good students, there were no problems with carousing or drinking—but he also wasn't aware of the full scope of what was going on.

Initially, the players were living close to St. Mike's in the apartment of an acquaintance of Frost: goaltending-school guru and instructor Jon Elkin. But Elkin, a single guy who worked a lot, wasn't around that much, so this largely unsupervised "billeting" wasn't working. In the span of less than a month, it was decided they would go "home." Except "home" in this case was back to Frost's house in Brampton.

All four spent more time there than at their actual homes. Barnes was from out of town, the only non-Brampton boy of the group, but according to Keefe, Barnes initially liked being part of the so-called "Quinte cult," a term Keefe didn't like or use then and finds even more cringeworthy now. Keefe maintained he still had a functioning family life, but cracks were starting to develop.

"My dad would get upset he didn't have much say with me anymore," Keefe said. "But my family was still supportive of me. They were still coming to watch my games. They were still giving me money. My whole time I played in the OHL, my parents were at games, I'd still go home, visit, eat dinner there."

Futa and the Majors had seen enough.

"It was a game where Barnes had taken what seemed like his 25th instigator penalty, and we had lost again," Futa said. "Other kids on the team and their parents were getting upset. You could feel it all coming apart at the seams. It was out of control."

St. Mike's decided to trade the four of them, but Frost wouldn't permit them to be broken up. It had to be a four-player package deal. Futa knew there was no way the Majors would get equal value for what they were giving up in terms of the quartet's actual hockey-playing ability, and he knew Frost would have to broker the deal with some other OHL team. Keefe had an incredible 37 goals and 74 points in only 38 games; Jefferson had 18 goals, 40 points and 116 PIM in 27 games; Cation had 9 goals, 30 points and 129 PIM in 36 games; Barnes had 11 goals, 25 points and a whopping 215 PIM in 31 games, including 24 fighting majors.

"We had made Jefferson our captain," Futa said. "It was entirely work ethic–driven. No one worked as hard as he did. Sheldon was the best player in the league going away, the top scorer in the league on a last-place team. Sheldon was a warrior, an absolute warrior. His knowledge of the game was incredible. The Professor, that's what he was called. I thought you could at times see him thinking through all of this. He knew this wasn't right."

At the OHL trade deadline in January 1999, St. Mike's traded all four to Barrie, getting back five players. It was not a good hockey trade for the Majors, but Futa was just relieved to be free of the lot of them. Mind you, even now, Futa still has a tough time reconciling how they could be so good and yet so bad; fiercely dedicated to improving as hockey players, but such terrible teammates and people.

"I can't say I disagree with any of that," Keefe said, looking back on those days. "It was crazy at times. I think anyone who would know me knew me as the guy who would speak up and disagree [with Frost] on something. I would say, 'This is stupid.' As I got older, I got more wits, became a little more independent. A lot of the things we were being advised to do by Frost just didn't make sense. The isolation [from our teammates], that was the biggest thing. He just didn't want us around other players that he perceived as bad influences.

"I also didn't like the signals from the stands. That was very stupid. He had certain signals for Jefferson and certain signals for me. Jefferson would follow them to a T. My signals were different, really basic—skate more, move your feet, shoot more. Quite frankly, I wouldn't look up. We would feud a lot because I wouldn't follow the signals. . . . I rebelled often, but I always stayed within the group."

Barrie brought more of the same. If anything, it escalated to even crazier levels than at St. Mike's.

Bert Templeton was the GM/coach who made the trade for Frost's boys. The feeling was Templeton, a legendary OHL hard-ass, a no-nonsense, tough-guy coach and manager, would tame the group. He tried. He battled with all four and with Frost as well. But when the Colts, with the second-best regular-season record in the OHL, lost to Oshawa in a seven-game, second-round playoff series, Templeton was fired, replaced as GM/coach by Bill Stewart.

Keefe, though, was rewarded for his productivity in his first OHL season by being chosen by the Tampa Bay Lightning in the second round of the 1999 NHL draft.

What unfolded in Barrie the next season, 1999–2000, is legendary—if by "legendary" you mean a gong show of epic proportions. It might be the single craziest season played in any league. Ever. There should be a book devoted entirely to the sheer nuttiness (not all of it, by any means, Frost-related) that transpired that season with the Colts, who on the face of it had a spectacular year, winning the OHL championship and playing in the Memorial Cup.

Early in the season, Cation was suspended 15 games by the OHL for his part in a brawl with Oshawa. In the same game against Oshawa, Ryan Barnes was suspended for 25 games for swinging his stick and breaking the fingers of Generals assistant coach Curtis Hodgins—who sued Barnes, the Colts and the OHL and was awarded damages of more than $20,000. Stewart was stripped of his GM duties by the league after he stowed a Ukrainian player, who didn't have the proper paperwork to get into the United States, in the equipment compartment under the bus to cross the border for a game in Erie, Pennsylvania. Colt defenceman Ryan O'Keefe was suspended for 24 playoff games for a slew-foot that fractured the ankle of an opposing player. The list could go on and on . . .

But it was also the year in which Frost's group of four became three. Barnes decided he'd had enough. His NHL team, the Detroit Red Wings, was obviously giving him guidance, but he'd grown weary of all that went with being in the so-called cult. Still playing on the same line as Keefe and Jefferson, for a time they wouldn't pass him the puck. They wouldn't talk to him. He was an outcast in their group, but was welcomed back into the Colts' team fold, where the rest of the players hated Keefe, Jefferson and Cation.

"I think [Barnes] got outside pressure rather than some awakening," Keefe said, looking back on it now. "Whether it was his family or the Red Wings, he said, 'This isn't working for me.' . . . Whatever it was, he made a good decision."

Barnes, who went on to play only two NHL games but still had a seven-year pro career, is a player agent in Ontario now.

"I haven't ever really talked [publicly] about those days, and it's probably best not to say anything now," said Barnes, who'll always be known as last into the "cult" and the first out.

Keefe said being hated by their teammates was eating him up, but he still refused to leave the group. Frost had this incredible hold over him and the others, though Keefe said his relationship with his family was still functional in his final year of junior.

"As a young kid, I don't remember thinking any other way," Keefe recollected. "We were having success, it was going well. But it was intense, it was hard, it was draining. Our teammates hated us; we hated them. There was so much friction. We thought we were doing things the right way. No one worked harder than us. We would do full workouts after the game. Frost made us. We couldn't say no—we were under his control. How does that happen? I don't have an answer. I don't know other than we respected what he was saying. I don't know the exact definition of a cult, but you could certainly say that about us. It was a following, and he had that influence on us to follow him, to isolate us from the rest of the team."

The problem, really, was that in spite of what was an untenable situation, at odds with everything the team game of hockey is supposed to be about, Frost's boys were individually having incredible success and their team was on the way to winning a league championship. Against all odds.

The old four-man power play from St. Mike's was a good example of that.

"In Barrie, we also ran a four-man scheme," Keefe said. "Barnes in front of the net, Jefferson down low, Cation on the point, me on the half-wall; the fifth guy might as well not have even been there because he wasn't part of it. We had the No. 1 power play in the league, or close to it, playing four on four."

Keefe shook his head at the memory of it, seemingly in equal parts amazement and disgust.

"I never knew this until after the fact, but [Bill Stewart] told the fifth guy, the other defenceman playing with us on the power play, that when we set up offensively, he was to skate back down into his own end and stand by the goalie. [Stewart] just wanted to show everyone in the rink how ridiculous it was that we weren't including him as part of the power play," Keefe added. "I didn't even know that had happened until after the game. I was so focused on the four-man group, it was irrelevant to me who that fifth guy was. I didn't even know he was missing. It's crazy, and it's even crazier we succeeded. It goes against everything. None of it makes any sense."

The totally dysfunctional Colts were a train wreck, albeit a winning train wreck. Stewart, who possessed a tremendous hockey mind, could be a crazy cowboy of a coach at times. The whole team behaved like idiots at the 2000 Memorial Cup, both on and off the ice. The organization had a season-long running battle with the league and OHL commissioner Dave Branch, who had suspended multiple Colt players and Stewart. The team walked out en masse from the Memorial

Cup banquet when Branch started to speak. They pulled all sorts of stunts on the ice, they were constantly in the news, ultimately losing in the Cup final to Rimouski. And while Jefferson was running his mouth nonstop at the Memorial Cup, garnering headlines for verbal attacks on Brad Richards and Ramzi Abid, amongst others, Keefe did something on the first day of the tourney that would haunt him.

Contrary to what has often been reported, Keefe did not refuse to shake Branch's hand when he was given the OHL championship trophy. He shook hands with the commissioner on that occasion before accepting the trophy. It was during the opening ceremonies of the Memorial Cup that Keefe went down the line of dignitaries, shaking hands, and refused to do so with Branch. It was on national television. It would be convenient to blame this on Frost or the "cult," but as Keefe recalled it, none of that came into play in his mind.

"It was a totally spur-of-the-moment thing by me, just me," Keefe said. "I made a split-second decision, a really stupid decision."

The Colts were a fractured, dysfunctional group, but the common bond they shared at the time, from the coach on down, was an anti-league, anti-Branch sentiment.

"One of the things our whole team had sort of rallied around was an 'us versus the world' mentality," Keefe added. "People don't realize this, but we had a big sign in our dressing room that season that said, F--- THE LEAGUE. We had so many run-ins with the league, so many guys suspended. People have always tried to tie me not shaking hands with Branch as part of the Frost influence, but with the mindset our whole organization had, it was nothing more than a spur-of-the-moment decision by me. It was foolish."

Looking back, the only word Keefe can come up with to describe that final junior season is "mind-boggling."

"We won the OHL, but no one liked us," he said. "We were a fragmented hockey team, and looking back on that now, I hate it, I hate it,

I hate it. It makes me really wonder [what we were thinking]. It also makes me have a lot of respect for Bill Stewart. To coach, and win, in that environment—that was an incredible job by him."

In the six-year, mostly mediocre, professional hockey career of Sheldon Keefe, there was never any time when David Frost wasn't a factor in his life. But the irony is, as pro hockey served to put some physical distance—as well as a smaller but steadily increasing measure of emotional detachment—between him and Frost, their relationship caused Keefe more personal aggravation than even during the most tumultuous times in junior hockey.

It's almost as if his bill came due for all that success in junior.

Keefe never played more than 49 NHL games in any of his three seasons with Tampa, playing parts of each year in the minors. He had a modest 12 goals and 24 points with 78 PIM in 125 career NHL regular-season games.

In the summer of 2002, Frost became a player agent certified by the NHL Players' Association, but even before that, from the time Keefe showed up in Tampa in the fall of 2000, Frost was "representing" Keefe. How Frost was certified by the NHLPA, given his track record and history, was the subject of much conjecture at the time, but most everyone assumed it was owing to his closeness with Bob Goodenow, executive director of the association. (In December 2005, when Frost's toxicity in the hockey community was high—and also, perhaps not coincidentally, after Goodenow had stepped down as executive director that summer—Frost "resigned" as an agent.)

Frost would regularly harass Lightning management, complaining about how the diminutive free-agent signee Marty St. Louis was playing more than Keefe for coach John Tortorella. In his book on Danton and Frost, Steve Simmons quoted Tampa GM Jay Feaster at length, saying how most everyone in the organization liked Keefe as a person, but the constant haranguing they got from Frost, and Keefe's reluctance to accept more development time in the minors, ultimately was the player's undoing in Tampa. The same sort of situation was playing itself out in New Jersey with the Devils, who had selected Jefferson 135th overall in the 2000 NHL draft, the summer after the Colts' OHL championship. Cation, by the way, never played pro hockey, heading off to a Canadian university career at St. Thomas University in the fall of 2000.

When Keefe's three-year entry-level NHL contract with Tampa expired, the Lightning retained his rights by making him a qualifying offer. He signed a one-year contract, but was put on waivers before the regular season began. Keefe was claimed by the New York Rangers, spent a month there, but never played in a game before being put on waivers again and being reclaimed by Tampa. The Lightning sent him to Hershey of the AHL, where he played the 2003–04 season. He "loved" it in Hershey, had a good season with the Bears, and with each passing year, Frost's pervasive influence slowly receded.

"It was extensive still; we spent time together in the summer," Keefe said, noting he and Frost bought real estate together (Frost owned a house and Keefe a cottage on a piece of property in Battersea, near Kingston). "But he was not at my games—some, but not many—and we spent more time talking by phone before or after games than seeing each other. It was a habit, but as I got older in pro, it started to become less. We talked less, he was involved less. I made more decisions on my own."

The same, Keefe said, went for his relationship with Danton. They would still spend time together in the off-season, talk or text occasionally during the season, but with each passing year it was getting to be less and less.

Keefe felt like he was maturing, planting the first seeds of becoming his own man, but he noted it came with a price.

"Not having any tangible relationships [in hockey] outside of

[Frost's] group, that really wore on me," Keefe said. "So anyone who played with me from 2002 to 2005, I think, would tell you I was a good teammate. I know I was a good teammate then; I was starting to become the person I wanted to be. Admittedly, though, I wasn't nearly as committed [as a player]. I wasn't driven like I was before. I was maybe putting myself a little too far out there as the friendly, team-oriented guy. I lost my focus a little bit. That definitely hurt me as a player, but I felt better about myself."

In the summer of 2004, after his "happy" season in Hershey, Keefe signed a one-year NHL contract with the Phoenix Coyotes. But the NHL lockout wiped out that entire season. Keefe went to play for the Utah Grizzlies of the AHL during the lockout, but four games in, he totally blew out his knee—MCL, ACL, the whole nine yards. He didn't know it at the time, but it was the end of his professional hockey career.

Nothing that happened on the ice in Keefe's six years as a pro was as life-altering as what occurred off it during that time, and beyond.

In 2001, the Frost story got national treatment when the photograph of Mike Jefferson's 13-year-old brother Tom, wearing only underwear and taped to a chair, surfaced and got into the hands of the Children's Aid Society. Frost and those who were in attendance, including Keefe, maintained it wasn't as it appeared, but Tom Jefferson said he was physically abused; among the allegations, he said Frost pointed a pellet gun at him. A year-long police investigation resulted in no charges being laid, but it still had a big impact on Keefe's personal life.

Up to that point, unlike Mike Jefferson with his family, Keefe said he had always managed to maintain a decent relationship with his parents, Brian and Roberta, but the sordid details and negative publicity arising out of the Tom Jefferson–Dave Frost police investigation, taken at face value, changed everything.

"My parents weren't trusting or listening to what I was telling them," Keefe said. "I told them, 'Don't overreact,' but they didn't side with me. They said, 'Is that what was going on all those years [with Frost]?' What was being investigated [by police] and what my parents were saying, it wasn't accurate. Looking back now, I don't blame my parents for feeling that way, because there was such miscommunication between us. But I was very, very angry. This wasn't just about Frost; I was part of the investigation and it was wrong. I had to go through a lot of crap."

Keefe didn't talk to his parents for the better of part of two years, during which he was totally estranged from them. But one day in the fall of 2004, after he blew out his knee in Utah, he picked up the telephone and called home.

"I was [emotionally] hurt [by the estrangement], I was nursing my injured knee, but my head was very clear," he said. "I called my mom and we cleared the air."

And he knows why he did, too.

"When I was younger [in junior], even going through that period where I didn't feel like I needed anyone, I was successful," Keefe said. "I had my [Frost] friends, I still had my family and I felt independent, even if I wasn't truly independent. But as I got older, my hockey was going downhill, I got a girlfriend, I had a lot more time to think about things, and I realized I just wanted to have a really good relationship with my family. That was very clear to me."

Keefe also, in the spring and summer of 2004, had to contend with the fallout from Danton's criminal conviction for what the FBI said was a failed to plot to have Frost killed in St. Louis, where Danton had been traded from the Devils.

"I didn't have much information on any of that, and what information I did have didn't make any sense to me," Keefe said of Danton's arrest and subsequent imprisonment. But that was also the beginning of the end of Keefe's relationship with Danton.

Still, through all of this, Frost continued to be part of Keefe's life, even after Keefe reconciled with Brian and Roberta. Maybe not like he was in earlier years, but Frost was a still a presence.

In 2003, at the behest of Kevin Abrams (who was part of the Quinte Hawks' ownership group in 1997), Keefe used $175,000 of his NHL money to become the sole owner of the Pembroke Lumber Kings Junior A franchise in the Ottawa Valley. Keefe said the plan was for him to own it, but while he was still an active pro player, Abrams would run it. And that's how things started. But Keefe came back to Pembroke after his knee surgery in 2004–05 and rehabbed there. In January, he started to become more actively involved in the operation of the team, helping Abrams, even jumping behind the bench for games. Frost was, with Keefe's blessing, also involved with the team as sort of an unofficial assistant coach. He wasn't on the ice for practices or on the bench for games, but he was in the stands and around the team a lot.

With the NHL lockout over and his knee rehabbed, Keefe's one-year contract with the Coyotes had rolled over to the 2005–06 season. He was hoping for it to be a big year on two fronts. One, a return to the NHL for himself. Two, Abrams had assembled a Pembroke team that was ranked as one of the top Junior A clubs in the country and was hosting the Fred Page Cup, which was the Eastern Canadian championship and only one step removed from the Royal Bank Cup national championship tournament.

Keefe went to the Coyotes' camp, but it was disastrous. He had trained all summer in preparation, but he didn't do a thorough job with his knee rehab. He was able to get through the skating portions of camp, but couldn't walk at the end of each day. The Coyotes assigned him to the minors before he had even played a preseason game. He refused to report to the minors, asked for a trade, raised the possibility of being assigned to Hershey, but he knew the end was at hand. His knee was messed up; his dedication to getting it back to where it needed to be wasn't there, so he didn't actually play a game anywhere in 2005–06, and then made it official in the summer. He was retiring as a hockey player.

"When it came to a decision of still trying to play [pro] or going back to Pembroke to run the team, it was easy for me, just like that," Keefe said, snapping his fingers. "I knew what I wanted to do [with his life]."

Keefe made that important decision after consulting with Frost and Abrams. Frost told Keefe he supported Sheldon's decision but would rather Keefe continue to play, but Keefe was adamant. He was quitting. Meanwhile, the Lumber Kings' 2005–06 season had gone down the tubes. Having Frost around the team hadn't gone well. Because of his reputation, his presence was attracting negative attention. Keefe said that at no time in Pembroke did Frost have—or try to have—a relationship with any of the players the way he'd had with the Brampton Boys, but he'd worn out his welcome there nonetheless. When Keefe sat down with Frost in the summer of 2006 to talk about his own retirement, Frost had already announced he wouldn't be back with the Lumber Kings the following season. That was not only fine with Keefe, but he knew it had to be, that Frost was toxic in Pembroke and would severely hamper, if not ruin, Keefe's desire to build a new life for himself as a junior team owner/operator and coach.

"[Frost] was originally part of the team with my blessing," Keefe said, "but I wasn't happy when all the negative attention was coming onto the team and the community. I couldn't have that. [Frost] had to go."

Little did Keefe realize, though, how quickly things in Pembroke would go from toxic to radioactive.

It was not lost on Sheldon Keefe that, at a time when he was embarking on a new life of sorts—finally trying to assert himself as a more independent young man, telling Frost in no uncertain terms he couldn't be in Pembroke or around Keefe's Lumber Kings team—a giant sinkhole opened up on the road to redemption. The past—Keefe's and Frost's—reached up and grabbed Keefe, pulling him right back into the morass.

It was during the Lumber Kings' 2006 training camp that all hell broke loose. On September 6, after an Ontario Provincial Police investigation, Frost was charged with 12 counts of sexual exploitation involving teenage boys and girls over a period from 1995 to 2001. Keefe's past life with Frost—specifically what went on in Room 22 of the Bayview Inn in Deseronto during the 1996–97 season, was back in the news.

It wasn't good news, but it was big news, a national story, that ran on front pages across the country and was the lead item on all the network news programs. Pembroke was crawling with reporters and news organizations. Next to Frost, no one was more squarely in the media's crosshairs than Keefe. And the people of Pembroke were not happy to be drawn into Frosty's world. Not happy at all.

"I really thought it was all over for me [in Pembroke] before it had even started," Keefe said. "Because of Frost, my name in town was mud. I was being shunned. Here I am, I'm in my first year coaching and running a business, with no experience, really, and there is this huge controversy in Pembroke. I'm in the middle of it all. There was a lot of cleaning up to be done."

Perhaps the most misleading aspect was that the charges against Frost publicly cemented or reinforced the long-standing bond between him and Keefe when—at least in his own mind—Keefe had already begun, both emotionally and physically, detaching from Frost. The testimony at Frost's trial was subjected to a publication ban, making it illegal to report on who said what. But that didn't stop many accounts from reporting that Keefe and the others testified at the trial and that the testimony ostensibly ended up being on behalf of or in favour of

Frost. Eight of the 12 charges were dropped, and Frost was acquitted of the remaining four in August 2009. Still, the court case and legal entanglements actually helped to solidify Keefe's estrangement from Frost. Keefe's focus, at that point, was on getting on with the new life he was trying to forge for himself.

"When he was first charged, I legally couldn't see or talk to him," Keefe said, "and I had already really cut back on talking to him or seeing him anyway. We sold the property we owned together. That was the last of our ties."

At the same time, Keefe was also moving on from his childhood friend Mike Danton. Keefe did visit Danton after the latter was incarcerated in 2004, and for a time, they continued to communicate by mail, but as with his relationship with Frost, it just ran its course and petered out.

"Mike became pretty bitter [with me]," Keefe said. "He didn't feel I was writing enough or supporting him enough when he was in prison. I felt as though I went through a lot of crap for how out of control the whole situation had gotten. I had a girlfriend. I had a business [the Lumber Kings]. I had started to live my own life and wanted to focus on my own life. I think he was bitter about that. Leading up to [Danton's prison] release [in September 2009, not long after Frost was acquitted on the four sexual exploitation charges], I had no communication with [Danton] at all. The last few years he was in prison, there was no contact. When he was released, I just decided it's not something I wanted to be associated with."

Often asked to pinpoint the exact moment when Frost was no longer a part of Keefe's life, he used the date of his wedding to wife Jackie—June 28, 2008—as the official marker.

"Everyone wants to know exactly when I last saw or talked to [Frost], and I can't tell you, not precisely, because I'm not sure," Keefe said. "There was no big blowup, no defining moment. Our relationship went from daily contact to weekly to monthly to a few times a year to nothing. I can tell you he wasn't invited to my wedding; he didn't attend my wedding. I know for a fact I haven't physically seen him since before [the wedding]. I know there was some sporadic [verbal] communication right around the time Danton was being released from prison [about 14 months after the wedding], but that was the end of it. My son [Landon] was born in 2010, [second son] Wyatt was born in 2012, and [Frost] has never seen or met my kids. We no longer have any ties. I was living in Pembroke during the season, living in Arizona [his wife Jackie's family is from Scottsdale] in the summers. There was no reason for me to communicate with him."

There was, however, huge incentive for Keefe to not be associated with Frost in any way. From the moment the fertilizer hit the fan in Pembroke in September 2006, Keefe knew his only hope to survive was to prove to everyone he was his own man. His entire future in Pembroke hinged on it.

"I remember a meeting in town with some of the most influential business leaders," Keefe said. "I was trying to get their blessing and [get them to] back me in the community, but it was a tough time. It was to the point where some of these gentlemen were going to pool their money to [buy me] out of there. I pleaded with them to have lunch with me, I asked them to understand my perspective, I assured them there would be nothing more to do with Frost, how I knew I had zero chance of success if I wasn't being honest. A lot of those gentlemen became major allies. One of them came to my wedding in Arizona.

"I knew I had to earn people's respect, literally one at a time. I had to be out in the community. I had to be visible. You know, it would have probably been easier for me to get out of hockey entirely, just live in Arizona and be out of the spotlight. But I'm competitive, I like hockey and I had what I thought was a wonderful opportunity. As much as

I was aware of my past and the hurdles I would have to overcome, I looked at Pembroke as a place where I could, with my family, put down some roots. I had lived in seven cities in four years in pro, I played for two major junior teams, two Junior A teams—I had no stability in my life. That's how I viewed Pembroke: a chance for stability."

What happened during Keefe's seven seasons in Pembroke was remarkable by any measure. With him as the owner, GM and head coach, Keefe's teams had a collective record of 265–76–20, making him the fastest coach to reach 200 wins in league history. The Lumber Kings won five consecutive Central Canada Hockey League titles, two Fred Page Cups (in 2007 and 2011) and a Royal Bank Cup national championship in 2011—also coming very close in 2007, when they lost to eventual champion Aurora in the semifinal. Keefe was also able to bring his friend Shawn Cation back into the fold. Cation, who had been estranged from Frost even longer than Keefe, was an assistant coach in Pembroke for a couple of seasons and continued to help Keefe out beyond that after moving to Ottawa for a job outside hockey.

Keefe took to Twitter and established the highly public profile of a happy family man who was a well-respected member of the community, running a model Junior A franchise and thriving business—not only developing hockey players to compete at higher levels (NCAA and OHL), but moulding teenagers into young men, a far cry from the image a Sheldon Keefe–David Frost word-association exercise would have yielded before 2006.

"He's a great coach," said Lumber King grad Ben Dalpe, who played two seasons (2011–12 and 2012–13) there. "He's a players' coach, you can talk to him about anything at any time, his door is always open, but if you need a kick in the ass, you're going to get one. He's so smart, but he's also so competitive.

"When I went there to visit Pembroke with my dad, we were aware of the stories about his past, the Frost stuff, and we knew he'd been through a lot in his life. But he was running one of the best programs in junior hockey and I wanted to be part of that."

Maybe that is the least surprising part of it all. The Professor always knew the game, processed and thought it on a different level from so many. And he knew that if he could, one by one, win over his players, fans and community leaders, he'd be known more for what he's doing and will do than for what he did such a long time ago.

"I'll bet you some of the players and families who left Pembroke after their time with our organization never even knew my story or anything about David Frost," Keefe said. "They came because they heard good things about Pembroke, there were zero incidents during my time as head coach, and they wanted to be part of something good. Then they would leave and spread the word. One graduate telling someone else, from staff and volunteers and players and their families. One by one. That's what it's about for me: I want to be able to make my mark, have stability and be in control of my own life."

Where there was once revulsion for Keefe, there were now the early signs of respect.

Keefe's success in Junior A, not only on the ice in terms of winning championships, but how his players and organization carried themselves off it, didn't go unnoticed.

After the Lumber Kings won the 2011 RBC national championship, Keefe was asked to be head coach of Team East in the 2011 Canadian Junior Hockey League's Top Prospects game. A year later, he applied to coach the Canada East team in the World Junior A Challenge, and while he didn't get the head-coaching position (it went to Greg Walters), he was asked to be Walters's assistant coach. Because the World Junior A Challenge is a sanctioned Hockey Canada international event, there was a high level of scrutiny. With it, though, came a figurative seal of approval from Hockey Canada. It was as if some counterculture kid who lost his way had been welcomed back into the establishment.

It was a step, a notable one—but it was just one.

Keefe suspected even then that not everyone might be so quick to forgive or forget his past, to give him the benefit of the doubt.

When Sheldon Keefe was a kid playing minor hockey, as focused and driven as he was, he never ever thought of it as a means to an end, a journey to the NHL. He wasn't a big dreamer. There was never any grand or master plan—not in his mind. He just liked to play the game and do whatever was necessary to be good at it. It was much the same once he started coaching in Pembroke. He didn't go into coaching there thinking, "This will get me to the OHL or the NHL."

"For one thing, I didn't know if I was any good [at coaching]," Keefe said. "For another, I'm well aware of my past, the hurdles I have to cross. I did eventually get confidence that I knew what I was doing [coaching] and I did think this is going to be a career for me [in Pembroke], but I didn't look at it and say, 'I'm doing this to coach in the OHL or the NHL.' I never thought of or expected that. To be honest, I thought I was too toxic for that."

That changed, though, in 2012. Putting together a winning program in Pembroke, surprising even himself by getting a little love from the hockey establishment—via the CJHL and Hockey Canada—and being able to mend a fence with Mike Futa allowed Keefe to at least consider the notion of moving up the coaching ranks. Futa, that 27-year-old rookie head coach who couldn't deal with Frost and his boys at St. Mike's, went on to become a respected OHL general manager in Owen Sound and then the well-regarded co-director of amateur scouting for the L.A. Kings. As Keefe got more and more successful in Pembroke, their paths would occasionally cross, with Futa looking for an opinion on a CCHL player who was eligible for the NHL draft. At some point, though, their talks got a lot deeper.

"My first thought was, 'Am I being manipulated or snowed here?'" Futa said. "I'm working in the NHL now and I'm not going to get played by anyone. I told Sheldon I would listen to what he had to say and give him advice, but if [Frost] is still in the picture in any way, I can't and I won't put my neck on the line for him. Not this time. Sheldon told me, 'Those guys [Frost and Danton] are out of my life.' Now, Sheldon had done nothing to earn my trust, but I wasn't the least bit surprised he was doing well as a coach and winning championships. He always was smart and he had a work ethic."

Futa, however, sensed Keefe was in earnest, that Frost was no longer in the picture. Futa also told Keefe, regardless of whether he wanted to coach at the next level or not, he had to make amends. Specifically, Futa told Keefe he owed a handshake and an apology to OHL commissioner Dave Branch. Futa went so far as to try to broker it, but suffice it to say Branch didn't immediately embrace the opportunity. Keefe was going to have to earn his way into people's good books with actions over words.

"The moment when I really knew Sheldon was different, that he was for real, was when I met his wife [Jackie] and kids," Futa said. "I was at a rink and I saw this woman and her children in the hallway, and [Jackie] came up and introduced herself and the kids to me. She knew who I was and she thanked me for helping out Sheldon. When I saw her and the children, when I saw how happy they were, that's when I realized Sheldon was for real. If he wasn't [for real], he'd be throwing away this [his family], and I just couldn't imagine him doing that. That's when I knew, that's when I felt really confident [about Keefe]."

Sheldon said he and Jackie met in Springfield, Massachusetts, late in Keefe's third pro season—or as Jackie quickly reminded him, April 16, 2003. Springfield was a shared farm team between Tampa and Phoenix. Some of the Phoenix-owned players in Springfield had their girlfriends from Arizona visit them that season. Jackie was a friend of one of those girlfriends, and she tagged along on a visit, meeting Sheldon.

They hit it off, but carried on a mostly long-distance relationship for a couple of years, Jackie back home in Scottsdale, Sheldon in Hershey the following season and Utah the year after that. They continued to see more and more of each other as time wore on. In the summer of 2006, when Keefe had retired and was going to make a full-time go of it in Pembroke, they got engaged, bought a house there and worked together to build the business.

"It was nice for me to have Jackie, because she helped to give me a sense of normalcy that had been missing in my life," Keefe said. "I'd always lived with all the 'noise' from the Frost situation, and from day one with Jackie, it was about establishing a life for ourselves."

Not that it was easy for the woman he married in 2008.

"When the dust gets kicked up [about Frost], it's stressful for her," Keefe said. "I can deal with it because I'm used to it, but it's much harder for her."

Backed by his wife, armed with more support from hockey people like Futa, Keefe allowed himself to dream of moving up. There were OHL coaching vacancies in Mississauga and Owen Sound that summer of 2012. And Keefe did apply, without success, for the latter. He had also previously interviewed for a job in the Quebec Major Junior Hockey League, but when the 2012–13 season began, he was still in Pembroke. And that was just fine by Keefe, especially with the World Junior A Challenge coming up in November.

If life was going well for Keefe in Pembroke—and it was—the same could not be said for Kyle Dubas in Sault Ste. Marie, Ontario. At the age of 25, hometown boy Dubas had been hired by the Greyhounds in April of 2011, amid much fanfare, as the second-youngest GM in OHL history.

In his first full season as GM, in November 2011, Dubas made a bold, blockbuster trade with Windsor, acquiring netminder Jack Campbell for two players and seven draft picks. The highly touted young American was in his final OHL season and was supposed to put a veteran-laden Greyhound team over the top. Instead, the bottom fell out. The Greyhounds not only finished ninth and out of the play-offs, but in giving up seven draft picks they also appeared to have gutted their future. It would get worse. On the eve of their 2012 training camp, three Greyhounds were charged with sexual assault (the charges were dropped after the 2012–13 season). Coach Mike Stapleton's team then stumbled out of the gate, going 13–14–2–0. Dubas fired Stapleton on December 3, 2012, replacing him with Keefe. But the young GM had been contemplating the move for weeks. He needed that much time to do his due diligence.

"I knew that if I screwed this up [firing Stapleton and hiring Keefe], I was not only likely to lose my job, but I might be out of hockey entirely," Dubas said. "I was under pressure to get it right, to make sure I was making a good decision for our organization. I felt like I was really putting my neck on the line."

Dubas saw Keefe at the World Junior A Challenge in early November. Quietly, knowing he would likely be making a coaching change, Dubas began calling around for references on Keefe. He was shocked at how positive so many of them were, especially from rival coaches and executives in the CCHL.

"I figured there would be jealousy and resentment from his peers because he was so successful," Dubas said, "but I was shocked to find out how well respected Sheldon was. They were basically saying to me that they thought it was a travesty he's not coaching at a higher level."

Dubas also went to former Pembroke players and parents, digging hard to find out if there was any dirt on Keefe. He couldn't find it.

"Even the kids who got cut by Keefe had good things to say about him," Dubas said. "It was remarkable."

Five days before the actual hiring, Dubas and Keefe met for six hours. A copious note taker, Dubas didn't write anything down. He just asked questions, listened and tried to judge for himself whether this man before him was worthy of being entrusted with an OHL franchise.

"What struck me more than anything else was how brutally honest Sheldon was about his past," Dubas said. "I knew after meeting him he was the right man for the job."

Still, Dubas knew there would be a backlash in the media and some parts of the hockey community. He had to sell his owners on the idea and prepare them for the possibility of negative publicity.

Toronto Sun columnist Simmons, who wrote the book on Danton and Frost, tweeted about Keefe's hiring that day: "I hope for the sake of players and parents on Soo Greyhounds, they have done thorough due diligence before hiring @SheldonKeefe as coach."

Keefe had his own message he put out on Twitter that day: "Those that base opinions solely on what they know from 7–18 years ago, your concerns are valid but give it a chance. U just might be surprised."

For the junior hockey cognoscenti, those familiar with Keefe's track record as a coach in Pembroke, the move made all kinds of sense. But there was all that baggage. For most people, Sheldon Keefe's name couldn't be mentioned without conjuring up dark images of David Frost or Mike Danton. Many in hockey believed if Keefe was coming, Frost couldn't be far behind, pulling all his strings.

It mattered little to some that Keefe made an immediate impact with the Greyhounds, going 23–12–1–3 to turn things around and get them into the playoffs, where they lost in the first round. Or that he followed it up with a tremendous 44–17–2–5 record and a first-place finish in the West Division in his first full season (2013–14), earning rave reviews and accolades from his players, including high-profile future NHL stars like Edmonton first-round pick Darnell Nurse. His .678 winning percentage, admittedly on a limited 107-game sample

size, was the best in franchise history. Or that he was named by Hockey
Canada as one of three head coaches for Canadian entries in the prestigious 2014 World Under-17 tournament.

Some skeptics, though, remained, uh, extremely skeptical.

"You know he's still seeing Frost, don't you?" an OHL owner said
during the 2013–14 season.

The owner was asked if he knew that for a fact.

"Well, that's what I've heard," the owner said. "If you look closely,
you'll see he still has ties to Frost."

One of them, depending upon your definition of a "tie," is Soo
Greyhound goaltending consultant Jon Elkin, who was hired by the
OHL team after Keefe was employed. That raised some eyebrows.
Elkin, you may recall, was an acquaintance of Frost's back in Keefe's
junior hockey days at St. Mike's. Frost had arranged for the Brampton
Boys to briefly live at Elkin's Toronto apartment when they played for
the Majors.

"They know each other, they had an association a long time ago
because of their hockey school businesses, but they've never had a relationship the way some people perceived it to be," Keefe said. "Jon knew
very little about what our relationship was like with Frost, and [as for]
what Jon did know, he served as an adult voice of reason to let Frost
know that the isolation that existed around us was not normal. It's so
unfair to make Jon any part of this. I think anyone who knows Jon
knows that he's his own man. He's also a very good goalie coach."

Indeed, Elkin has an impressive hockey resumé. He's worked for
the Calgary Flames and numerous OHL franchises, as well as with
countless individual goalies. When the Greyhounds called to do a
background check on Elkin, they found a goalie coach/consultant with
solid references from previous employers. And maybe most important
of all, when the Hounds decided to hire him, Elkin was already the
personal goaltending coach of Greyhound goalie Matt Murray.

"I know Jon to be the best goalie coach in North America, he had a previous relationship with Matt Murray, and we felt he could really help Matt," Keefe said. "We interviewed a number of people, and when it came time to make the decision on the best candidate, I separated myself from all of that and let Kyle handle it. There's been no issue— not with any of the teams Jon has worked with in the past, and not with the Greyhounds, either. None. Jon has been a tremendous addition to our staff."

The other connection to Frost, though, was a much thornier one for Keefe. It's his younger brother Adam. Even though Adam never had the same type of all-consuming relationship with Frost as Sheldon, Adam Keefe remained friends with Frost—and for that matter, with Danton, too. It was a source of some friction between the brothers.

"I have only selfish concerns," Sheldon Keefe said, "[about] how it affects me. Adam knows I'm not thrilled about it. I have no relationship with David Frost. None. My brother does. It doesn't impact Adam negatively. You have to understand, Adam's relationship with Frost was never anything like mine. Adam's was very casual. He got to know Frost and his family, and on occasion, from time to time, maybe once a year Adam will see them. I don't feel great about that relationship, and when I bring it up to Adam, he comes back with he wasn't around for all of my stuff and his own experiences have been positive.

"My brother is a quality guy, and I have to respect that with him. My parents know all about it. When Adam comes home from playing overseas in the summer, he lives with my parents. He's very much his own man, he makes all the decisions in his life. Adam still also speaks with Mike Danton. Adam did support Mike in prison when I didn't. Adam is a very caring guy; he's sensitive to what Mike has been through. That's Adam's life, not mine. We don't talk about that [anymore]. It's nothing to do with me. It's out of my control."

If someone wants to draw the inference that, because Adam Keefe occasionally consorts with Frost or Danton, Sheldon Keefe must be doing the same, Sheldon said there's nothing he can do about that.

"I can only control what I can control," Keefe said. "So that's what I'm doing [in Sault Ste. Marie], one person at a time."

If there's one thing that stands out above all others when Sheldon Keefe tells you his story, it is how he's willing to take ownership of much of what he has done or said in his life. He's not blaming anyone but himself—not even Frost, really—for how things went. But if only briefly, Keefe did allow himself the forgiveness some others may not be prepared to offer.

"As a young guy, in many senses, I may have been somewhat more a victim than an accomplice," Keefe said, "and I'm not sure anyone looked at it in that manner."

That's as close as Keefe came to feeling sorry for himself or deflecting. He had no problem with those who have a problem with him, but if you listen carefully, there's also a message in there.

"If there is anyone who feels negatively toward me because of the player I was, because of what I did back then, if I see them now and they still feel that way towards me, I understand that," he said. "I deserve that. If someone wants to live in the past, I fully understand why they would feel about me the way they do. But if they have contact with me now, if they have gotten to know me in Junior A or the OHL or even my last couple of years I played pro hockey, I think they would come away with a more positive experience, certainly not what my reputation was."

Keefe certainly won over Mike Futa.

"I really believe he's found his way," Futa said. "If I were asked, 'Give me the name of someone we should be looking at for an AHL coaching job,' there's nothing in my mind anymore that would prevent me from saying, 'You need to consider hiring this guy.' I believe this is a good story."

Even though Keefe coached in the OHL, and stood on a bench across the way from Guelph Storm assistant coach Bill Stewart, as of 2014 the two had not spoken since Keefe played for Stewart.

"It's a strange dynamic," Keefe said of the non-relationship with Stewart. "Bill has many reasons to be bitter at me, but I can say I'm happy to see him back in the league. He's an outstanding coach."

In March 2014, just days after this interview with Keefe was conducted, Keefe finally met with OHL commissioner Branch in Thorold, Ontario, the first time they had been face to face since the 2000 Memorial Cup handshake snub.

Keefe extended his hand, shook hands with the commissioner and said to him, "I've been waiting a long time to shake that hand."

They then shared some conversation.

"My view is that Sheldon was a young person, and young people sometimes make interesting choices or decisions," Branch said. "But that's part of being young. We get older and we see things differently. Sheldon and I had a very good talk, a good discussion, and I am happy we had it."

Symbolically, it was a big moment for Keefe.

"It was important for me to get some closure," Keefe said. "The situation with Branch was one that really ate at me for a long time. It's not how I wanted to represent myself. It's a constant reminder of how messed up a time it was for me."

The good citizens of Pembroke didn't just forgive and forget Keefe for those Frosty times in the fall of 2006, they honoured him like a conquering hero of the Ottawa Valley. On October 4, 2013, Keefe and his whole family, as well as a surprise appearance by the entire Greyhound team, were in attendance for a pre-game ceremony when the Lumber Kings, CCHL and city of Pembroke paid tribute to him in a banner-raising ceremony, listing his accomplishments there. He also received the key to the city from the mayor.

Keefe went from being shunned in Pembroke to getting legend status in the arena rafters.

Not everyone is sold on Keefe, though.

Simmons, the newspaper columnist and author of the Danton-Frost-Jefferson book, can't get there and maybe never will.

"I wish I could believe that Sheldon Keefe has completely turned his life around, and from everyone I talk to in the junior hockey world, he's a terrific coach, maybe an NHL coach one day," Simmons said. "But there's a part of me deep down that wonders about him. Maybe I know too much about his past . . .

"Yes, all of that was years ago. And sometimes we change and grow up and leave our pasts behind. But if I was a parent of a player going to Sault Ste. Marie to play, I would have a boatload of questions for Sheldon before allowing my son to do so. I would want him to answer for some of the things he's never answered for. And despite all the good things I've heard about him from parents whose kids have played for him, I would want my own answers, I would want to look him in the eye and trust my instincts. Because I would never want to expose a child to the hockey life he grew up in. I've seen the damage that can be done to a family, and I wouldn't wish for anyone to ever experience that again."

Keefe said he understands why some may feel that way about him.

"I wouldn't consider taking on such a role in hockey if I wasn't willing to spend time to put people at ease if that's what they need," Keefe said. "I estimate I've coached over 200 players, and I would provide the names and phone numbers of every one of their parents to even my harshest critics."

Keefe said one of the things he treasures most is a scrapbook full of letters from Pembroke players and parents he received at the City of Pembroke celebration.

"It's a reminder of how much things have changed," he said. "It makes me feel good about the mark I've left on people's lives, one at a time. Ultimately, I can say whatever I want, but it's all irrelevant. The people I encounter, the experiences they have with me, determine whether I'm worthy. That's all I can control now."

Keefe's thankful to be in a position to get the opportunity. He's even a little thankful, in a manner of speaking, to Frost.

"He's legitimately left me alone for these many years and stayed out of my life," Keefe said. "I'm grateful he's allowed me to live my life with no intrusions."

But what if? What if, one day, David Frost shows up at an OHL game being coached by Sheldon Keefe?

"I think about that sometimes—not a lot, but once in a while," Keefe said. "In one sense, it wouldn't change anything. I don't have a relationship with him. That part is never going to change. But I would hope we let sleeping dogs lie. He's living his life, I'm living mine."

If it should happen that all is not as it seems in Keefe's new and improved world, it's obvious who stands to lose the most.

"A lot of things in my life would fall apart if Frost were back in the picture, and my marriage is one of them," Keefe said. "My wife doesn't understand the whole hockey culture, but I've explained enough of what went on for her to know it wasn't a good time in my life. Everything in my life that means something to me—my marriage, my kids, my parents, my career—would go totally south if things went back to the way they were. That can never happen. . . . I've got two sons, and if they ever want to know about my life growing up, there's plenty of documentation out there for them on that. But I'm hoping they will see me as I am, as someone who moved on to better things, and be proud of their dad.

"I know some people believe [Frost] is still there, pulling strings, calling shots, but he's not. To my knowledge, in my eight seasons as a head coach, he's never seen me coach a game. To anybody who knows Dave, to think I would be giving an interview like this, talking about him like this, that could never happen."

The Professor likes to think he's finally figured things out. He's going about his business, living his life, doing the right things, he said, but also now doing them, maybe for the first time, for all the right reasons. Keefe's considered a rising star in the coaching ranks, someone who could end up behind the bench of Canada's national junior team one day, or maybe even an NHL club. He's well aware that any new appointment he gets will require him to answer for his previous life all over again. He said he's never been better equipped to do so.

"When I played, I only wanted to prove people wrong," Keefe said. "I was small, I was the outcast. I was a bad teammate and won an OHL scoring title and championship. My motivation was always about proving people wrong. And even when I first started coaching, I was still doing that. I was the outcast who was proving I could succeed on my own, still trying to prove people wrong. But these last few years, I no longer care about proving people wrong. I'm more into proving people right. I have a lot of people in my corner now, a lot of people I have a positive relationship with, people who have gone out on a limb for me, helped me to get where I am. I am working now to reward their faith in me.

"I know there were a lot of days I used to wake up and I would constantly think about the way things were in my life. I would wonder, 'What is David Frost thinking [about me]? What is he saying [about me]? What is the media perception [about me]?' Now, I have next to no days when any of that enters my mind. I wake up in the morning, I kiss my wife, I hug my kids, I take my son to preschool, I go coach hockey for a living and I just be me."

Regrets?

Well, in October 2013, Keefe retweeted a message from a motivational/inspirational Twitter account. It read as follows: "No regrets. Just lessons learned. Accept your past with no regrets, handle your present with confidence, and face your future with no fear."

Words to live by for Sheldon Keefe.

CHAPTER 11

The Joy of Life

*Crazy Jari's Amazing Odyssey to Become the Skating
and Skills Coach to the NHL Stars*

———

Steven Stamkos quite likely saved Jari Byrski's life.

Or, at the very least, the goal Stamkos scored for Team Canada
at the 2008 World Junior Championship created a life-saving spark, a
little ray of light into what was an otherwise dark, bleak and dangerous
state of depression that had engulfed the normally ebullient skating
and skills coach to the NHL stars.

It was January 2, 2008, another seemingly hopeless day in Byrski's
luxurious 33rd-floor condo unit—the same place where, on June 15,
2007, the love of Byrski's life, his soul mate, business partner and wife-
to-be, Ania, died after a long and difficult battle with cancer.

Jari's grief and guilt over Ania's death became too much for him
to handle. So, a few months after her passing, in the fall and winter of
2007, he shut down in every way imaginable—physically, mentally and
emotionally. He virtually locked himself away in his condo on Lake
Shore Boulevard West. He rarely showered or shaved. He barely ate.
He communicated with no one, not even with his dearest friends or
famous NHL clients like Jason Spezza or Brent Burns or their families,

whom he'd known since they'd come to him as young kids, age 11 for Spezza, age eight for Burns.

Jari Byrski just went off the grid and into a deep pit of despair.

"I went down, down, down," Byrski said. "It was horrible. My guilt was overwhelming. I wasn't able to do anything, see anyone. There was too much pain to go back to the rink and talk about it, to talk about Ania. I just couldn't cope with the pain."

There were many days in that fall and winter of 2007, during what amounted to a four-month moratorium on living, when Byrski thought he would be better off dead. He would go to the apartment's solarium, open the door to the balcony and look down the 33 floors to the ground below and wonder if that was all that was left for him.

"I can't tell you how many times I said, 'This is it, I'm going to jump.' I already felt as though I had died. I already felt as though I had already landed on the ground. I was already dead inside. Ania meant so much to me. I was not comfortable with the guilt I had. All my love could not help her with the cancer. The doctors gave her three months to live; it turned out to be 13 months. But to see her suffer like she did, the last two or three months, it was awful. She wanted to die at home, but I did that all wrong. It was terrible. I had guilt about that. I worked too much when she was alive and healthy. I felt guilt for that. So much guilt, about everything."

Byrski isn't sure why he didn't jump off his balcony to end it all, doesn't know exactly what held him back. He's not even sure why he happened to have the TV on that day after New Year's Day in 2008. But there he was, sitting in an almost catatonic daze on his leather couch, seemingly incapable of caring about anything. But then he heard a familiar voice coming from the television, an old friend, talking about Team Canada at the World Junior Championship and, in particular, a goal by Stamkos, who had first come to Byrski for skating and skill instruction when he was just 10 years old.

Something twigged inside him.

"I knew the person who was analyzing the game [on TV], I knew the boy who scored the goal . . . I don't know why, because I had no interest in anything, but I took some interest in this, so I kept watching, getting more interested," said Byrski.

The Stamkos goal—scored at 2:20 of the third period, the third of Canada's four goals in a 4–3 quarter-final victory over Finland at the 2008 WJC—rekindled a fire within Byrski. Slowly but surely, he started to care again. He was actually inspired. He could feel energy returning to his body and soul. It was during the next few days of that tournament that he went back to one of his great passions in life: painting, expressing himself through art.

Byrski painted a picture of Stamkos, his arms aloft after scoring "The Goal," set against a backdrop of a big Canadian flag, with a smaller inset depiction of Stamkos shooting the puck, a gold medal and the flags of the participating countries on little pucks.

On the reverse side of the painting, Byrski penned a deeply personal poem, not only as a tribute to Stamkos, who was months away from becoming the No. 1 pick in the 2008 NHL Entry Draft and bona fide pro hockey superstar, but as an expression of gratitude for the young man unknowingly saving a life, his life:

> *You stood at the top of the mountain,*
> *Wrapped in a golden and joyful fountain.*
> *Admired by the world around,*
> *Bringing and sharing the moment with us so profound.*
> *With a smile on youthful face,*
> *Touching us all in your embrace.*
> *Reaching with grace to your dream,*
> *Being part of something greater than teams.*
> *When your life with that spark,*

Can bring the light to what was dark,
Can bring the feeling of being part
Of your talents, gift and open heart.
Giving your warmth to the world that became too cold.
Thank you . . . Jari.

Not long after he completed the painting and inscription, Byrski, back from the brink, met with Stamkos and gave him the painting.

"I gave it to him, I think it was in February or March," Byrski said, "and it was at that moment I decided I'm going back to my life. That was the turning point. There was no looking back. . . . I decided then that's who I am, that's who I have to be."

Stamkos was well aware his friend Jari had experienced difficulty dealing with the death of Ania, but never could have imagined the depth of it, how desperate and depressed Jari had become. Stamkos, at age 17, couldn't possibly have known how important the painting and poem were in restoring a shattered life.

"When I hear that [story] now," Stamkos said, "I get chills thinking about it."

Jari Byrski, at one time or another, has taught skating, stick-handling, shooting and skill development to upwards of 100 NHL players, maybe 200 by the time you factor in his work with NHL teams such as the Ottawa Senators and Tampa Bay Lightning, player agencies (the Orr Hockey Group) or the NHL Players' Association's All-Canadians Mentorship Program for Canada's elite-level 14-year-olds.

If asked which players he's worked with, Jari will casually scroll through his phone contacts . . . Bryan Bickell, Brent Burns, Mike Cammalleri, David Clarkson, Andrew Cogliano, B.J. Crombeen, Michael Del Zotto, Steve Downie, Trevor Daley, Cody Hodgson, Aaron

Johnston, Manny Malhotra, Mike Kostka, Brian McGrattan, John
Mitchell, Rick Nash, Jamie Oleksiak, Alex Pietrangelo, Jason Spezza,
Jeff Skinner, Steven Stamkos, Raffi Torres, Antoine Vermette, Stephen
Weiss, Daniel Winnik, Wojtek Wolski . . .

"It's hard to keep track," Byrski said, "because some come and
some go and some come back again. Some come a lot, some come a
little. . . . I'm honoured to be involved with all of them. It's a privilege."

There are a handful, though, who have special "favoured son" status—
including, but not limited to, Spezza, Burns, Stamkos and Wolski.

Much of what Byrski has accomplished in terms of an NHL-level
profile traces back to that long-ago Saturday night at Chesswood Arena
in Toronto when an 11-year-old Jason Spezza first attended Byrski's
SK8ON school.

Rino Spezza, Jason's dad, was coaching the Toronto Marlies team
made up of players born in 1983 and had heard about this "European
Jari guy" teaching kids skills and skating in an innovative and unusual
way.

"I certainly wasn't equipped to teach the kids specific skill development," Rino Spezza said. "So I took the whole team to Jari. Half the
kids liked him, the other half didn't. That's how it is with Jari. Either
you get him or you don't. Jason was in the group that did. Jason just
took to him right away. The drills were tough, they were really challenging, but Jason liked that."

"There were all these kids, and only one of them, Jason, was asking
me questions I've never been asked before," Byrski said. "He's 11 years
old, he's asking me questions that are challenging for me to answer. I'm
like, 'Whoa, who's this kid?' And you could see he was very special, his
skills and ability. I always remember Rino coming up to me after the
first time, and he said to me, 'My boy liked this, we'd like to come back,
see you next week.'"

It was the start of a special relationship. Jason Spezza has continued to use Jari for skill development ever since, and that opened doors for Jari at every level.

"Jari really took me under his wing," the Dallas Stars centre said. "I just enjoy him as a person, and he has such a positive outlook and tremendous energy. I owe him a lot."

It was Byrski's relationship with Spezza that led to Jari working with Spezza's representatives, the Orr Hockey Group, at its annual summer development camps. It was the Spezza connection that led to Byrski working the Senators' summer prospect development camp since 2006. That resume paved the way for the NHLPA All-Canadians program. And so much more.

"My first meeting with Jari was when I was overseeing the summer development of a young Jason Spezza," said Senators director of player development Randy Lee, who started as the team's strength and conditioning coach. "Jari's energy on the ice and passion for encouraging young players to develop their high-end skill left a huge impression on me. The level of energy he brings to every on-ice session is contagious. The players who worked with him over the years believe in him as a coach, but more importantly as a person. He's been a big part of our development camps and really created a strong bond with the players."

It's a popular refrain. When Tampa Bay Lightning head coach Jon Cooper was coaching the Bolts' farm team in Syracuse of the American Hockey League, he was looking for someone to teach specialized skills. His assistant, former NHL player Steve "Stumpy" Thomas, told Cooper about Jari, with whom Thomas's son Christian had worked during his minor hockey days in Toronto. Byrski started by working for Cooper in the AHL and then moved up to conduct the skill side of the Lightning's summer prospect camp once Cooper was promoted to the NHL.

"Jari's energy level is off the charts," Cooper said. "Guys just gravitate toward him. The problem is he's busy; he's a hard guy to nail down. Everyone wants a piece of him. Even now, we'll use Jari's drills at times when he's not here. But we do not have his lingo down, which is hilarious. He's unique, just a special person."

Cooper and Stamkos will often marvel in practice at a player performing a beautiful toe-drag deke and roofing the puck for a goal. The two will look at each other knowingly, nod and simply say to each other, "Jari."

Stamkos wouldn't think of ending any off-season without at least a few weeks of daily skill instruction from Jari.

"Once the [regular] season begins, there's basically no time for skill work," Stamkos said. "None. It's all travel, play games, practice when you can, but the practices are not anything to do with skill development. It's great to get time with Jari, work on your hands and your feet."

The only difference from the time when a 10-year-old Stamkos showed up to SK8ON is that it's now Steven, not his dad, Chris, who tells Jari what areas need to be worked on.

"Chris Stamkos came to me the first time we met," Byrski recollected, "and said, 'I know more about hockey than you, but you're going to teach my son because he won't listen to me.'" He laughed. "Chris would tell me to work on turns, that Steven was slow on the takeoff out of the turn, and I'd say, 'Okay, Steven, your dad wants us to do turns,' and Steven would say, 'That's so boring,' and I would say, 'We'll do turns for a while and then do something else fun.'"

Now, in August, Stamkos will show up to Jari with a very specific list of things he wants to improve on.

"Typically, it's a 50-minute session," Jari says. "Two stickhandling drills with momentum of movement. One drill for acceleration, hard feet and monster hard work and conditioning. One drill with just pure hands in a small space. One drill for dynamic shooting, one drill for stationary shooting."

Jari will employ pylons and pucks and sticks and shooting boards and PVC pipe to go over the stick shaft on stickhandling drills. Whether it's Stamkos or Spezza or Skinner or Cammalleri, "the player will tell me he wants more of this or less of that. The players, they keep getting better; they want more speed in their drills, more complicated drills. We keep coming up with new gadgets and equipment, always pushing, always more, more of everything."

The bond Byrski has formed with some of his players is beyond tight. The Spezzas and Stamkoses consider him a member of the family. With many of his clients, summer isn't officially over until Jari comes to their homes for dinner or a BBQ just before they leave for NHL camp.

"That's our tradition," Chris Stamkos said. "We share laughs and stories. Jari is a special guy—a little eccentric, but special."

"That's our 'airing of the grievances,'" Steven Stamkos said, laughing. "Jari is so much fun."

For many years, Rino Spezza actually used to get out on the ice and be one of Jari's helpers. And Byrski's eyes positively light up at the mere mention of Brent Burns's name. The hairy San Jose Sharks behemoth came to Byrski as an eight-year-old, and Jari instantly took to the lovable goofball in what's become an enduring relationship.

"He was so young, only eight," Jari said. "Like a flamingo bird—passion in his eyes, so much desire, a smile on his face. I fell in love with this kid and his family. Now, he has all these animals he keeps in his house, all these tattoos . . . we're both a little crazy, maybe that's why we like each other. I worked in Minnesota with him and Derek Boogaard. I've had so many good times with Brent: his crazy military and Navy Seal training, his groomsmen, racing his bike Tour de France style, all those animals and snakes in his house. What's he got, like, 600 snakes? I don't like snakes. He tells me when I stay at his house not to worry, I'm in a safe room. Hah! There is no safe room in a house with 600 snakes."

There's a special place, too, for Wolski, who shares Polish heritage with Byrski. He's another one who came to Jari at a young age, made the NHL and remains a lifelong friend. When he made it, Wolski gave

Byrski a Rolex watch with the inscription: FROM 8 TO 8. Wolski wore No. 8 in the NHL in honour of Byrski's SK8ON.

"I tried to convince Spezza and Stamkos [to wear No. 8]," Byrski said, laughing. "Not happening."

Byrski could tell stories about his "boys" all day long.

Like the summer of 2011, when he got a written message from his new office assistant that read, "Ann wants to invite Jari for dinner." Jari was perplexed. He didn't know an Ann, and he certainly wasn't prepared at that point to begin dating again. He asked the assistant to call the woman back, pass along his "thanks, but no thanks," only to find out a couple of weeks later that the assistant hadn't followed up with this Ann. So Jari decided he would call her himself and personally apologize. The call went something like this:

"Hello, Ann, it's Jari Byrski—"

"Hi, Jari, you missed the party. What happened? I invited you."

Ann turned out to be Ann Bickell, the mother of Chicago's Bryan Bickell, and she wasn't phoning Jari for a date—unless you count inviting him to a Stanley Cup party in Orono, Ontario, as a date.

"The Stanley Cup," Byrski moaned. "I've never been to a Cup party. I missed it. I got some Kleenex and I cried in the corner like a baby."

Fast forward to the summer of 2013. Byrski's assistant—a different one this time, a woman not too familiar with hockey—left him a written message: "You're invited to dinner with Stanley."

Jari racked his brain, trying to remember which Stanley he knew who would want to have dinner with him, when, suddenly, all he could remember was: "Ann wants to invite Jari to dinner."

"Hah-hah!" Byrski bellowed. "I wasn't missing it this time. I was being invited to Bryan Bickell's day with the Stanley Cup. 'Dinner with Stanley.' I love it."

Byrski won't ever forget that day with the Cup he shared with

Bickell, or what it means to have worked with a teenage kid and seen him grow up to be a Stanley Cup playoff hero.

Byrski has had more than one opportunity to put aside the helter-skelter lifestyle of working with so many players and teams for a less harried and potentially more profitable existence, working with just one entity, but he couldn't bring himself to do it.

U.S. billionaire and entrepreneur Nelson Peltz sent his four sons to Jari's summer hockey schools for years, and if they couldn't make it to Toronto, Peltz would fly Jari on the private jet to his mansion in Palm Beach, Florida (cited by *Forbes* magazine as one of the most expensive homes in the U.S.), or his estate in Bedford, New York, which once belonged to Mariah Carey, where Jari would get on the ice and work with the Peltz kids. Eventually, No. 352 on the *Forbes* 400 list of the richest people in North America in 2013 offered to hire Byrski full time not only to school his boys in hockey but to run a hockey-related company for Peltz—equal time on and off the ice, but at a far more leisurely pace and much more lucrative rate of pay than what Byrski was used to.

"Mr. Peltz was very good to me," Byrski said. "He and his family are incredible people. I still talk to them, but I never seriously considered it. He told me, 'Don't be crazy, you're going to make money you will never make here, you will never have to work so hard again.' But I couldn't do it. I had two issues. One, how can I turn my back on some of the biggest talents in the game? Two, it's not about the money. This is my body of work, the realization of my passion. Not just those who play in the NHL—the children. I love working with children. And then I look at the sweaters, the pictures I have on my walls of my guys, that stuff symbolizes the relationships I have with them. I just couldn't walk away from all of that."

Imagine how all this might have turned out if Jari Byrski had actually ever played hockey. Because he didn't—not really.

Jari Byrski's life story could be the stuff of a Hollywood epic.
Think of some twisted hockey version of Warren Beatty in *Reds*. This
one would have to be called *Blue and Yellow,* though, as homage to
Byrski's Ukrainian roots.

Byrski was actually born in the Polish village of Szczecin. At
age five, he moved to Puszczykowko in rural eastern Poland, where
his mother's family resettled after being driven out of their Ukraine
homeland by the Stalin regime. Jari's mother Bozena met a Polish man,
Kazimierz Byrski, in the little Polish village. Jari was born December 7,
1961. The marriage only lasted a few years, and while Jari's father made
efforts to see him, he had to move away for work and Jari was primarily
raised by his working mother and his grandparents.

He grew up dirt poor in a small village in the middle of the
Wielkopolski national park in eastern Poland. There was no electricity,
no running water, no indoor plumbing, no television—no real comforts
at all. His home was lit by kerosene lanterns and heated by an old stove.

"It was a tough way to grow up," he said. "I had no friends at school.
I was different. I was a minority. We were very poor. I was very small. I
felt inadequate. At ages six and seven and eight, I was left on my own a
lot as my mother was working in the city."

During the winter, though, Jari would see the bigger boys playing hockey on outdoor rinks, and he immediately fell in love with the
game. He so wanted to be a part of their games, but had no skates. His
mother told him they couldn't afford skates. So, left on his own in his
family's little back garden, he improvised. He took snow and water,
created a small hill of frozen snow and ice and made what amounted
to a little patch of ice and a ramp of sorts. He took a pair of shoes,
fashioned some plastic to the bottom as makeshift blades, and would
spend hours alone on the little patch, making turns and manoeuvres
that had to be tight because his space was so limited. He had no hockey
stick; he used a tree branch. He had no puck; he would use whatever he
could find to hit around the ice with the branch.

When he was eight, though, his mother surprised him with a gift of skates, something he had constantly pestered her for. He excitedly opened the box, and what he saw mortified him. They were figure skates. White figure skates. Girls' skates.

"Imagine my trauma," Byrski said. "Figure skates. I said to my mother, 'What am I supposed to do with these? I can't play with the guys.' I got into big problems with my mother for not being appreciative. She didn't know the difference between figure skates and hockey skates, and she went to great trouble to get them and I wasn't appreciative."

Jari took the white figure skates, went to his grandfather's tool shed and used sandpaper to take the white finish off the leather. He put black boot polish over the scarred, sanded leather, and the result was a terrible coagulation of black, brown and white. But they were skates, and Jari would spend hours on the little patch of ice in his garden. Finally, he worked up the courage to go to the outdoor rink with the other boys.

"I was never part of their group, but they let me play," he said. "I was the butt of a lot of their jokes. I couldn't play very well in those skates. I kept falling, I couldn't make proper turns. One of the boys told me to file off the toe picks on the blade, which I did. I still couldn't turn as well as others because the [figure skating] blade is so much longer, but I was becoming a very good skater. I was tiny, but very agile. I learned lots of little tricks on my blades."

At the state-run school in communist Poland, though, the administration would decide which sport or activity best suited each student. Jari badly wanted to be a hockey player, but was told his aptitude was as a figure skater, an ice dancer.

"Can you imagine the scope of the jokes I faced from the other boys?" he said. "Having to dance on ice with a girl, at age eight or nine? I resisted it. I showed no figure-skating prowess."

The school figured he was a lost cause. It basically gave up on him. He was allowed to be on the hockey team, but not really. He was the youngest and smallest, so he mostly just sat on the bench and continued to be an outsider, bullied by the older, bigger boys.

"I wasn't growing, I was shy and embarrassed, and they were always laughing at me, making jokes about me. I was very late to puberty. Even in Grade 9, I was still under five feet tall. It turned me off. I didn't want to be part of any sport or part of anything, really."

His focus changed from athletics to academics. While he continued to skate on his own when he could, he became a voracious reader. At age 14, he was reading Joyce, Faulkner, Dostoyevsky and Proust, anything he could get his hands on. He would read in his unheated bedroom on the second floor; the inside wall would be covered in frost and he'd cut the fingertips off his gloves so he could turn the pages of his precious books, only to rue his creativity the next day when he would wear his gloves outside and his exposed fingertips would freeze.

Reading allowed him to realize there was a large world beyond his little corner of communist Poland. He was raised with a hatred of communism and totalitarianism, fear and distrust of all things Russian.

"My family on the Ukrainian side were all rebels, sent to camps and died," he said. "As a young boy, my family would sit around the fire and drink their vodka and the stories would come out—horrible stories about what the communists did to our family. My eyes were opened wide. I was anti-communist. Everything from the east I hated, everything from the west I loved and glorified."

Jari was doing well in school. His mother wanted him to be a lawyer, but there was far too much bouncing around inside his head to focus on law or school. Raised as a devout Roman Catholic, Jari turned to Buddhism. He grew his hair and became part of the burgeoning hippie movement. He set off on a journey of self-discovery, backpacking through the mountains from east to west. He took a vow of silence on that literal and figurative journey, never speaking, living in mountain huts and, by writing notes, begging for food from locals. He wanted to be an artist or a sculptor, like his father, who used to do cartoon illustrations. But he ultimately returned home and went to university.

This was around the same time as the rise of Lech Walesa's Solidarity movement in Poland, amidst general strikes against the government, civil unrest and martial law. The students at the university, including Byrski, locked down the university for several days of protest until they were forcibly ejected by military police.

Jari had seen the violence in the streets, the tanks, the police and the army shooting at unarmed protestors. He'd seen enough to know he wanted no part of it. He was able to secure a travel pass to go to a region of Poland on the Baltic Sea—a quieter, more serene place—which gave him time to think about what he wanted to do with his life. That choice, though, was effectively made for him not long after he returned to school.

At university, Jari met a woman, Dorota, and he got her pregnant. Soon after, in the spring of 1983, they were married, and in October of that same year, their son, Matthew, was born. Jari was now trying to raise a family while attending university, majoring in psychology. He would attend classes by day, perform diaper duty after class and tend to Dorota and Matthew at night. Then he would meet a friend from school; they would study in a janitor's closet at the university into the wee hours and smoke strong Polish cigarettes with no filters to stay awake. He'd only get a couple of hours' sleep, be up at 4 a.m. to line up for rationed food, toilet paper and other necessities of life that were in short supply because of the general strikes and civil unrest in Poland.

He excelled at school in the psychology department, having particular success working with children and art. While at school, Jari befriended two American exchange students from the University of Florida who were studying in Poland. They regaled Jari with stories of America and freedom. He met more American students who encouraged him to go the United States, telling him they could help arrange a scholarship for him there. It all sounded too good to be true.

So, on his own, leaving his wife, Dorota, and baby son, Matthew, behind, promising to return after completing his studies abroad, Jari touched down in Atlanta in the spring of 1985, took English as a second language and studied psychology at a local college.

"As soon as I got to America, I was like, 'Whoa!'" he said. "I knew I would not be going back to Poland."

Jari Byrski's first contact with Canada came after the 1972 Summit Series with the Soviet Union. He hadn't seen any of it when it was actually played, but he was aware of the outcome from listening to Radio Free Europe on his grandfather's little battery-powered transistor radio. When he finally did see some replays of those eight historic games, he immediately fell in love with the Canadians for beating the hated Russians and playing the game of hockey like he'd never seen it played before—so roughly, so physically. And yet, even though he would never forget Poland beating the Russians in the 1976 World Championships on Polish ice in Katowice, he still couldn't help but be awed by the Russians' speed, skill and precision passing and team play, especially that of little Valery Kharlamov, the diminutive Russian superstar.

"He was small," Byrski said. "Like me."

As fate would have it, Byrski was perhaps going to get a chance to go to Canada. Missing his wife and child back home in Poland, Byrski went to American authorities to see if they would permit him to bring his family to be with him in Atlanta. But he was told his student visa wouldn't permit that. It was suggested to him, though, that if he went to the Canadian consulate, there was a chance Canada would allow the whole family to immigrate there. Byrski was told by Canadian authorities that they could approve his immigration status in three months, his wife and child's in one year.

While studying in Atlanta, Byrski had become a huge fan of the NHL. He worked odd jobs to make money, and two of his best American friends were a pair of rabid Philadelphia Flyer fans.

"Crazy men," Byrski said. "Absolutely crazy. They would fight each other if they had disagreements over the game while watching it. We would go to bars to watch the games. I've never seen this kind of hockey. Fighting, hitting, yelling at the referees. I loved it. I told my friends about me going to Canada, and they told me all about it—one of their fathers went to Canada during the Vietnam War."

Canadian immigration authorities gave Byrski the option of settling in Montreal, Toronto or Vancouver. He chose Toronto because he was blown away watching Wendel Clark hit, fight and score for the Maple Leafs.

"It had to be Toronto because of Wendel," Byrski said. "He was my hero. He embodied something that was missing for me. He was smaller than most, but not afraid. He was confident and tough and passionate."

So in 1987, Byrski touched down in Toronto. Within a year, Dorota and Matthew joined him. They had another mouth to feed with the arrival of son Bart. Jari worked odd jobs to support the family—painting houses, working at a funeral home, driving a truck—but mostly he was drawn to hockey, not only for himself as a fan but as the father of five-year-old Matthew.

"I'm taking Matthew everywhere to skate," Jari said. "Pleasure skating at the community rinks, ponds . . . we would find outdoor ice and every day after work, for two or three hours, I would have Matthew out there, teaching him. I'm starting to do a lot of the drills and exercises I did as a young kid, I'm using my figure-skating training. Matthew and I would be exhausted, but we loved it. Dorota thought I was cuckoo."

It must have been quite the sight at Oriole Arena or Fenside Arena in Don Mills: Jari, with his little boy, doing everything but the conventional counterclockwise pleasure skating. They would zig and zag all over the ice, kicking their legs high in the air, doing the same edge work drills he would one day show to NHL superstars.

"The guys in the orange vests, the rink attendants, they would say to me, 'Sir, you can't do that. Sir, please stop that.' It got to the point they would see me walking in and tell me I couldn't go on the ice. The arena manager said to me, 'Sir, why don't you take your son to hockey school?'"

Hockey schools were too expensive. He had no money for that. But then he thought he might be able to trade his services as an instructor for Matthew's lessons. He started checking out all the hockey schools in Toronto and settled on one that he could identify with. It was run by Dr. Yasha Smushkin, an old-school Russian who reminded Jari of his own teachers back in Poland. Smushkin was something of a minor hockey legend in Toronto. He would wear a big Russian fur hat and fur skate covers over his black figure skates. He would have a microphone and amplifier on the ice and would bark out orders to his students in a thick Russian accent.

Jari and Smushkin came to an agreement: Matthew would get free skating lessons and Jari would be one of Smushkin's instructors/demonstrators. Matthew continued to excel at skating, and Jari was getting noticed for his ability to relate to the kids and teach. Matthew started playing AAA minor hockey with the Don Mills Flyers, but Jari noticed that as well as Matthew could skate—he was on the ice hours each day—his hockey skills and understanding of the game were lagging. That was when Jari realized it wasn't enough just to teach skating— that shooting, stickhandling, deking and game situations needed to be incorporated into the instruction. As time wore on, Smushkin started paying Jari for his work. Jari had an expanding role and was becoming popular with many of the minor hockey players and their families. Maybe too popular.

It was clear to Byrski he had found his calling. He loved working with kids, he was good at it and he was passionate about it. But his utter devotion to it was also fracturing the relationships in his life. Jari's marriage was disintegrating; by 1993 it was over. His relationship with Smushkin had become strained, and in 1992, Smushkin dismissed him.

He was no longer married, a father of two, out of work but still looking for a hockey school for Matthew. Jari went to former NHLer Martin Maglay, the Czech goalie who started HockeyTech, a well-known Toronto hockey school at the time. Maglay told Byrski it was time for Jari to strike out on his own. So in 1993–94, SK8ON became reality. By day, Byrski would drive a truck for a carpet company. By night, he would try to establish himself in the competitive Toronto hockey school/skating instruction landscape.

"It just felt right," Byrski said. "I had Matthew out there with me, which was important to me. The first three to six months was tough. I would go on the ice at Chesswood, after the HockeyTech sessions before me, and there were people there watching, they would stand at the boards and laugh at me doing my teaching. They would call me [a] clown. People would say to me, 'Who are you? What did you do in hockey? How many goals did you score?' What could I say? I played no pro hockey. I played very little hockey at all. I finished my career when I was 14, and it was not much of a career."

It was almost as though he was back to being the smaller, outcast kid in Poland once again. But Jari figured if Wendel Clark could prevail in a big man's world in the NHL, he could make his way on the ice in Toronto, too. And he did just that.

It didn't take long for word to spread about the crazy Ukrainian—most assumed Jari was Ukrainian, not Polish, because his SK8ON colours were blue and yellow. There were a variety of reasons why he was becoming so popular with young hockey players and their parents.

First, his skating drills were like no others. Intricate and highly complex, focusing on edge work, they were challenging to the point of being, for many, impossible to complete.

"I think that's what first made me like going to Jari," Spezza said. "It was so challenging. It was so hard."

Elite players in Toronto minor hockey seemed to gravitate towards

Jari, but his background—that of a bullied child and a teacher with a major in psychology and a love of art—made going to SK8ON something far greater than a place for elite-level players to thrive. Many parents took their kids their because Jari was known for doing wonders with kids lacking confidence and self-esteem.

If some kids were overwhelmed by the complexity of the movements, Jari made sure to entertain them. He would sing and dance in front of the kids, make crazy faces and blurt out random catchphrases—"CONFEEEEDENCE!" or stealing Leonardo DiCaprio's line from *Titanic:* "I AAAAAAM THE KING OF THE WORLLLLLLD!"—laugh like a madman, often poking fun at himself but sometimes mixing it up with the kids.

As a kid who was bullied, an outcast, he knew what it was like to lack confidence, and as technical as many of his skating drills and movements were, they were mostly about instilling confidence, making kids reach outside of their comfort zones and feel good about themselves for trying something difficult and getting a hug from Jari and stick taps from their peers. Jari would get shy kids to sing in front of the group, disarm everyone by good-naturedly poking some fun at the elite, confident kids. The parents who turned out in droves to have Jari teach their kids could not have known how Jari's difficult childhood in Poland and his natural passion for teaching and psychology played into everything he was doing on the ice.

"I was the outsider kid when I grew up," Byrski said, "so I am always thinking of the small kid or the quiet kid or the kid with no confidence. There's a little kid inside of me, and I know some kids wonder, 'Does anyone like me? Does anyone love me?' So when I see a kid, I want to teach them what I know about skating, but I want to give them a safe place, a hug, sing with them, laugh with them. . . . I'm taking my own experiences and what was missing in my life, and that's my passion. I love kids, I love teaching them."

Maybe it was serendipity, but at the same time that Byrski's hockey school career was taking off, he hired a secretary who turned out to be the love of his life. Her name was Ann Lebeuf, a Québécoise from just outside of Montreal, and she had an incredible impact in every aspect of Jari's life and business. In short order, Ann became Ania—"she loved the European pronunciation of her name," Jari said—and she ran the business for him.

"She's the one who really built the business," he said. "She would spend hours talking to clients. She would take care of everything. She was the missing ingredient."

While Ania would drive the business and keep it all organized and running smoothly, Jari was constantly seeking new teaching and training methods. He saw a team doing skating drills while jumping over stick shafts and he could only think of the many ways that the drills could be adapted for stickhandling and agility training. The next thing you knew, he was walking into Chesswood Arena with bundles of stick shafts. He would go to Matthew's games and technically break down the movements required to take a puck from the corner and drive to the front of the net, constantly seeking to make his instruction practical and current with what was happening in the game. Between the pylons, stick shafts, mini-boards and pucks all over the ice, his sessions looked like a hockey yard sale. With a large staff of assistants, large groups of kids would flow from one drill station to another seamlessly. It was equal parts precision timing and art form of sorts, all set against a backdrop of fun and laughter and unbridled enthusiasm.

In its heyday in the late 1990s and early 2000s, Jari would mark the end of the hockey year with a celebration for his students and their parents, a gigantic skills competition: hardest shot, most accurate shooter, faster skater, puckhandling agility. There would be two one-hour sessions, with 125 kids on the ice in each session. It was poetry in motion, a flawlessly choreographed exercise that would put an NHL

All-Star Game skills competition to shame. Afterwards, all the kids from both sessions and their parents would have an awards banquet. Boxes of skates and dozens of sticks and pairs of gloves and equipment would be on display as the kids waited with eager anticipation to find out who would go home with the prizes.

"That was all Ania," Byrski said. "She got sponsorships, organized everything, she did it all. It was amazing."

But so, too, was the way Jari doled out the prizes. The skates and sticks and equipment were awarded by random draw. The elite players who won the various skill events went home not with expensive gifts, but links of smelly sausage, a bag of onions, a jar of pickles, a gigantic package of toilet paper. The presentation of these prizes would draw guffaws from the other kids and parents, which was Jari's idea. As he said back then when asked about the bizarre prizes, "No one can brag about winning a bag of onions." Winning the skills event was its own reward.

SK8ON's business was thriving, but it was hard work, too. Time-consuming. Jari would be on the ice all day all summer long, running camps from morning to night. During the hockey season, he'd give private instruction in the mornings or afternoons as well as regularly scheduled classes each night of the week. There was never any doubt he was a workaholic, but it was a business that needed to be tended to, and for as much as Ania and others did to help it run smoothly, Jari was the show, the centrepiece. Without him and his Crazy Jari routine and unique skill and skating drills, there was no business.

So life was good, but life was busy. And then, when Ania was diagnosed with breast cancer in 2000, life got complicated and life got hard.

Ania underwent chemotherapy treatments. By 2002, she was declared by doctors to be in remission. But the treatments and illness took their toll on her. She had never been a big fan of living in the city, and she wanted to move to a more peaceful setting. So in 2003, she moved to Lac Joly near Mont Tremblant, Quebec. Jari and Ania lived apart, but every Thursday he would make the eight-hour trek—it often took 12 hours if it was snowing—to spend weekends with her. But in 2004, she began to complain she wasn't feeling well. In 2005, doctors told her the cancer had returned, and it was not only in her breasts but in her lungs and bones, too. She was terminal. She returned to live out her days in Jari's condo, her bed set up in the 33rd-floor living room, with its beautiful view across Lake Ontario. Doctors gave her three months to live; she lasted 13 months, dying in her bed in the condo on June 15, 2007.

In the immediate aftermath of her death, Jari went back to work. He was at the Ottawa Senators' prospect development camp in early July, he went back to his summer camps with the young kids in July and August, but he knew he was cracking. He couldn't stand to be around the kids. The grief and guilt associated with Ania's death were eating him up. He gathered some of his big-name clients—Stamkos, Michael Del Zotto and Alex Pietrangelo, amongst others—and told them he couldn't be there for them, that he needed some time away from the rink, time to sort out his life.

And that's when he went off the grid and into a deep pit of despair and depression.

Jari and Ania were to have been married on August 8, 2008— the eighth day of the eighth month in a year ending in eight, which only underlined Jari's utter fixation with the number eight. (In Chinese culture, eight is associated with prosperity and confidence, which is why the opening ceremonies of the Beijing Olympics took place at 8 p.m. on that date. Jari's obsession with it started because 1988 was the year in which he and his family were reunited in Canada.)

Jari and Ania had planned to be married in a mountain hut in eastern Poland, near his birthplace. Instead, after Ania died, he took her ashes there and spread them on the mountain in Poland, and did the same in Lake Louise, Alberta, which was one of Ania's favourite places they had visited together.

But even after Ania's death, he wasn't about to let his planned wedding date of 08/08/08 go by without marking it in some special way. So on that date, a Friday, he invited eight of his NHL clients to join him on the ice for a skating and skills session. The eight who were able to be there that day included Spezza, Stamkos, Wolski, Cammalleri, Andrew Cogliano, Steve Staios, Manny Malhotra and Alexei Ponikarovsky.

"We knew that day was special to him, and we were flattered he wanted to spend it with us, on the ice," Stamkos said of the 08/08/08 session. "We all knew [after Ania's death] that Jari was hurting, that he was going through a difficult time, but I don't think anyone knew how bad it was. It was great to see him back doing what he loves."

It wasn't lost on Byrski that he did, on what would have been his wedding day, something Ania likely would have objected to.

"I'm a workaholic, nonstop, that's who I am," he said. "I've had some regrets about that, but I have to be content and live with my decisions. I wasn't able to balance my passion for work and my personal time. I should have been spending more time with Ania and my own kids, but at the end of the day, my passion was to love hundreds of kids but maybe not spend enough time with my wife and own family. . . . My professional life and my passion for it kind of burned everything around it."

It's funny, though, how things work out.

In the early months of 2008, after Byrski came out of his deep, dark depression and was in the midst of rebuilding a business that, outside of his pro clientele, had largely fallen apart, he was having lunch with his sons, Matthew and Bart, talking about hiring a new secretary to get things up and running again.

"Matthew said to me that day, 'Why don't I try to help you?' So

Matthew comes in, and next to Ania, he's the best person I've ever had in that job. And I said to him, 'You're a great skater, you know how I teach skating. You should be on the ice with me.'"

So SK8ON once again became a thriving enterprise, with much of the load being shouldered by Matthew Byrski, on the ice pretty much all day long and overseeing much of the company's administration.

"It's an incredible circle of life," Byrski said of working and spending so much time with his eldest son. "Matthew is doing a great job of running the business, and I'll always want to be involved in some way. You know, a lot of the parents ask, 'Is Jari going to be on the ice with my child?' so I'll still come on the ice for a few hours each day and be the crazy old man. I'll sing, be my Crazy Jari self, and they're happy, but I can't tell you what it means to be father and son working together and for Matthew to one day take over the business."

Byrski knows times have changed. The kids all still come to learn, but it's not the same as it was for that decade, framed by Spezza and the 1983 birth year at one end and Jeff Skinner and the 1992 birth year at the other, when Jari developed special bonds with kids like Spezza, Burns, Wolski, Bickell, Stamkos, Del Zotto and Skinner, amongst others.

"The elite kids now, there's no time for extra skating and skills," Byrski said. "AAA teams do it as a team. The coaches who get hired to coach these teams do it themselves or have someone to do it. Some kids would like private instruction, but they just don't have the time. I still love working with children, having fun, teaching them, but it'll never be like it was with Jason [Spezza] or Brent [Burns] or Wojtek [Wolski] or Steven [Stamkos]."

Byrski cherishes those relationships, looks fondly at the wall in his SK8ON office (in his condo) at all the signed photographs and many autographed jerseys from his NHL "boys."

"It's very touching to me," Byrski said. "I stepped on the ice in Canada for the first time in 1988, and this is the country that gave birth to hockey. It gave birth to Jean Beliveau and Rocket Richard and Gordie Howe and Bobby Orr and Wayne Gretzky and Mario Lemieux . . . This country is like a church, a holy land of hockey, and for me, a young boy from Poland with Ukrainian roots, to come here and start SK8ON and wear my blue and yellow, to expose my creativity and ability to everyone and be so scrutinized by people who know so much about hockey . . . and to develop the relationships I have with so many who have gone on to be stars in the NHL, I am blessed."

But Jari Byrski won't soon forget the darkness and despair of Ania's passing, or the guilt he carried for allowing his professional life to overwhelm his personal life. He deals with that every day, and probably always will.

"I'm slowly making peace with myself on that," he said.

When he's not on the ice at the rink, or working in his home office on SK8ON business, Jari has his paintings, his artwork. His living room looks like an art studio. Many pieces hang on the walls; others are in various states of completion on the floor of his condo. Most of them are impressionistic, abstract.

One of the pieces, hanging on the wall, is special. It's the T-shirt Ania was wearing when she died. It's been laid flat, stretched over a frame and painted over in a multitude of colours, pieces of broken glass incorporated for what Jari calls the "life experience," as well as imagery of her heart, her veins. There are others pieces, too, lovely and colourful abstracts with layers of texture and intrigue, not unlike the man who paints them. He'll often paint one and give it to an NHL client who's getting married or having a baby, his art work on the front, an inscription or meaningful poem on the back, similar to the one he gave Stamkos in 2008, the one that in no small measure helped to save his own life.

"These pieces of art," Jari Byrski said, "I call them by a title. I call them 'The Joy of Life.'"